Time and Form

Axl Books
www.axlbooks.com
info@axlbooks.com

ISBN 978-91-86883-27-0

Time and Form
Essays on Philosophy,
Logic, Art, and Politics

MARCIA SÁ CAVALCANTE SCHUBACK
LUIZ CARLOS PEREIRA (eds.)

AXL BOOKS

Contents

Introduction

Time and Form is a collection of essays on philosophy, logic, art, and, politics based on courses held by Swedish and Brazilian scholars between 2006 and 2013, in the realm of the Linnaeus-Palme exchange program supported by *Internationella programkontoret för utbildningsområdet* (Sweden), under an academic cooperation agreement signed between Södertörn University (Sweden) and Pontifícia Universidade Católica do Rio de Janeiro (Brazil). The agreement was led jointly by the Departments of Philosophy in each university, but scholars from other disciplines such as Theory of Literature and Aesthetics have also participated in the program. The aim of this academic cooperation was to foster a reflexive dialogue between two very different cultural, theoretical and pedagogical traditions with regard to pressing questions of our contemporaneity. In times of globalization, where traditional forms of life as well as established theoretical approaches are shaken in their most fundamental grounds, the search for new modes of co-existence and reflection becomes a matter of special urgency. The different approaches and questions discussed in the present volume mirror this search for new forms of life and of theory: they are pursued here both as the subject of reflection and as the way to reflect upon traditional philosophical issues. In this sense, the question about the relation between time and form can be considered the common thread that connects the different contributions.

Times of globalization are times dominated by technology, conceived not merely as new sets of technical inventions but as the very condition and the very mode of being and existing. Times of globalization comprehend the globalization of time, in which local becomes global and global appears locally. Singularities now tend to be dissolved in their "unidimensionalization," recalling n expression by Herbert Marcuse, and new forms of subjectivity begin to appear. In the opening essay of the present collection, Hans Ruin deals with these questions by addressing Martin Heidegger's thoughts on the relation between technique, time and existence. In Heidegger's writings on the essence of technique, one of the main questions is about how to think in the age of planetary or global technique, that is, about the direction and destiny of philosophy itself, when the thinking subject no longer knows of its position in the world and becomes the subject of a loss of grounds. The second essay, by Marcia Sá Cavalcante Schuback, presents the thoughts of the Czech phenomenologist Jan Patočka about a thinking subject that having lost its grounds is no longer able to rely on the modern idea of an autonomous and self-sufficient subject –thoughts developed by Patočka in terms of an *A-subjective Phenomenology*. Here the question about the responsibility of an a-subjective philosophy becomes central and gathers different aspects of Patocka's late philosophy. Nicholas Smith's essay, "Association in Husserl and Freud – passivity and the unconscious," addresses further another issue concerning times of globalization: if these are times of grounds lost, the question about the sensibility of the subject imposes itself as very central. Passivity in the etymological senses of passive tense and of being passionate, of being beyond the control of consciousness as Freud has elaborated it in his doctrine of the unconscious, is a main issue in the phenomenological tradition inaugurated by Edmund Husserl. Smith discusses passivity and the unconscious with regards to both Husserl and Freud.

Times of globalization are times in which both individual and collective subjectivity are shaken and turn into radical questions. A discussion about forms of collectivity in connection to George Simmel's Mass Theory is presented by literary theorist Stefan Jonson in the essay "Forms of Collectivity. George Simmel's Mass Theory and the Transformation of Social Philosophy in Weimar Germany." Jonson's essay formulates the decisive social-historical background to be contrasted to the experience of new meanings of the collective and of democracy in global societies. Fredrika Spindler's reflections on Spinoza's philosophy in the essay "Multitude and Democracy" are also concearned with the question about new senses of the collective in contemporary society. In her essay Spindler is attentive not only to the challenges of global democracy and of multitude but also to the urgency for transforming forms of thought when political philosophy can not be entirely separated from what could be called philosophical politics. This question is further developed by Luiz Camillo Osório in his essay "What can Art do? Politics, Experimentation and Museums," an outcome of his course at Södertörn University and of his seminary at the Modern Museum in Stockholm. Departing from Jacques Ranciére's thoughts on the relation between arts and politics, Osório reflects upon artistic ways of resistance to global strategies of control and their tension with art institutions such as museums. At the center of his discussions is the work of the Brazilian artist Elisa Bracher and her way of challenging artistically both the aesthetization of the public sphere and the monumentalization of artistic practices.

Times of globalization are not only times of complexity but above all of paradoxes. Traditional oppositions such as those between nature and technique, individual and collective, identity and difference, segregation and integration, and their dialectical relation seem unable to account for the increasing paradoxes of the times. When technique becomes part of nature, when nature itself becomes technical, when individuality can no longer be separated from the collective, when private and public spheres are intrinsically mixed, when differences appear as forms of identification and the very integration segregates whereas segregation produces other ways of integration, dialectics and the logic of oppositions become a question in itself. Discourses on cultural differences and traditions and the open question about the meaning of global democracy presuppose logic and dialectics already operating in language. This central issue is addressed in the second half of the volume, which begins with Charlotta Weigelt's essay "Aristotle's logical Analysis of Motion in Physics I." The central question of the essay are the challenges that movement present for logic and hence for attempts to grasp discursively movement in its moving force. In its moving, movement is related to its past and to its future, to its necessity and reality as well as to its possibility. But in which sense should the possible be thought in terms of its truth or, to put it in other terms, what is the truth of the possible and of its modes of possibility? These are some central questions addressed by Luiz Carlos Pereira in the essay "On the constructive notion of Truth and a New-Sea Battle Problem." In these discussions about Aristotle, the movement and possibility of language is reflected with the attempt to find a language of movement and of possibility in which the dialectics of oppositions discovers new dimensions. The limits of oppositional logic and dialectics is also discussed in Luisa Buarque's essay "Aristophanes in the *Cratylus*," that summarizes main topics discussed in her course on Plato's dialogue *Cratylos*, held at Södertörn. In her readings of this platonic dialogue, "the comic" appears as a vital element in the critique of traditional philosophies of language, throwing new lights upon central problems of modern linguistics such as the relation between the significant and the signifier, the name, the nameless and the unnamable. In contrast to Plato but equally in relation to the main problems addressed by Plato is the discussion on Samuel Beckett's experience of language presented in Helena Martins' essay "The Dust of Words." Focusing on Beckett's relation to philosophy and particularly to Descartes philosophical thought, the article presents a reading of Beckett's "literature of the unword" in which language is said at the limit of language of saying and of the saying of language. Martins' reading of Beckett presents the encounter between literature and philosophy by turning to the points and lines of its impossibility. Here the impossibility of communication between different realms of experiences, between different cultures and traditions emerges as a soil of possible other meanings. This topic of the possible grounded in the impossible has already been discussed in early German Romanticism. Pedro Duarte's text "Neo-Post and Anticlassicism. Modernity in Early German Romanticism," also based on his course on the same topic, proposes a reading of these questions in German Romanticism, showing the romantic roots of Modernity. Concluding the volume, Sven-Olov Wallenstein discusses the relation between Poetry and Thought as a relation of vicinity, vicinity that has its own figures and movements. Departing basically from Heidegger's discussions on this vicinity, Wallenstein's article points back to the beginning of the volume, discovering in the questions left open by Heidegger signs for new forms of thought in a time where new thoughts on form and transformation are being requested.

Written after the teaching visits of each scholar in the other's country and hence after having met the students and the academic culture of these two different countries and histories, the essays incorporate, each one in its way, the challenging meeting with otherness, and the search for letting the other remain other. The *lingua franca* of this collection is English but in reality four languages were present during these years of exchange: English, but also Portuguese, Swedish, and French in which some courses were held. The most important language and thought was however the language and thinking of the in-between. We would like to thank all teachers and students that have taken part in this exchange for their engagement, enthusiasm and gifts of thoughts. Last but not least, we would also like to thank Maria Priscilla Coelho and German Lourenço Mejia for for help with editing the texts.

Stockholm / Rio de Janeiro, 2014
Marcia Sá Cavalcante Schuback
Luiz Carlos Pereira

Technology, Time, and Existence. On Heidegger's Thinking of *Techne*

Hans Ruin

The goal here is to interpret and analyse a theme in Heidegger's philosophy that is of increasing importance today, namely that of *technology*. In his last written public statement in 1974, that he sent to a conference in America dedicated to his work, Heidegger declared that the most urgent task today is to think through the destiny of technology and the predicament in which it has placed man: a predicament which he designated as *Ge-stell*, often translated as "en-framing" in English, *composição* in Portuguese. It is also a theme of urgency for us: to come to terms with and to learn to reflect on the historical situation we know as technological. Technology has reshaped our human living conditions in monumental ways. Technology is changing the actual face and nature of the planet. It still holds in its potential the extermination of all life on the planet. It enables us to move with greater speed, in natural and in virtual space. It transforms our bodies, making them into mixtures of nature and art. In and through technology the human being can admire the capacities of his intellect and his hand, and in technology it can also see himself as the great destroyer of worlds.

Today we can look at the devastation of the earth, the coral reefs, the rain forests, and the oceans. Traces of the activity of humanity are everywhere. The standard answer to the problems facing us with greater urgency is to rely on more technology, and on new technology. We often find ourselves asking where is this development heading? Towards what new fields of technological fabrication, action, exploitation, and pleasures are we moving? These are urgent questions for everyone on the planet today, in a world increasingly mediated through and maintained by technology.

But what does it mean to *think* the technical? Obviously, it means many things. Today technology is thought everywhere, in science and technology studies of various kinds. But what does it mean to practice philosophical reflection in relation to technology? First of all it is not to concern oneself with the history of technical developments. Nor does it primarily have to do with establishing the limits between good and bad technology or to aid technology in any of its specific challenges. Rather is has to do with making technology an object or topic of reflection, and thus to articulate its meaning, as well as what it means to live in a technological predicament. This can also be described, with Heidegger, as bringing out its "essence," its "being," or as he will eventually say: its "truth."

Today the philosophy of technology constitutes a large field of research. Within this field Heidegger's famous essay from 1953 "Die Frage nach der Technik," is still a widely read and discussed contribution, with ever new repercussions. Here I will work my way towards the explication of the argument of this text. But in doing so, I will also trace a path through the development of his thinking. Thus I shall also use this text and its question as a lever to try bring us in contact with some of the guiding themes of his philosophy. A first step will be to rehearse the argument in his main work *Being and Time*[1] (1927), focusing on its question of "the meaning of being," and on its methodology. This will include a discussion of the distinction between authenticity and inauthenticity, of historicity and the hermeneutic, of the problem of truth as well as the question of time. The analysis will then proceed to his interpretation of *Antigone* from his *Introduction to Metaphysics* (from 1935) and the famous essay from the same year on "The Origin of the Work of Art." Through these texts we can probe the double nature of

---

1. *Sein und Zeit*. (Tübingen: Niemeyer, 1986).

the Greek word *techne*, as both "technology" and "art," and how the difference between them gradually obtains a decisive role in Heidegger's thought. Following this analysis, I shall discuss the relation between science, technology, and philosophy as articulated primarily in the essays "The Time of the World Picture" from 1938 and "Science and Reflection" ("Wissenschaft und Besinnung")[2] from 1953. Against this background we shall finally be in a position to move toward the heart of the matter, a close reading and explication of the 1953 text on technology and its conception of the *Ge-stell*.

I

Being and Time seeks a new access to the ancient question of being or reality, by insisiting on the need to open it again as a genuine question. Against a modern conception, according to which the question of being is either meaningless, tautological, or simply inaccessible, Heidegger insists on the need to ask again: what does it mean to be? In order to open the question anew we have to first address, from where and by whom – in short through what type of being – the very question of human being, of thinking, is first made into a question. This leads him to the problem of the being of man, of thinking, and of understanding. In the terminology of *Being and Time*, this is the question of *Dasein*, existence or being-there, in the translation of Sá Cavalcante: *presença*. We humans are the ontological place and occurence where being obtains its meaning. Dasein does not "found" being, nor is being simply "projected" from Dasein, rather Dasein is the ontological site where being occurs, and obtains its meaning. For this reason, any general ontology must start with an exploration of the existential ontology of human Dasein as a "fundamental ontology." Since Dasein is both the object and the subject of this exploration, the whole methodology becomes inevitably circular, a phenomenological-herme-

2. "Wissenschaft und Besinnung," in *Vorträge und Aufsätze*, (Pfullingen: Neske, 1954), 41-66.

neutical excavation of the everyday comportment, or ways of being, of Dasein. Only thus can a freer path be obtained to the question of what it means to be. In the course of this project it must also struggle against its own inherent tendency toward self-concealment. For, as Heidegger says from early on, Dasein not always philosophically closest to itself, but often most distant, and thus inclined to misrepresent its own being, and to interpret it in terms of what it encounters. This is what it means to be "inauthentic." In the context of Being and Time this is not a moral concept, but rather a philosophical-epistemological concept, having to do primarily with the conditions for conceptual access to our own being.

In view of the tendency toward mis-representation, it is only through critical, "destructive" interpretations of given patterns of understanding, that a more genuine understanding can be achieved. The criticism has to be directed not only toward misconceptions in the present, but also, and more importantly, toward the traditional patterns of understanding. In virtue of being a temporal and historical being, Dasein always also interprets itself from the tradition that it inherits.

Dasein is not a subject distinct from the material world. It is not a transcendental foundation. It is essentially a being-in-the-world, an *In-der-Welt-Sein*. To explore Dasein is therefore to explore this entire structure, of being-in-the world. But what is *world*? The modern scientific attitude has an answer: it is a constellation of entities, of objects, of a very small nature, but a composite structure. This is the "modern" conception: Galilean, Cartesian, Newtonian. According to common sense metaphysics this world of objective entities in a given, mathematically calculable constellation is the *real* world, that which really is. Besides this we have the experienced or subjective world, with all its flavors, colors, loves and hates, a world of values, of qualities, etc. In a traditional empiricist conception the first world is the primary, and the other a secondary world, whose characteristics can be explained in terms of the workings of the first world.

4

It is this traditional understanding of world that Heidegger will here place in question and which he will expose to a phenomenological destructive critique. How does he go about this? He asks the question: how is the intuition underlying the conception of the first and objective world first formed? This intuition is in fact not a primary given, but a secondary given intuition, based on a very particular way of encountering things. It requires that the ordinarily given world for different reasons has become estranged for us, that we have in a sense lost our immediate dealing with it. The primary example is the one that Descartes refers to in his famous thought example in the *Meditations*, with the lump of wax. He asks the question: what is the essence of matter? From handling the wax he draws the conclusion: It is extension in space, it is a separate, individual, unconditioned *res extensa*. But in order to draw this conclusion he must already have detached himself from the everyday dealing with the wax, where it is a part of his everyday context of equipment, where it is immediately meaningful to him as wax.

Science and the very idea of an "objective" knowledge of nature has often been seen as requiring precisely a certain distancing of oneself from the everyday concerns of existence, in order to be able to engage in theoretical and abstract contemplation. Heidegger agrees with this conception. But the problem arises when this specializing attitude and the relation it establishes to its surroundings is subsequently made into the basis for a metaphysical theory of reality. When we analyse things phenomenologically we must be attentive, not only to how things appear to our theoretical gaze, but also how this appearing takes place, as a relation between ourselves and the appearing. Phenomenology implies a secondary, reflexive level of experience. From this perspective the theoretical-scientific attitude can be seen and thus also analyzed as one attitude among other possible attitudes, and one that discloses beings from a particular angle.

What then could be more primarily given than reality for the naturalizing gaze? In *Being and Time* Heidegger will say that the object as primary given is the object in the form of a

Zuhandenheit, a "present-to-hand," as immediately meaningful in an implicit contextual setting, as part of a world of human concerns. The object that science treats is a *Vorhandenheit*, "present-at-hand," which then appears as a secondary category in the order of being. The task of a critical destructive phenomenology is to open an access to those levels of meaningful experience that otherwise risk being blocked out, when the standard theoretical interest dominates. Thus phenomenology in Heidegger's version comes forth as a theorizing, that attempts to go with the things themselves, to follow in the direction of the formation of meaningful experience, and thus to explore the foundations of scientifically and technologically mediated reality.

In order to illustrate this procedure, we can turn to another example of how Heidegger questions our ordinary intuitions about how things present themselves. This is the phenomenon of *truth*. What is truth? This question has haunted philosophy and metaphysics ever since its beginnings. The common answer is that truth is correspondence or correlation, *correspondentia*, between fact and judgment, between the world and the word. This is how Aristotle tentatively describes it, and this is how it is formulated in Aquinas and also in Kant. Truth is correspondence between thing and intellect. But according to Heidegger this standard conception does not reach the deeper foundation of the phenomenon of truth. Again, he says, it is a secondary intuition, which hides a more fundamental phenomenon of truth, which is that of a thing's immediate disclosure, its coming into presence as and in itself, its showing, in and through language. But when language reaches out to capture that which is, it does not portray it. It does not first see what a thing is, and then create a linguistic entity, which depicts what it has seen. The principal event of truth is the very act of disclosure, which is what the Greeks sensed when they designated the event of truth with the word *aletheia*, which means: not-forgetting, or non-concealment. Truth is a letting something out of its concealment, permitting it to stand forth.

How then has truth in this supposedly more original sense been transformed into truth as *correspondentia*? Just as in the analysis of the experience of the object, Heidegger develops a critical-genealogical argument, by means of which he wishes to show how this secondary experience has arisen from a supposedly more original one. The key move is what happens when a specific truth is communicated. When the description of an event or an artifact is transmitted by means of language, a person will receive this as the image or depiction of the state of affairs. He can then look up the phenomenon in question, and confirm whether or not it is indeed the case, in short if it is "true." If things turn out to be as they were described, we say that it was a true or correct description. Its truth would then seem to consist in the fact that it correctly corresponds with how things are. But this truth of truth is in the end only a confirmation of the *communicability* of experiences. It does not give us the answer to what it means for a phenomenon to become present and available as such, or disclosed, as Heidegger would say. This event of disclosure is something which Dasein constantly lives: Dasein is disclosure, it takes part in, and is itself appropriated by such a disclosure. Dasein is the in-between, the *Zwischen*, whereby the world appears and becomes meaningful. When we try to think and conceptualize truth, we are also in fact trying to conceptualize an opening within which we already find ourselves, as the precondition for any specific "true" judgement.

From these two examples of Heidegger's phenomenological analyses, we have seen how he works in a critical-genealogical spirit to uncover layers of meaning of being, of how things are, while at the same time providing arguments for how this covering over has taken place. It is to show how being to some extent generates its own covering over, its own disappearance. The examples have not been chosen randomly. They constitute central elements in the analysis of *Being and Time*. But more specifically, they constitute significant steps in the analyses leading up to the articulation of the problem of technology, as a disclosing covering-over. For this is eventually how he will describe its operation: that it reveals, and in revealing also covers up, and thus leads to a certain form of forgetfulness.

As a third and last station in this brief reconstruction of the argument of *Being and Time*, let me point to one more theme, which also has an immediate bearing on the specific problem of technology. This is the question of time and temporality. The whole second part of the book is devoted to this problem and its complex developments. But there is one particular aspect of his analysis that also confirms the general direction of the reading I have suggested so far, namely the analysis of the emergence of a so called "vulgar concept of time." To begin: What is time? With this question philosophy has struggled as long as with the problem of truth and being. What is time? *Is* time something at all? How can we reach an experience of time that can permit us to address its mode of being? From the phenomenological perspective we cannot satisfy ourselves with the common sense notion of time as the general medium or fourth dimension of events that is measured with clocks and calendars. Time should instead be sought out in its primary givenness. So where and how is time given? Time is given to Dasein as the open *possibility* of its being, as its not yet, and thus as its constant coming into presence in and through future. The primary phenomenon of time is the event of givenness as such, as events come about and also open our existence to our *past*, as ultimately coming toward us from the future. The past comes to us from the future toward which our existence is always already moving ahead of itself. And this lived time is something finite. It is not eternal, but a mortal time, the temporality of mortals.

As a description of something we could call lived time this finite temporality has an immediate validity. But what is its relation to the objective, overall medium of measured time, of historical time? Heidegger's response to this question has important and immediate bearing on the whole problematic that we are here approaching. For in his analysis he brings in the question of *technology*. It is not the actual word "technology" that is activated, but it is in and through the technics of time that existential temporality is critically explored. His argument goes as follows: from within the shared horizon of finite possibility, Dasein invents points of orientation according to which it can organize its communal existence. The establishing of clocks has this function. The first clock is simply the most distant and stable phenomenon than can be envisioned, namely the sun, the moon, and the stars, the most "objective" and stable entities there were for ancient man. In relation to these natural phenomena man can orient his activities with regard to others, and thus establish a shared space of temporal orientation. The genuine existential significance of this temporal orientation is not the measurement of something that is outside or around man, but rather to establish a stable, repetitive movement in nature, in relation to which life can be organized.

Time is not what is measured by the sun or the movement of the earth. This can be shown by the simple question: how long does it take for the earth to rotate around its own axis? The standard "correct" answer – 24 hours – is in fact a tautology. The twenty-four hour span is just another name for one rotation of the earth around itself. Ultimately every measurement of time is circular. As the clocks are established, from the natural to the gradually more sophisticated artifacts, up until the contemporary so called atom clocks, correlated to the oscillation of the cesium atom, they become ever more stable devices according to which humanity organizes its daily living. In the course of this process they initiate a secondary sense according to which what they are doing is in fact measuring and keeping track of *something* which exists, namely the very pulsating sequence of nows. What the clock says is ultimately now, now, now – to the point of making the human being listen to its calling as if it indeed it were measuring something objective. But once we reach this level of articulation we have come to the so called "vulgar" concept of time in Heidegger's terminology. Time is then implicitly understood and interpreted on the basis of the artifacts, and thus of the technical administration of lived temporality of human existence, in its ultimately incalculable happening of future. Thus, through its natural and spontaneous use of artifacts, of signs, and of technical devices for administrating, organizing, and measuring life, human Dasein produces a sphere of meaning, that discloses the world in a way that also tends to cut itself off from a free access to the more elementary experiences which enabled these artifacts to come into being and presence in the first place.

The purpose of the existential analytic is to bring to articulation the foundational layers of the meaning of being, which are covered over through the very praxis whereby Dasein inhabits its world. It is to remedy the forgetfulness of being, which is an inherent legacy of being itself, and thus to regain access to the possibility of posing the question what the meaning of being could actually and ultimately amount to.

II

The question of technology and the technical in Heidegger's writings undergoes a series of transformations over the course of his work. In *Being and Time* there is no sustained discussion of the technical, the word itself is almost absent. One of the few occurrences of "the technological" is found however in §7, an important section dealing with the method of phenomenology and of the whole book. It is a remark made in passing but nevertheless worth noticing for its implications. When discussing how phenomenology as a method is to be understood he writes that the more genuinely a sense of method is developed in correlation with the matter at stake, the less it has to do with what we think of as a "technical manual" (*technischen Handgriff*, 27). Here "the technical" is implicitly understood as something that follows a predefined course of action, and therefore as less attentive to the movement of the things themselves. This is not a philosophical definition of the technical, but simply an indication of how Heidegger uses it as a name for a stubborn and non-flexible course of action, a manual, which does not belong to the genuine work of philosophical critical exploration.

This general, vaguely negative sense of "the technical" is a heritage of modernity, where technology during the 19th century gradually obtains a negative ring. I will not here try to trace the emergence of this semantic field of the technical, but it would be interesting to do so at some point, and one can find such attempts already made in the literature. Instead I will make a brief excursus into the semantics of the Greek understanding of *techne*, in order to give us a background which can eventually lead back to Heidegger's appropriation of this term.

The word *techne* has a rich connotation in the Greek language. The different forms of the related verbs constitute a broad semantic field, of *technazo* and *technaomai*, verbs signifying contriving, employing, devising with skill and cunning. As the capacity for devising, it is an admirable trait, but sometimes with the sense of being tricky and even deceptive. At one point in the Odyssey its author refers to the net by means of which Hephaestus captures Ares in the act of seducing his wife as a *technas eisoroosin*. In the *Politics* Aristotle recounts the famous story of how Thales, in order to prove that philosophers can indeed use their wisdom to make a worldly profit, established a monopoly on olive presses. This was something that he, in Aristotle's words, *etechnasan*, brought about in a clever way. Generally it seems to have designated an ability to create skillfully what was not there before, and thus to bring about what is new and notable.

In the famous Choral ode to man in *Antigone* Sophocles mentions *technas* as the general name for the knowledge possessed by he who is *sophos*, and also *mechanoen* (line 365f), in the Portuguese translation someone with a *habilidade inventive*, which also shows how the words designate skill and resourcefulness in general. The activity of *mechanaomai* or the art *mechane* also designates the capacity to build and create, and it has entered our modern languages in the words having to do with "machines," the *machinae*, as a cleverly construed device.

If we turn to *techne* again we can see how it designates various crafts, especially metalwork, as in the Odyssey, where the blacksmith's knowledge is depicted as his *techne* (3:433). Etymologically, however, the word *techne* is originally believed to be related to the *tekton*, the carpenter or wood worker who joins materials together, sometimes explicitly contrasted to the metal worker (*chalkeus*). But *tekton* can also mean a craftsman in general. There is also a possible etymological connection to the verb *tikto*, meaning the begetting of children (as the *teknon*), the bringing forth into a world, as the capacity both of the father and the mother, but in particular of the mother, who literally brings forth new beings into the world (an etymology of which Heidegger was also aware, as he mentions it in his Heraclitus lectures).

So what did the Greeks understand by *techne*? I think we should be cautious when trying to answer such questions, more cautious than Heidegger sometimes is. For there can be no single and correct answer to such a question. The Greeks are not one entity. And the word and the term itself can obviously mean many things.

If we seek a philosophical, or at least a philosopher's, answer to the question what *techne* is we can at least begin by consulting what is presumably the only elaborated Greek philosophical attempt to define *techne* in relation to other human capacities. This we find in book 6 of Aristotle's *Nicomachean Ethics*. Aristotle here mentions *techne* as one of five intellectual capacities, or virtues of the soul, *aretas psyches*, or simply one of the basic intellectual comportments, *hexis*. It is as one of these five intellectual comportments that he discusses *techne*, normally translated as *art*, from the standard latin translation *ars*, which also recurrs in all the latin languages. The German and Scandinavian counterpart *Konst/Kunst* comes from a verbal root with the connotation of knowledge (kunskap/vetande).

Referring to his own previously stated central distinction between *action* and *production*, between *praxis* and *poiesis*, Aristotle here insists that two different types of rationality are here also in play. The comportment vis-a-vis the logos of *praxis* is different from that of the logos of *poiesis*. The logos of *poiesis* has to do with the capacity for making, whereas art as *techne* is "a rational quality concerned with making" as the English translation reads of the contracted *hexis meta logou poietike* (1140a). Indeed all art, all *techne*, is precisely this rational quality concerned with making. Thus his definition of *techne* reads: "a rational comportment concerned with making, guided by true reasoning," *hexis meta logou alethous poietike*. Its opposite is *atechnia*, artlessness, which is to act according to a faulty or simply false reasoning, *pseudos*.

A few words are called for also in regard to the relation between *techne* and *technologia*. The latter word, which is found, e.g., in Aristotle's *Rhetoric* in the verbal form *technologeo* (p 1354b17) designates for the Greeks a set of rules for a specific *techne*, e.g., that of rhetoric or grammar. Later it can also mean the study of a *techne*. In English, the German word *Technik*, which is what Heidegger usually refers to, is generally translated technology, which is etymologically somewhat misleading. *Technik* comes from *technike/os*, that which is done in an artful or skilful way. In the Latin languages we can separate between *technica* and *technologia*.

Aristotle emphasizes that *techne* has to do with becoming, with *genesis*. To pursue it is to deal with bringing about what is new, as its source and cause. It is distinct from the production that is inherent in nature, which has its cause within itself. If we reflect more freely on this passage it is important to note two things in particular. Through the common term of *techne*, Aristotle invites his readers to reflect on the nature of the human capacity to bring forth the new, and to do so in accordance with thought and reflexion. *Techne* is a peculiar form of rationality, inseparably connected to the capacity for making things. As such a theoretical or intellectual skill it also has a relation to the true and the false. This brings us to the question: what more precisely is its relation to truth, to *aletheia*? In the introductory section to the sixth book of *Nicomachean Ethics*, we read the sentence: "Let it be assumed that there are five qualities through which the soul achieves truth in affirmation or denial, namely Art (*techne*), Scientific Knowledge (*episteme*), Prudence (*phronesis*), Wisdom (*Sophia*) and Intelligence (*nous*)" (1139b, *esto de hois aletheuei he psyche to kataphanai e apophanai pente ton aritmon*). The mind achieves truth in five different ways, or through five different comportments, not just through theoretical knowledge (*episteme*), but in different ways, one of which is *techne*, as a special form of po(i)etically oriented rationality or reason. Intellectually it reaches into how it is, in and through its very poetical activity. Or this is at least one way of interpreting this enigmatic passage, which has puzzled many interpreters.

There is a reason why I stop here and point to this specific passage. No single passage in Aristotle's writings is more significant for Heidegger's subsequent development, not only of a philosophy of *techne*, but also for his understanding of *truth* in general. This one line, and his interpretation of it, guides not only what he will later often claim to be "the Greek conception of technology," but also his own understanding of the ontological meaning of technology as such. Indeed, in the essay *Die Frage nach der Technik* from 1953 the argument hinges, as we shall see further on, partly on the reference precisely to this passage.

In order to truly judge the importance of this passage for his thinking, I want to point to an early text that was often referred to as the "blueprint" or outline for the whole composition and orientation of *Being and Time*, namely the so called "Report on Aristotle" or "Natorp-report," as the full title reads in German, "Phänomenologische Interpretationen zu Aristoteles. Anzeige der hermeneutischen Situation," published posthumously in *Dilthey Jahrbuch 6* (1989), an essay that Heidegger sent to Paul Natorp in 1922 to document what he was working on. This text contains in great concentration most of the themes that will eventually constitute Heidegger's philosophical horizon. Yet, the guiding question here is not the meaning of being in general, but the meaning of *life*, of human existence, and how this was conceptualized in Greek thinking generally, and in Aristotle in particular. Heidegger argues that within the nascent vocabulary of Greek metaphysical conception we must pay close attention to the guiding models and motives behind its ontological framework. What is substance, *ousia*, in Aristotelian philosophy? It is being understood along the lines of what is fabricated, in *poiesis*, and placed at hand, *hergestellten, umgänglich in Gebrauch genommenen Gegenstände* (253). Being, he concludes, is *Hergestelltsein*, being fabricated or produced, and grasped in language through its *eidos*, its visibility, how it presents itself. Theoretical knowledge of things or entities is only one way of revealing their nature, another way of relating to that which can be different, and by means of being executed, treated or produced. And this way of making being true, of *Seinsverwahrung*, is *techne* (254).

The argument is directly linked to the passage already referred to from the *Nicomachean Ethics* book 6, which is here recalled as a key text for understanding Aristotle's whole ontology. Heidegger does not read it primarily as a treatise on virtues. Instead he focuses on its significance for developing what we could call a phenomenology of the different intentional structures of world-disclosure, the principal *Vollzugsweisen*, or simply ways of making true, or of "disclosing" being. *Techne*, as the first mentioned among them, is here presented as the *verrichtend-herstellendes Verfahren* (255), a performing-producing procedure. To summarize his point: the Greek, or rather Aristotelian, metaphysical conceptuality is a reflex of a specific human poietic activity. More specifically the Aristotelian account of *techne* in itself provides a key for understanding how this mode of comportment can be interpreted phenomenologically as a mode of intentional world-disclosure.

In his analysis, Heidegger does not make the explicit connection to the way in which technology comes to characterize the attitude of modernity, nor to the attitude of modern science as it comes to the fore in Descartes and onward. Still, the analysis of Aristotle can here be said to point exactly toward the critique of modern technology, as a shaping of the world according to the model of a fabricated object. What is also noteworthy in the early analysis of technology is that it is not yet connected to a sense of a critique of modernity, but in a more neutral way to an explication of the genesis of Greek metaphysics from within an interpretation of how the Greek thinkers understood the nature of *techne*. This particular analysis of what we could call "the technological genesis of substance metaphysics" is not recalled in *Being and Time*. In this work he appears instead to be more positive with regard to the possibilities of retrieving from the Greek inheritance new possibilities for the future. The parallel criticism of substance metaphysics as the metaphysics of a naive objectivism, is instead connected to a modern gesture, the work of Descartes, and implicitly modern natural science.

If the Greek-Aristotelian inheritance in the end comes forth as something that we need to transcend, we can at the same time see how Heidegger is looking elsewhere and further down in the Greek tradition for another understanding of the technical. I am thinking here of what could perhaps be called a more tragic sense of *techne* where it becomes a manifestation of the finitude of man, an opening towards a deeper sense of destiny where nature is revealed as the overpowering force within which finite existence finds itself thrown and struggling. This is at least how we could read his analysis of Sophocles in the lecture series *Einführung in die Metaphysik*[3] from 1935, and its interpretation of the Choral Ode from *Antigone*. Here the words *mechanoen* and *technas* (line 365f), which he translates as *Machenschaft* and *Wissen*, knowledge, are understood very differently from in the analysis of Aristotle, not as figures of a metaphysical representation of being as something fabricated, but on the contrary as terms designating the violent transcendence of Dasein with respect to nature, whereby it reveals nature as an overwhelming destiny, precisely through the violence of *techne*. In other words, in the interpretation of a Greek tragic sense of *techne*, there is no sense that the technical should be implicated in a forgetfulness of being, rather the contrary.

In the Antigone reading the interpretation of technology as *Machenschaft* in the "negative" sense as forgetfulness and covering over, and as a domination of life and nature, is absent. Also in first part of the great Nietzsche interpretation (*Nietzsche I*: 96ff), *Der Wille zur macht als Kunst*, he operates with a similar understanding of *techne* as in the lecture on *Introduction to Metaphysics*, stating that at first, or originally (supposedly referring to the a

3.   *Einführung in die Metaphysik* (Tübingen: Niemeyer, 1953).

Sophoclean context) *techne* has the meaning of a form of knowing that places man in the midst of the opening of beings, not a making or fabricating, a transformation which he locates in Aristotle, and which is contrasted to the former as secondary.

The explicit critical confrontation with the question of technology, as defining the modern predicament, emerges gradually within the context of his extensive work on Nietzsche. Gradually he shifts from an initially more positive retrieval of Nietzsche's thought, to an increasingly critical conclusion. At the end of this work, which goes on for almost a decade, he will pass a harsh judgement on the outcome of Nietzsche philosophy, as ultimately a metaphysics of the will, where "the will to power" comes forth as the culmination of a long tradition of metaphysical thinking.

An important reference for his understanding of technology during this time is his reading of Ernst Jünger's *Der Arbeiter*, in which Heidegger sees the culmination of Nietzsche's philosophy in a literary style. The conception of the modern will to power coalesces in the figure of "the worker" in Jünger's sense, as someone who abandons himself entirely to the rule of technology (cf. Gesamtausgabe vol 90). This criticism of technology as a culmination of the rule of subjectivity in the form of a will to power, is then developed most importantly in the two great and posthumously published works *Beiträge* (GA65, from 1936) and *Besinnung* (GA66, from 1938), to begin with in and around the concept of *Machenschaft*, in English rendered as *Machination*. It is in the volume *Besinnung* (completed in 1938), §63, that we find the argument fully developed that will later be articulated in public in the Bremen lectures from 1949, which are then reworked in the lecture and essay on "Die Frage nach der Technik" from 1953.[4] In this section he writes: "Technology is the fabrication of beings themselves (nature and history) in the calcu-

4. "Die Frage nach der Technik," in *Vorträge und Aufsätze* (Pfullingen: Neske, 1954): "The question concerning technology," trans. W. Lovitt, in *Basic Writings* (London: Routledge, 1977); "A Questão da técnica," trans. E. C. Leão, in *Conferências e Ensaios* (Petrópolis: Vozes, 2008).

lable machinability, the through-machinating machinability of the machination" (*die Machsamkeit durchmachende Machenschaft*). Additionally, technology is said to share the same essential space as that of Metaphysics. Here, I would say, the ideas and arguments that will later characterize his post-war writings on technology are essentially in place. I simply recall it here, as something that would deserve to be developed further.

Another characteristic of this period in Heidegger's thought is his deepened interest in the role and meaning of art and the artwork. While *techne* in one sense gets ever more associated with precisely that which increases the forgetfulness of being, by encapsulating it in the figure and Gestalt of the do-able and manipulable (*Machenschaft*); the other side of the Greek *techne*, namely art, *Kunst*, in the sense of a *poiesis* which not only portrays and imitates, but which brings forth the truth is upgraded in his thinking, to a level where art almost seems to take the place of philosophy, as a privileged means of disclosing being. It is this idea that I shall now examine a bit closer in a reading of "The Origin of the Work of Art" with a specific view to the question of *techne*.

Its basic philosophical motivation is to challenge a traditional aesthetic definition of art as a work of form and matter, designed for aesthetic pleasure. Ultimately the work of art should be understood as a unique way of making sense and thus of bringing about truth in the sense of a "disclosure" of world. In this text we can see Heidegger returning to the position that animated his analysis in the early text on Aristotle. For here he says that the traditional, Greek metaphysical conception of the object as such – as a fusion of matter and form – is in fact constructed along the matrix of a tool, made for a purpose. This matrix cannot really grasp the essence of the material thing of nature, which is characterized by a certain inexhaustibility and spontaneity, a *Selbstwuchsigkeit*, or *espontanea* in the Portuguese translation. Nor can it truly grasp the nature of the artwork. In the artwork the material component is not consumed, not simply used as the instrument for an expression. Instead it stands forth in its very materiality precisely in and through the work. Ultimately the artwork points in the direction of the event of disclosure in and through which both matter and form, and earth and sky, are revealed as such. The artwork thus transcends the framework of a fabricated object serving a purpose, and permits us to experience and think purposefulness as such.

Toward the end of the text Heidegger addresses the question of the "technical" nature of art, recalling the often repeated remark that for the Greeks there was no clear distinction between art and craft. The artist was also a craftsman, and both of them were named *technites*. But in an important argumentative move he adds that this should not lead us to understand that art must in the end be understood on the basis of craftsmanship. For in the end, *techne* means neither one of them: for *techne* is a mode of knowing, *eine Weise des Wissens*. Even though the passage from Aristotle's *Ethics* is not mentioned explicitly here, he is clearly referring again to its understanding of *techne*. This becomes even more clear as he goes on to say that *techne* ultimately means a bringing forth of beings, and further down that this is a "work of truth."

Here we thus seem to stand before a presumably original and genuine *techne*, which should permit us to look beyond the conventional model of fabrication and its effects. The argument is slightly deceptive, in the sense that it in one brush erases the very same distinction between art and technology that he is at the same time working to establish. But a way to read it is that it is possible to go behind and beyond the technical construction of reality and the technically engendered modern metaphysics, precisely in reflecting on the technical itself through its realization as art. In art the latent potential of the technical is released in and for its essence, as long as art and the artwork is not understood in a technical way in the restricted sense where it is reduced to form and matter, or to an artefact with aesthetic value and as a commercial good.

In the poietic activity thus lies both the danger and the saving possibility. It is not by entirely leaving the technical that art can constitute an alternative disclosure of world and nature, but rather by moving closer to its own technical-poietic-aletheic nature. In the end it results in what we could call a double *poiesis*: a poiesis of the maker, as well as a poiesis of the revealing, disclosing, and the letting be. It is this second poiesis which will be the work of language in its ideal expression as it lets things be in their being, without usurping them. But this more original non-instrumental dimension of poiesis can also be elicited from artworks, as well as in certain form of technology. The essay on the artwork thus contains a kind of meta-concern, which reflects back on philosophy. The question to which it responds is: can language avoid the objectifying effect of construing the world along the model of an artefact? Can it let things appear in their own, innermost essence, in a way that does not domesticate them according to fixed patterns?

III

From the early thirties we can see in Heidegger's work the development of an explicit confrontation with technology as a defining aspect of modernity, in which everything is brought in under the horizon of a calculating rationality. Everything is made the object of instrumental reason, in the end also man himself. At this stage of the development of Western thought Heidegger claims to see how an old metaphysical aspiration to name and articulate the basic nature of being gets drawn into the movement of a will to power, and human subjectivity oriented towards a control of the earth.

A good book on this topic is Michael Zimmermann's study *Heidegger's confrontation with modernity*, from 1990, which – with the help of a somewhat earlier study, J. Herff's *Reactionary Modernism* – traces the background of how the question of technology emerges as a defining issue from the beginning of the 20th century, primarily in Germany. Among the many voices that take part in this discussion we find Spengler, Cassirer, Dessauer, and Ernst Jünger. A defining experience for this whole generation was the First World War, in which an entirely new technology of airplanes, machine guns and grenades made obsolete the still-surviving medieval forms of warfare. Man had definitively entered into a new historical era, in which industrialization and mechanical warfare characterized his situation. In this complex discussion technology is both seen as the fundamental destiny of western man, as a threat to previous life forms, and also as a necessary development, which must be affirmed.

The basic intellectual topology of this situation, with its extreme alternatives of affirmation and escape, is still operative. I will not go deeper into this historical and social background of the general concern with technology at the time when Heidegger picks up and develops the issue. It is important, however, to be aware of how urgently this question was felt at the time, and that it was really a defining issue of cultural critical concern for the intellectuals of the mid-war period, not, as it is sometimes believed, something which emerges on the horizon only after the Second World War, where the atom bomb, the space programs, the energy crisis, and the development of information technology, and most recently genetic engineering, has given new impetus to this discussion. The general positions and diagnosis is in place during this time already.

When trying to freely analyse and understand the sense of this movement and transformation, philosophy finds itself in an ambiguous position. Philosophy is itself implied in this very aspiration to raise man to the position of master of the world through reason, where everything, and ultimately man himself, becomes a part of this great scheme. That this great transformation of the earth takes place cannot therefore simply be mended by means of a humanism, which ensures that human values are respected, since the very idea of the human is in itself implied in this transformation. This is essentially the argument in the famous Letter on Humanism that Heidegger writes in 1947. This is not a text that I will explore further here. Yet, the basic dilemma colours his confrontation with science and technology from the mid-thirties onward. Here I want to look more closely instead at a text from 1938, entitled "Die Zeit des

Weltbildes,"[5] "The time of the World picture" ("O tempo da imagem de mundo") and also at the later essay "Wissenschaft und Besinnung," "Science and Reflection" ("Ciência e pensamento do sentido") from 1953, the same year as the text on Technology that will be addressed subsequently.

As an introduction to the more specific theme of Heidegger and science, we first need to say a few words about the somewhat complex relation between science and philosophy. A long story could be told, from the Platonic dialogues and onward, about the intimate relation and also rivalry between science and philosophy, between *episteme* and *sophia*, up until German romantic and idealistic philosophy, where in the work of Hegel and Schelling we can see the hope of uniting science and philosophy under a shared horizon. This was the great dream of a speculative science of nature, which the young Schelling in particular sought to develop. But after this dream was over, the whole of the 19th century saw an increasing antagonism between these fields. In the great methodological debates during the end of the 19th century, in which Dilthey, Rickert, Windelband and others participated, the problem was whether or not there was a particular methodology for the human sciences, or if the same method which had proved so successful in the natural sciences, which were the great winners of this century, in close cooperation with an expanding technology – was to dominate also in the human sciences. For 20th century Vienna positivism, the answer was clear. Philosophy should be a service to natural science and limit its concerns to the clarification of the structure of scientific knowledge. For the most radical minds of this movement, philosophy as a distinct discipline was even doomed to wither away, to perish, as science gradually usurped its traditional problems giving them a rational and experimental form. In the contemporary field of cognitive science, this ethos is very much present, where traditional questions concerning the na-

---

5. "Zeit des Weltbildes," in *Holzwege,* GA 5 (Frankfurt am Main: Klostermann, 1954).

ture of thought, the mind, and epistemology in general, are re-formulated in scientific terms.

In this strengthening of the (natural-)scientific spirit which has characterized the past century, phenomenology occupies a very interesting position, one which is often misunderstood and misrepresented. Husserl's famous paper from 1911, "Philosohie als strenge Wissenschaft," "Philosophy as a rigorous science" recalls the sense of science in the ancient Greek sense of a systematic rational quest and exploration. Yet this is not done in the same spirit as in the manifestos of the Vienna positivism. For Husserl there is also a problem precisely with the way in which science is now conducted. Science as experimental natural science has lost its connection to the ancient Greek tradition. It has lost the genuine sense of *theoria*, becoming a method by means of which nature is domesticated. In doing this it has also entangled itself in metaphysical confusion. This becomes most clear when we look at how science treats the problem of the mind or the psyche. Here its naturalistic prejudice becomes apparent. It cannot address the problem of the relation between mind and nature, for according to its basic outlook, there is only nature. It thus suffers from a certain self-blindness or metaphysical naiveté. Only on the condition that science integrates a philosophical-reflexive perspective can it again become true to its original calling, as the highest work of the spirit. This is in very brief terms the argument of Husserl. I recall it here, also, because I think we can see a similar move in Heidegger. In his repeated criticism of the development of science, and its misguided aspiration to provide a kind of modern-rational metaphysics, it displays precisely this self-forgetfulness.

Heidegger is not critical of the scientific attitude as such. In his texts, at least the earlier ones, we also often find a strong commitment to a scientific spirit, but in a specific philosophical-speculative sense. In his controversial Rectoral address, which he gave at Freiburg University on becoming Rector in 1933, he works hard to convey a philosophical sense of science, which is to serve precisely as a guideline for all scientific pursuits, but only on the condition, that it can see and re-actualize its roots in the ancient tradition of *theoria*. Against those who want to make science into a national or racial project, he defends a kind of existential commitment to the idea of Greek *theoria*. For both Husserl and Heidegger, there is a positive sense of science and also a sense that at some point it went astray. For Husserl in the posthumously published "Crisis of the European sciences" from the mid-thirties, this gradual loss of meaning in the sciences comes out of the modern scientific revolution, symbolized by Galileo. At the same time as science really emerges out of traditional scholastic philosophy, and obtains its modern experimental approach, it also loses something, which will eventually form part of the spiritual crisis of the West. This is, in brief, the argument that we find in different forms both in Husserl and in Heidegger. But in the latter this is also directly connected to a critical reflection on the ensuing technologization of knowledge itself, including that of philosophy, together with the sketching of a new mode of theoretical knowledge that is neither scientific nor anti-scientific, but which ideally can let the meaning of the scientific become present as such. This is what he explores increasingly from the mid-thirties onward under the label of *Besinnung*, "reflection" or "mindfulness," *pensamento do sentido*, or *meditacão genuina*, in the Portuguese translations.

In the essay on the world-picture from 1938 he starts precisely by defending a sense of *Besinnung*. What is in need of *Besinnung*? Science, he answers, and also machine technology, as two interrelated phenomena. Machine technology is not a simple consequence of science, but something that requires it. Ultimately they are both rooted in modern *technik*, which is identical with modern metaphysics. Here we have in concentration the idea that he will elaborate also in later texts.

Heidegger's critical remarks on modern science are partly based on an analysis of how it is performed. Modern science, he writes, should not immediately be compared to Greek science, for it is something different. Essential to modern science is research, in the sense of the establishment of a mathematical model for the repeated movements of points of mass. Its exactness comes from the nature of its knowing, its method. The historical sciences are no less exact, they are simply organized in a different way. This discussion of the methodological rivalry between the humanities and the natural sciences had been going on for almost a century. But for Heidegger it is not just a question of securing the specificity of the human sciences, as was argued by, e.g., Dilthey. He is more interested in coming to terms with the scientific mode of disclosing the world as such.

The principal gesture of science is to secure its domain of research, and to specify the conditions under which it can have certain knowledge. Heidegger's example of how this works is taken from physics, which is an exact science in the sense that its findings and results can be expressed in mathematical language. But mathematizability has already from the start defined what can become an experience and a phenomenon within this science. In a sense its method has already defined the nature of its progression: the analysis of "an enclosed system of movement of time-spatially related point of mass." The exactness of this science comes from the way in which it has already attached itself to its field of objects. In relation to this form of science, the human sciences should not be seen as deficient, but simply as constituting a different relation to their domain.

What defines science apart from its exactitude? It is the *experiment*. But what does it mean to perform an experiment? Science, Heidegger writes, does not become strict by conducting experiments. On the contrary, the experiment will only be possible and meaningful to perform once science has reshaped itself as the mathematical treatment of nature. The experiment in the modern sense, does not add certitude to science. Instead its accomplishment is part of what defines science and also what separates it from Greek science, which did not make use of the experiment in this way. Aristotle's physics is not experimental in the modern sense, but this does not mean that it does not try to establish patterns and structure of movement in and of nature. But it is only when nature is conceived as following (mathematical) laws that the experiment in the modern sense becomes meaningful and can be established. "To perform an experiment means: to imagine a condition, according to which certain connections of movements can be traced in their necessity, and thus also become calculated and controlled in advance." Equally, in the historical sciences there are certain frameworks and qualifications that constitute their domain, primarily that of a critique of sources, in order to secure correct interpretations. Science in this sense is a domain of work, a *Betrieb* (*empresa*), organized in institutions, and necessarily specialized, in order to secure its progress. The modern researcher, has replaced the "savant," *Der Gelehrte* (*o erudito*), in order to become part of the academic trade.

It is at this point of the argument that "the technical" makes its appearance: for the researcher here necessarily enters the sphere of "the technician." As such he/she obtains his/her place within the modern world, as someone who works to produce results for the university as an establishment, an *Einrichtung*. Science thus enters a sphere of common work, and the production of results, and more so to the extent that it is organized in the form of efficient institutes. The historical sciences also form part of this development. Both nature and history become objects of explicatory representation, of *Vorstellen* (*objeto do representar explicativo*), a conception that he traces back to the beginning of modernity, to the Cartesian conception of certitude. This is the age when the subject, or the conception of man as subjectivity makes its appearance. It may seem puzzling to call our age the age of subjectivity, in view of the great leap toward objectivity and an intensified preoccupation with the controlling of reality through technology. But Heidegger's point is that the subject emerges as a foundation in relation to which all things are judged. In order to understand the nature and content of this transformation we must look closer at what characterizes our historical situation and predicament.

A common way of framing the problem in German is to ask for the current *Weltbild*, our *image* of the world, *imagem do mundo*. This was also the title for the series of lectures at the university, in the context of which Heidegger was invited to give his talk. But instead of simply accepting this title, and to proceed to articulate what is our world picture, Heidegger makes the framing of the problem into a problem in itself. For what does a "world picture" – an *imagem do mundo* – really mean? It means a representation of the world, of the entire system of beings, as an image, and thus as something that can be contained and mastered. World picture means not just an image *of* the world, but the world understood *as* image, *o mundo concebido como imagem*. To put it differently: the very phrasing of the problem by the organizers of the lecture series is thus interpreted as itself symptomatic of a problem; namely that the world has become a challenge of how to represent it as image for man to contemplate.

Even though this is said to be characteristic of our modern age, it is already anticipated, he writes, in the Platonic *eidos*. Yet it is only following the modern Cartesian conception of the world and of subjectivity that something like the constellation that Heidegger claims to have seen becomes visible. The conception of the world as image and representation is parallel and mutually implied by the understanding of man as subjectivity, as the being that represents its world to himself. To Heidegger this transformation of man into a representing subjectivity does not contradict the tendency to define the individual in collective terms. In other words: the two great rivalling ideologies, liberalism and collectivism (or communism/fascism) are somehow joined on a deeper level, in the configuration of the modern subject, which can begin to ask itself if it is essentially singular or essentially tied to a community only on the basis of a first understanding of itself as subjectivity. It is a very general and generalizing argument, but central for his thinking of both subjectivity and politics at this stage. Finally, this is also why "humanism" can emerge as an ideology for modernity, as also a branch of its fundamental "subjectivism."

In this age of the representing and calculating rationality, which seeks to make the world into an image and a manageable object, man tends to lose contact with that which cannot be calculated and which withdraws into the shadows. Some will seek to close their eyes to the present and to seek refuge in the past, in a "tradition." But this, Heidegger says, is only a closing of one's eyes to the actual historical moment. To really approach the present and confront it requires that we find a way of questioning, of creative, poietic questioning, a *schöpferische Fragen*, and *echte Besinnung*, genuine reflexive thinking, in the Portuguese translation um *perguntar e configurar criadores, a partir da força de uma meditação genuína*. Only through such a transformation of our intellectual comportment can we have a knowledge of and sense the truth of this incalculability. In listening to it, man belongs to being, while at the same time also being a foreigner, *ein Fremdling*, an *estranho*. In the last section of the text, Hölderlin is recalled, with a poem addressed "To the Germans," and in which he speaks of the limited scope of our gaze, and of our "mortal eye."

To this text Heidegger added a number of very interesting notes that he did not read at the time, but which were published with the essay in the collection *Holzwege*. In the first of these he exemplifies the attitude of *Besinnung* precisely in terms of how we can relate to technology, saying that it is not a question of simply abandoning oneself to what is taking place, but rather to establish a reflexive understanding through which its meaning, as a meaning of being itself, can come to presence. Also in note 9 he has an important additional remark that points directly to the subsequent essay on technology. In the modern theoretical-technical-scientific approach to beings, he writes, these beings are no longer what comes to presence in themselves, but rather what is placed over and against a representation, as something objectified. To represent is to place in front of oneself precisely as something placed, *gestellt*. In the Portuguese the whole sentence reads: *O ente já não é o que está presente, mas só o que está posto em frente no representar, o que é ob-jectivo*. This idea of a "*posto-em-frente*" of representation is precisely what he will later describe as the "essence" of technology, and of its way of making true or disclosing a world.

IV

In the essay on the world-image the spiritual-cultural situation of modernity is captured in terms of a how the world has become an image and a representation for a subject and its concerns. The way that science is done and administrated in this predicament is part of the situation itself. Therefore science, as normally performed, can no longer provide a critical point of reflection on the totality of what is happening. For this reason there is a need to develop another kind of reflection, that can cautiously take in and formulate the situation of modernity as a predicament where modern techno-science is an integral part. This kind of thinking is philosophical in some sense of the word, yet as we saw already Heidegger prefers to give it another name, namely "reflexive thinking," *Besinnung, meditação* or *pensamento do sentido*. It belongs to its character that it preserves a certain critical distance to how philosophy and rationality have developed from the ancient metaphysical tradition, and in particular to how philosophy has developed in modernity, following Descartes and the great project of a modern metaphysics of spirit and nature. In the text *"Wissenschaft und Besinnung"* (*ciência e meditação do sentido*) from 1953, this contrast and the need to establish such a reflection is explained further and deepened.

Now, however, it is time to approach Heidegger's most famous text on technology, and also the single most quoted essay in the field of philosophy of technology, namely "Die Frage nach die Technik" (*A questão da técnica*) from 1953. The text originated in a lecture he was invited to give at the school of polytechnics in Munich in November 1953, the overall title of which was "The Arts in the Age of Technology." But already in 1949 he had given a series of lectures in a local cultural club in Bremen, one of which was entitled simply "Das Ge-stell" (which was published posthumously in 1994, in volume 79 of his *Gesamtausgabe*,[6] together with the texts "Das Ding," "Das

---

6. "Bremer Vorträge: Einblick in das was ist," in *Bremer und Freiburger Vorträge*, GA 79 (Frankfurt am Main : Klostermann, 1994), 5-80.

Gefahr" and "Die Kehre"), where the basic argument of the essay is already in place.

When analysing this text it is important to first reflect on its method and goal as described in its opening passage. The task, Heidegger writes here, is to construct a way or a path of thinking toward technology. In other words, we are not simply seeking to develop a theory *about* technology, how it has emerged and evolved and how it affects our lives today. We are also seeking to perform something with thinking in thinking, and thus of doing something *in language*. All thinking goes through language, *passa pela linguagem*. In seeking in and through language, we seek to establish a relation to that which is thought, a relation which he qualifies as "free." This is very important to note from the beginning, and to keep in mind when we try to understand what he is trying to say here, namely that *what* is said is inseparably connected to *how* it is said, if we are to achieve something like a *free* relation to the phenomenon in question. Heidegger often speaks of technology in terms of a "destiny," *Schicksal* or *destino*, and often he is described as having a theory of how technology rules over our contemporary situation beyond the will and control of human beings. But here he says and declares from the outset that the whole purpose of the meditation is to establish something like a free, or at least freer relation to technology. As philosophy seeks to discover general patterns of meaning and being, its work is also a work of freedom and of liberation.

Why is the question of freedom important here? And why is it especially important in relation to the question of technology? A reason for this is that the technical often appears as something to which we do not have a free relation, as something to which we experience ourselves as tied. Heidegger even uses the strong metaphor of being "chained to," *gekettet*, which is stronger than the Portuguese translation *ficar preso a*. This characterization is taken to apply whether we affirm technology or deny, avoid, or escape it. In our ordinary comportment vis-a-vis technology, we are somehow contained and restricted by technology. Following this analysis it is then the work of philosophical reflection to establish a more free relation, by going beyond the conceptual matrix of technology itself. And this it can do, Heidegger claims, by seeking a *truth* about technology in the form of an "essence" that is not in itself technical. In and through the articulation of this essence in language, it should be possible to establish a different and more free relation to technology itself.

What then is the essence of something? From its traditional scholastic definition, à essência means *what, aquilo,* something is, in other words its definition. What then is technics or technology? There are two standard and partly overlapping definitions: first, that technology is a *means,* a *Mittel (meio)* for certain ends, secondly, that it is action itself, *Tun, atividade,* the capacity and realization of human acting. They are intertwined in such a way that technology is both the actual practice of action, and the means or tools by means of which this action is practiced. As such, technology is also understood as that which one wants to control, to get in one's hands so to speak. We want to have more control over the world, also over technology, and for this reason we also want more control over technology itself. This is the logic of the instrumental definition of technology. This understanding is in one sense indisputable. For this is how we think about and understand the technical. Heidegger also says that it is a "correct" definition. But that a definition is correct does not necessarily mean that it has reached into the essence of something. For this happens only, he says, when the truth happens, *das Wahre sich ereignet, acontece o verdadeiro.*

This is a surprising statement. What does he mean by separating "the correct" from "the true"? If the definition is correct, is it not also true? And if it is not true, how could it be correct? Heidegger here relies on a distinction, which is by no means obvious, and in many people's eyes unacceptable. In our tentative discussions earlier about truth and the happening of truth we have a background that can permit us to address and hopefully understand this distinction in a way that the text itself does not really help us provide. We saw for example how Heidegger already in *Being and Time* criticized the common conception of truth as correspondence and correctness, with reference to a more fundamental phenomenon of truth as "disclosure," the more original opening up of beings that take place in and through the understanding of Dasein of its world. Equally, in the essay "The Origin of the Work of Art" we saw how he continued to elaborate this distinction in its discussion of a "happening" or "event" of truth. The artwork was described as having a part in the opening up of a world.

In the present context we can hear the echo of these reflections. Here he also seems to speak of it in such a way as to indicate a kind of stratification of disclosure, a disclosure on different levels. Whereas the "correct" definition in a certain sense says what technology is, it does not open a relation to it in and through which we can receive it freely. So here "truth" in the more fundamental sense has to do with how the way something is understood also conditions our relation to this phenomenon. This means, in Heidegger's view, that we take the "correct" understanding and submit it to a deeper critical philosophical reflection. Another way of expressing the distinction between a correct and a true definition in Heidegger's sense is that between a limited and a broader, more self-reflexive understanding.

If technology is usually understood as an instrument, this then means that we expose the instrumental itself and as such to a critical phenomenological analysis. What is the instrument? It is that which brings about an effect, in other words that which has an effect which it causes. Thus we are immediately led to the problem of causation. This motivates Heidegger to recapitulate the Greek Aristotelian and Platonic analysis of causation, in terms of the four causes, elaborated at greatest length in Aristotle's *Metaphysics*. The core meaning of this analysis of causation from the viewpoint of the Greeks is to affirm two things. Firstly, we should not let ourselves be limited by the modern conception of effective causation, which is in fact only one of the four of the Aristotelian categories (beside material, formal and teleological). Secondly, to cause something in Aristotle's sense has to do with bringing it about, in other words with *poiesis*, and thus also of revealing and disclosing something, in other words of making true, *aletheuein*, or simply *alethes*.

Where have we ended up, Heidegger asks rhetorically? We started out from the problem of technology and we found ourselves with the question of truth. Again, and on the basis of the foregoing analysis, we can sense from where he is coming, if we recall the previous discussion of the Aristotelian definition of *techne* as a truth, a way of disclosing, and the great importance which Heidegger attached to this definition, already in his very first writings from the early twenties. Technology, he affirms again here, has to do precisely with disclosing. He secures this sense by reminding us of the etymology of the word, and its double meaning in Greek, of both crafts and art, and thus with a direct relation to *poiesis*. But more important is its connection to different modes of knowing, of *episteme*. Following this he recalls again the reference to the definition of *techne* from the *Nicomachean Ethics* discussed above.

What then is the relation between the understanding of *techne* in the ancient sense of *poiesis* and disclosure, and modern technology? Does modern technology also have to do with truth? Heidegger's answer is yes, and that it is important to understand in which sense this still remains part of its essence. In what way is modern technology also a "making true"? And how, more precisely, does modern technology *make true*? At this point it is opportune to take a somewhat critical distance from Heidegger's text and to examine how he constructs his argument, which is not entirely clear. Ancient *techne* has to do with *poiesis* and *aletheia*, since is has to do with bringing something about, and thus bringing it into its presence. This would seem to be easily applicable also to modern technology in the sense that the creation of a hydro electrical power plant, for example, also means bringing something in the open which was not there before, and as such letting the concealed into its unconcealment. But the truth which characterizes modern technology, Heidegger says, is not such a *poiesis* of disclosing, but a different kind of disclosure, characterized by a *Herausfordern*, an "exploiting," *exploração*, which demands from nature to deliver energy, *que impôe à natureza a pretensão de fornecer energia.*

Thus, the truth of *techne* in modernity does not concern the specific object of technology in its coming to presence, but with the more general nature of the whole situation within which it comes into presence. It is not obvious that these two levels of truth-making are comparable. There is a slipping in Heidegger's way of arguing here, where the concept of truth seems to serve two different purposes, in combining the ancient sense of *techne*, as a mode of knowing and truth-making, and the modern sense, in which it constitutes part of a whole way of disclosing nature, and man's relation to that nature, as that from which he demands that it deliver its resources in the most efficient way. Should we not perhaps say that the modern power plant is simply the extension of previous instruments, and their purposes, such as, for example the windmill? Heidegger answers this question with a categorical no. But how can he be so certain? Why is the windmill not also an example of the most efficient way of obtaining force from nature? His only answer, given in somewhat metaphorical terms, is that it does not draw streams of energy from the wind, but somehow goes with the wind. But what would he have said of the more recent attempts to develop wind-power plants, in the form of huge parks of windmills, which are now being widely developed especially in Germany and Spain, and also the USA? Are they also more true to the wind, or have they succeeded finally in making also the wind into a resource to exploit? This is a topic that deserves a more lengthy discussion.

From our earlier discussion we can sense the echo of a distinction introduced in the Artwork essay, between how the tool in a way *uses up* and *consumes* nature, whereas the artwork lets it be and discloses it in its material inexhaustibility. Here the distinction is not between the artwork and that of the technical tool, but between two different eras or epochs in the instrumental, where the modern one contains in its whole display or construction a certain relation to nature, in which it is precisely taken up in and consumed by the object. It is somehow made to stand forth and to be disclosed as that which the instrument does with it.

At one point the attempt to specify the limit between a technology which exploits nature and one that does not, risks watering down the whole argument into a question of imprecise and in the end impossible distinctions. Is there another perspective from which we can have a more clear perception of where Heidegger is going and what he is seeking? Over the next page he continues to enlist other ways in which the supposedly modern technological form of disclosure becomes visible, first in the agricultural industry and also in mining industries. What these different practices accomplish in regard to nature, is that it places it, *stellt*, *dis-põe*.

The remark is an important step toward the full development of what is arguably the most important concept in this text, that of *Ge-stell*, *com-posição*. We have seen this theme emerging above, and from the very start, already in the text on Aristotle written for Paul Natorp in 1922, where he defined Greek substance metaphysics as based on a technical comportment, from the point of which nature appears as that which is *her-gestellt*, fabricated, in the sense of being given a place. Also in the notes to the essay on the World-picture, on which I touched briefly earlier, nature in the age of the world-picture was described as that which is placed in front of the subject as image, *Ge-stellt*, translated as *posto-em-frente*.

In the Technology essay Heidegger builds a long chain of words around the same stem, so as to convey in language the interrelation of different phenomena around a common core. He is searching in language for possibilities of conveying the intuition guiding his exploration. He continues to say that this placing also displays, *heraustellt*, nature (*ex-põe*). Furthermore it is displayed so as to become *commendable* and demanded or ordered, *Bestellt*, which means *encomendar*. In order to preserve the elaboration of the same stem, the translator renders it as "ficar a postos para se *dis-por* da energía." Through this *posing* or *positioning* of nature within the construction of the instrument, nature itself ultimately becomes part of what is commanded, *Bestellt*, so as to *aparece como um dis-positivo*. In a powerful image Heidegger captures this phenomenological aspect of nature within technology by saying that as a contrast to the old bridge the power plant is not built into the river, but *the river is built into the powerplant, instalado na usina*. Again we can see the reference to the earlier analysis in the Artwork essay of how the tool in a sense draws nature into itself and conceals it in its self-grown being, its *ser espontâneo*.

This transformation in the relation between man and nature, whereby it appears as commanded and placed before us so as to deliver, is something that on one level results from the increased capacity of man, of his plans, decisions and knowhow. At the same time, Heidegger emphasizes that it is not something over which man has a simple choice, to do or not to do. The compulsion to dominate nature comes from the situation itself, in which he finds himself as someone that is commanded to command, *herausgefordert die Natur herauszufördern*, a correlation which is not preserved in the Portuguese translation which has *desafiado a explorar*. A version syntactically closer to the original would be *explorado a explorar*, or perhaps *exigido a exigir*. The standard translation is not incorrect, but the philosophical point Heidegger wants to make by this connection and which he develops in the whole passage, is that man in his willing, his projects, and his understanding of himself stands in the same position as against that which he has before him. Man is drawn into the whole system of demanding a result, and of himself as delivering it. Heidegger's examples are taken from modern European mechanized wood industry and agriculture, where man is drawn into it as a resource among the natural resources. He is observing, we could say, the metaphysical implications of an increasingly effective capitalist economy.

From the perspective of Brazil, one could also say that what he is describing is also the consequences of a colonial slave economy, where nature is explicitly apperceived as a resource to exploit for maximum profit, and within which the worker is a human resource, a tool to be used, to maximize its profitability. This is a line of reasoning that, to my knowledge, has never been explicitly elaborated in relation to Heidegger, but which seems to be a pertinent example of his thesis, deserving further reflection.

The demand, which man not only directs towards nature, but which he experiences in and on himself, is a demand to command nature – *das Sichentbergende als Bestand zu bestellen, o apelo de exploração que reúne no homem o dis-por do que se des-encobre como dis-ponibilidade*. This, he says, is what we shall call Ge-stell, *composição*. The passage is not easy to read, as it uses language, drawing its etymological and homonymical resources, to reach for a meaning of that which cannot easily be conveyed. What then is *Ge-stell*? It is a demand, an *Anspruch, apelo*, something which directs itself to us, and in directing us takes hold of us before we can voluntarily control and chose it. This is an unusual way of using the term, as Heidegger also acknowledges. *Gestell* in German can mean a rack, like an *estante de livros*, or even a skeleton, *esqueleto*, but certainly not a demand on man to demand.

So how can we defend this awkward and idiosyncratic way of using language? Heidegger asks the question himself, and he responds that this is nothing compared to what Plato did, when creating the philosophical language that we still use today, out of the everyday Greek language. By means of this term he seeks to designate a mode of disclosing the world, which hides in the essence of modern technology, but which itself is not technical. How could we translate this into something else? What is he looking for? A mode of thinking? A mode of acting? Yes, but also something more: namely a mode of thinking and acting that also implies a way in which the beings which we think and act upon are revealed and brought to presence, namely as resource, *Bestand, des-encobre o real como dis-ponibilidade*.

Technology is misunderstood if it is seen as only the practical extension of modern natural science. On the contrary, it is science that is already implied in the *Ge-stell*, in the sense that an experimental natural science is directed toward the demanding gathering in a commanding disclosure, that it *reúne e concentra o desencobrimento da disposição*. Therefore we must look for the technical not simply in its applications, but ultimately in a certain mode of disclosing nature, which is already present in the way that natural science posits its object, as an object of experimental research, aimed at making its movement calculable and managable.

The *Ge-stell* is a way in which both nature and man are revealed in their interconnectedness. This is something that happens, as a "sending" of being, in other words as a *Geschick* or destiny, *destino*. How should one understand Heidegger's repeated references to technology as destiny, in particular in relation to the initial commitment to reaching a more "free" relation? To what extent and in which way is it even meaningful to speak of freedom in this space? Man always finds himself within a space of disclosure that he has not chosen, as an epistemic situation, from which his understanding of things takes shape and emerges. This was the idea already in *Being and Time* where Heidegger defined the historicity of Dasein as being "thrown" into a predicament from within which it must then act. It does not however, appear as an exterior force, a fatality which forces, *fatalidade de uma coação*. Instead it is that in relation to which man can first become free, but only to the extent that he belongs to it as someone that *hears* and *listens, hören*.

In the Portuguese version this very important line is translated: *Pois o homem só se torna livre num envio, fazendo-se ouvinte e não escravo do destino*. To speak of "slavery" here is interesting, as I suggested above that there is an implicit problem of slavery to be elaborated on the basis of Heidegger's account. But the German original has another expression that plays on the distinction between *gehören* and *hören*, belonging and listening. We can belong so as not to listen, but in listening to our belonging, we also open a space of freedom in relation to this belonging. This does not mean that we are entirely released from it, as the slave who achieves his freedom (in the ideal case), but that we can constitute a kind of distance within this very belonging. This inner, listening distance is the space of freedom.

For this reason, it is also, Heidegger says, inadequate to speak as we often do of technology as simply a destiny and as the unavoidable fatality of our time. Such common sense expressions of how we cannot avoid the progressive movement of rationalization and development of ever newer and more sophisticated technology, does not capture the sense of the destinal as Heidegger understands it. To open ourselves to the destinal in technology in his sense, is precisely to become engaged in a more free conversation with its demand. For at this point its demand, its *Anspruch*, can become a liberating one, indeed *um apelo de libertaçâo.*

This openness to the liberating appeal is a possibility. But another possibility, which is part of the destiny of *Ge-stell*, is that this opening is *not* preserved, that on the contrary it is closed off, subjugated to the same blind, or rather deaf urge to control even itself. To the *Ge-stell* belongs also the concealment of its own condition, and the position of man within it. In this situation, where man seeks to expand his reach over the earth, and become its master, he no longer sees himself, and his own inclination. He never confronts himself, as Heidegger writes, *nunca pode encontrar-se.* The *Ge-stell* does not only constitutes a mode of disclosing the world, it also implies a mode *próprio de desencobrimento,* of disclosing it, so as to conceal that this disclosing is taking place. To put it in other words: it tends to hide from itself its nature of being a possible disclosure, and it mistakes itself for the world as it is in itself.

As Hölderlin has written, and as Heidegger quotes in several of his later lectures, "close to the danger is also the saving." What then is the *saving* here? The saving is the opening of the essence, the bringing out of the essence of that which is happening, so as to establish a freer relation to it.

All of this means that technology, in its essence as *Ge-stell*, is fundamentally ambiguous, as Heidegger explicitly also recognizes toward the end of the text, *de grande ambigüidade.* For in its very nature as disclosure, lies the threat as well as the saving power, both *o irresistível da dis-posição e a resistência do que salva*. They are both aspects of the same constellation, as stars moving over the sky, which is another metaphor used here. The essence of technology contains the threat of making everything part of the commanding, but it also holds the key to precisely a *Besinnung*, which at this stage in the Portuguese text is translated in yet a third way, as *consideração do sentido*. This mode of relating to the world is also made possible by opening ourselves to that other side of the ambiguous technology, which, as we have seen earlier in the course, was contained already in the word itself, *techne*. So here in the very last lines of the text, art, *Kunst*, *arte*, is called upon again, to release us from the other side of its own common heritage, *techne* as control and as demand.

Here we can thus see also how the two lines in Heidegger's thinking of *techne* that we have followed in our lectures, come together, in an opening toward that will enable a future, but only on the condition that art is not understood in its modern sense of aesthetics, of that which produces the beautiful for its consumption. Only by preserving its relation to the shining and the appearing, to truth, can art serve as guide towards what he is seeking. In this process we should not simply think that we will be saved from the dangers and miseries of modern technology by becoming artists, or consumers of art. For art in itself is not something to which we have a clear and simple relation today. In the world of technology art also has a stable place. Yet if we are able to remain in the philosophical, questioning, and reflecting attitude, art will also have to be estranged, become strange, in order to – possibly – be recovered, as we also seek to recover the essence of philosophical reflection as such.

Negative Responsibility

Marcia Sá Cavalcante Schuback

> "Nothing" is the force
> That renovates the world.[1]
> *Emily Dickinson*

In *Donner la mort*, Jacques Derrida presents Jan Patočka as a philosopher of responsibility. In his readings, Derrida is looking for the heretical (or un-thought) meaning of Patočka's essays on the philosophy of history. Heresy as the un-thought, or the un-thought as heresy is what seems to seduce Derrida's to the text. Derrida attributes the heretical meaning, that is to say, the meaning of the heretical in these essays to Patočka's discovery of the knot of "orgiastic irresponsibility" living as a secret within responsibility. Orgiastic irresponsibility appears here as the secret force of responsibility. Responsibility awakens by means of incorporating, repressing and disciplining this "orgiastic irresponsibility," that is to say, this secret. Derrida listens to the question of responsibility presented in the *Heretical Essays* with Heideggerian ears – or, to put it more correctly, with ears used to interpreting Heidegger in a certain way. These ears listen to Heidegger's *Being and Time* as a treatise about the awakening of the "becoming oneself," that is, about the becoming of the subject as *Dasein*, understood as the birth of freedom, authenticity and the proper – in short, as the birth of existential responsibility. Derrida reads and listens to Patočka as a modulation of this understanding of the existential analytic of *Being of Time*, a modulation that may "correct" improprieties of Heidegger's presumed search for the proper and the authentic. He reads the

---

1. Emilie Dickinson, *The Complete Poems*, ed. Thomas H. Johnson (Boston/ Toronto: Little Brown, 1960), 650.

43

secret of responsibility in Patočka as the two-sided story of the genesis of egological subjectivity through the incorporation, repression and discipline of "orgiastic irresponsibility," the expansion of diurnal responsibility through the contraction of nocturnal irresponsibility. Derrida reads and listens to Patočka as a philosopher of transcendental subjectivity, a philosopher to whom the awakening of responsibility can only be understood as a certain way of self-relation, namely, as reflective self-relation, as self-reflection in which self-transcendence takes place. The awakening of responsibility can therefore only be understood here as the awakening of philosophical consciousness. Responsibility is presented not only as a matter for philosophical discussion but as the core of the philosophical attitude. Derrida will insist that there is no responsibility without dissidence and an inventive rupture with tradition, authority, orthodoxy, rules and doctrines, following the path of tradition in which philosophy assumes for itself a dissident responsibility towards history. A lot can be said about the way Derrida presents and interprets Patočka's heretical essays and a lot, too, about the way in which he assumes the secret meaning of responsibility in his readings of Patočka. I will leave these questions for another occasion and move away in the sense of putting into question the underlying conviction of Derrida's readings that the question of responsibility in Patočka is connected to "the very idea of a genesis or a history of egological subjectivity."[2] The purpose of the following notes is to indicate that for Patočka responsibility is neither a concept, nor responsibility for and of a concept. Responsibility is rather a task, the task of transcending subjectivity as self-relation and philosophy as self-reflection. Responsibility appears then as the very task of "a-subjective phenomenology."[3] It appears as negative responsibility; or more precisely formu-

2. Jacques Derrida, "Donner la mort," in *L'Ethique du don* (Paris: Métaillé/ Transitions, 1992), 37. Eng. transl. *The Gift of Death,* trans. David Willis (Chicago: University of Chicago Press, 1995), 19.
3. Jan Patočka, *Papiers phénoménologiques* (Grenoble: Jerôme Millon, 1995), 288.

lated, it appears as responsibility *for* the negative.

A-subjective phenomenology takes as its point of departure a critique of Husserl's subjective phenomenology. The *alpha privativum* in the expression "a-subjective" has several meanings. One of them – which can be considered the propaedeutic meaning – is that of a denegation of Husserl's subjective phenomenology. It is a denegation rather than a negation insofar as the hyphen in the term regards and sustains a tension with subjective phenomenology, with subjectivity understood as self-relation and self-reflection. Transcendental subjectivity cannot be overcome from out of a philosophical position as if it could be eliminated or sublimated through philosophical ordinances or dictates. Overcoming subjectivity is, for Patočka as much as for Heidegger, a historical task; and, as such, it becomes a question at the point at which epochal and existential history can no longer be separated from one another.

Patočka's critique of Husserl's subjective phenomenology can be summarized in his critique of the way the latter grasps "appearing as such" and hence the very meaning of phenomenology. Patočka considers that the most radical discovery of Husserl's phenomenology was already the idea of a "transcendental a-subjective phenomenology," understood as the discovery of the "field of the self-showing" (*sich-Zeigen*),[4] which Husserl discovers but also loses. The discovery that Husserl made was the field of the showing itself from itself in the different modes in which something appears for someone, that is, in experience. This discovery was not about a new field of objects and objectivity unknown before, but rather about the field in which the difference between the showing itself and what is shown appears. It is the field of a difference that Heidegger conceived of and elaborated as "ontological difference" between Being and beings, and that Patočka will rephrase as the "phenomenological difference" between the appearing as such and appearances. Husserl

---

4. Jan Patočka, "Epoche et reduction," in *Qu'est-ce que la phenomenologie?* (Grenoble: Jerôme Millon, 1988), 257 ff.

discovered the field of self-showing, "the phenomenal sphere."
To quote Patočka: "Husserl discovered the phenomenal sphere,
the sphere of appearances in their appearing – something that
the tradition had never taken before into view when reconvert-
ing it into the structures of appearances in their particularity. In
an enterprise close to Descartes', Husserl aims to put this sphere
into relief and to secure it methodologically."[5] However, in expressing this discovery in terms of "self-appearing" and "self-
showing, (*sich-Zeigen*), Husserl somehow lost sight of his own
and most foundational discovery. As Patočka insists, although
"the (phenomenological) intention views the appearing as such
– the phenomenal sphere – it (this intention) remained circumscribed insofar as (Husserl) used terms coming from the sphere
of the subjective.[6] The terms of the subjective sphere are not
only the "ego" and "consciousness" or "self-consciousness" but
the very pronoun "self" active in the expressive "it-self." Placing
the accent on the *self* of self-appearing, Husserl remained – according to Patočka – a prisoner of the chains of the "self." This
is the core of Patočka's critique of the subjectivism of Husserl's
phenomenology.[7] Remaining too "subjectivistic," Husserl both
misses the "as such" of the appearing and the transformation of
the very understanding of human existence that derives from
a phenomenology of "appearing as such." Patočka will make a
similar critique of Heidegger's understanding of the field of "appearing as such" as "comprehension of being" from out the ontological difference, by considering that when Heidegger insists
on "Being itself," he also remains enchained in an understanding of Being as what is "itself." In that he is too non-subjectiv-
istic, Heidegger also falls into the chains of selfhood of Being

5. "Le subjectivisme de la phénoménologie husserlienne et la possibilité
    d'une phénoménologie a-subjective," in *Qu'est-ce que la phénoménologie?*, op.
    cit., 206.
6. Ibid. 207.
7. See particularly Patočka, J. "Le subjectivisme de la phénoménologie
    husserlienne et la possibilité d'une phénoménologie a-subjective" and
    "Le subjectivisme de la phénoménologie husserlienne et l'exigence d'une
    phénoménologie a-subjective," in *Qu'est-ce que la phénoménologie?*, 89-243.

itself. The central critical point is the "enigma" of the reflexive-pronoun, of the "self" in the expression "it-self," active in both Husserl's and Heidegger's ways of expressing the "as such" of appearing, the former in terms of *self-showing (sich-Zeigen)* and the latter as *Being itself (Sein selbst)*. Phrased as "self-showing," "what shows itself from itself," "the appearing as such" loses it intransitivity, its fundamental meaning as "gift" – "*Es gibt*," "*il y a*" – a gift without generosity, that is, not only without "the farce of giving and receiving"[8] as Samuel Beckett expressed it, but beyond the place from which the distinction between giving and receiving can be made. Phrased as "self-showing," the appearing "as such" becomes subjected to the identity of a self, to a meaning of being as what is itself according to itself, *to auto kath'auto*. Awareness of identity, the categorical act in which the identity of the "itself" is experienced in the "transparency of its opacity,"[9] exposes the ambiguity of the reflexive pronoun "it-self" that operates in the expression "showing itself from itself" and aims to grasp the field of the appearing as such, that is, the phenomenality of the phenomenon. In doing so, Husserl's and to a certain extent Heidegger's phenomenology both betrayed phenomenology.

In *Reflections on Europe*, Patočka affirms that "Husserl's project is grounded on the idea of the "*self-responsibility of knowledge*," knowledge acquired through intellectual life as grounded in self-understanding, rooted in self-relation."[10] Only from within the covering up of the phenomenological discovery of the appearing as such, as it is reconverted into self-appearing, can philosophy be defined as self-knowledge based on self-relation and in this sense as self-responsibility. Patočka will describe this reconversion, or betrayal of phenomenology in terms of the "will to self-responsibility." He says: "the will to self-responsibility would

8. Samule Beckett, "Masson," in *Proust and Three Dialogues with Georges Duthuit* (London: John Calder, 1999), 112.
9. Renaud Barbaras, *Le désir et la distance. Introduction à une phénoménologie de la perception* (Paris: Vrin, 1999), 82.
10. Jan Patočka, "Reflexion sur l'Europe," in *Liberté et sacrifice. Écrits politiques* (Grenoble: Jerôme Millon, 1990), 188.

have no meaning if there did not also exist the possibility of irresponsibility that manifests itself alongside the purely technical conception of science."[11] Philosophy is, for Husserl, self-responsability in the sense that it makes evident the irresponsibility of the modern meaning of science as irresponsibility towards self-appearing, that is, towards the phenomenal sphere. Philosophical self-responsibility arises for Husserl from self-knowledge, self-inquiry and self-relation, in which the meaning of what appears appears in the way in which *self-appearing* and *the appearing of the self* as personal-embodied existences relate to each other. In this Husserlian sense, philosophical self-responsibility or philosophy as self-responsibility is responsibility for "Being in it-self," for "things in them-selves" insofar as one becomes responsible for "being one-self." It means committing oneself in return to "Being in itself," to "things in themselves" in the sense that only in being oneself does it become possible to give an account of "being in itself," of "things in themselves." Self-responsibility here takes up the etymological sense of responsibility, an expression derived from *respondere* as a process of reference and self-reference, in which one renders the reckoning, makes an account and lays the grounds for ones' own being in Being itself.

Patočka's a-subjective phenomenology can be grasped in the way he brings self-appearing back to its original phrase, which reads: the "appearing as such." The phenomenological task assumed by Patočka is the one of bringing back phenomenology to the mode, to the "as such," "*als solche*" of the appearing. Indeed, phenomenology is thought as a return, a re-phrasing of "self-appearing" into "appearing as such," where the "self" becomes re-expressed as the "as such," into the modality of being. "As such," the appearing appears negatively. The appearing as such, in its mode, that is, in its *event*, appears as *non-appearance*, as *non-being, non-thingness, non-selfhood* or *non-selfness*. It does not appear "*as*" appearance, in that it has no appearance. It appears

11. Ibid.

"as such." This means that it appears without appearing *in* everything that appears. But insofar as the appearing as such is neither something that appears in itself – an appearance – nor something other than the appearance, than things, than something in "itself"; because the appearing "as such" *is* being and non-being at once, then its mode, its "as such" is neither identity nor difference, and even less indifference. Its modus is rather one of non-alterity, of *non-aliud*, an expression that Patočka borrows from a treatise by Nicolas of Cusa.[12] Understood in this manner, which for Patočka means experienced in this way, the *appearing as such* is in tension with everything that *appears in itself*, that is, as appearance. Carrying still further the distinction between "as such" and "in itself," it becomes possible to uncover another meaning of the "subjective," one that is no longer that of the "self-responsible rational subject" grounded in self-reflection and self-relation. "As such," the appearing does not appear, either for a constituted subject or for itself. It appears a-subjectively.

Patočka described this a-subjective meaning of the "subjective" as "a much simpler meaning." It is the meaning of the subjective as "ontological movement" or "movement of existence," which I would like to suggest to be understood as the simple meaning of the gerundive *is-being*. It is the meaning of a *sum* that exposes itself as what the Latin *sum* cannot fully express – the simple *existing* in its gerundive form. This other meaning of the subjective is "a-subjective" because it exposes the subjective as existence in its gerundive existing, as existing *in* existence, as moving in the movement of life, and not simply as existence *tout court*; it exposes the subjective as exposed and ek-static in the very movement of existence. Patočka's theory of the movements of ex-

---

12. Patočka translated Cusa's *De li non aliud* in Czech but the translation appeared under the name of J. Sokol, cf. Jan Patočka and Pavel Floss, *Mikuláš Kusánský* (Praha: Vyšehrad 2001), 123-243 [Floss, P. *Mikuláš Kusánský. Zivot a dílo* (Praha: Vyšehrad, 1977), 205-340]. For a very inspiring discussion about the world as the *non aliud* in Patočka, see Filip Karfík, "Die Welt als das *non aliud*," in *Unendlichwerden durch die Endlichkeit. Eine Lektüre der Philosophie Patočkas* (Würzburg: Königshausen & Neumann, 2008) 55-68.

istence is a reformulation of Heidegger's understanding of Being and of human existence as ek-static temporality, re-conceived in terms of movement in the event of its moving. Existence is ek-static in that it is existence in its gerundive existing, movement in the moving of the movements of life. Patočka will describe the is-moving of the movements of existence as *"energeia ateles,"* activity without direction, possibility for possibilities, neither self-relation nor relation to something other than itself; thus, here, the "self" and the "other" are nothing but moving movements. In relation to different philosophies of existence,[13] Patočka's theory of the three movements of human existence reformulates the meaning of existence in showing how existence is ontological movement, in the sense that it only exists 'existingly', gerundively, so to speak. Ontological movement, being as movement, says movement in the *meanwhile* of its moving, says the event of moving. In its meanwhile-ness, in the event of its moving, movement is both always already moving and still to begin to move. In the moving, movement is past, present and future at once without dissolving these differential ecstasies into the void of a permanent, non-moving eternity.

The three movements of human existence describe analytically what is to be understood as intertwined. Patočka affirms the analogy with Heidegger's description of the ek-static temporality of Being and of *Dasein.*[14] It would be mistaken to read the three movements as progression or edification of states in life. The linearity of the movements presented by Patočka corresponds to the linearity of time in talking about time. How, then, to say the contemporaneity of temporal ecstasies in words without impoverishing them into linearity and successiveness? Moreover, which word would be able to say the time that is needed to say time? Patočka describes the three movements in

13. Cf. Patočka's critique of existentialism in his "Zweifel am Existentialismus," in *Ausgewählte Schriften: Die Bewegung der menschlichen Existenz,* ed. K. Nellen, J. Němec a I. Šrubař (Stuttgart: Klett-Cotta, 1991), 509–514 [přel. P. Sacher (v. 1991/2)].
14. See also Paul Ricoeur's Preface to the *Heretical Essays in the Philosophy of History.* Op.cit.

the following way. The first movement is the one of acceptance, of throwing down roots and anchoring existence in the earth of the world. The "coming to a home" that constitutes the main dimension of this first movement, describes more than anything else a being with others. Community and society appear here as the true meaning of "home"; home, thus, is essentially "protection."[15] Human existence is movement and not a thing in movement: it is existing and only therefore can it search for "home," for "rest" and "protection." It is, from the beginning, displaced and un-placed. The old metaphors of human existence as journey and trip, as existence in exile from God, show the being already in movement of existence, shows it as moving-together-with-others, that is to say, as e-motion and co(m)-motion. The second movement corresponds to the attempt to reproduce existence for the sake of remaining in existence. It is the movement that moves against movement: life becomes the means of survival, a kind of dispersive and fragmentary movement, in which movement flies from movement. It is the movement of escaping from movement, a will to remain existent and not to continue the moving movement of existing. It is the movement of encapsulation in a "self," in a time, in a space, the movement towards reification and instrumentalization of existence, of an ontic separation between self and others. The third movement is the movement that shakes movement itself. It is the shaking movement where every home and ground, every selfhood and otherness, every determination loses ground. Movement moving towards non-movement, movement fleeing from movement, movement shaking movement: this is a possible description of the three movements from out the moving of movement.

The transparency that emerges in the third movement is what I am calling the transparency of the *gerundive existing* as

15. In Portuguese, there is a beautiful word for protection, meaning a piece of cloth that warms, a sweater or scarf, which is *agasalho*. This word, used already by Camões, has a Celtic-German origin, coming from *gesell, Gesell-schaft*.

moving ground and therefore as what has no ground, no cause, no "why." The grammatical expression "gerundive," *gerundivus modus*,[16] here used by Patočka, comes from the verb *gero*, meaning to carry, to bear and has several derivations such as gesture and gestation, (having similar connotations to the German *gebären*). It unfolds a semantic of *the possible as what is actual as possibility* and not as actualized possibility. The carrying and bearing is itself moving and unstable, as in gestation, and not the solidity and stability of a soil or ground. The distinction between *moving ground* and *solid ground* describes the distinction between *a-subjective existing* and *subjective existence*. In its gerundive form, that is from a grammatical point of view, 'existing' is a verb form that expresses the meanwhile-ness of an action as its ground; it says the impossibility of separating the before from the after, the here from the there. It says the "nudity of existence," as Patočka explains, quoting Paul Valéry, who writes of "Life entirely nude, life regarding itself clearly, having no other substance than life itself and neither a further ground than the clairvoyance of the living being."[17] The groundlessness of the gerundive meanwhile-ness of existing as moving movement defines the 'such' of 'appearing as such'.

The third movement is the moving in which human existence discovers itself as existing in the gerundive mode; that is, in groundlessness, pure transcendence, as the freedom of negativity. But this is possible not only because existence is shaken, but also because the points of reference of and for existence – the very "ground" upon which existence moves suffers a seismic upheaval. The third movement, the movement of losing every stability of a "self," either one's own or another's, is the move-

16. Derived by grammarians from the passive future participle *gerundus*: the mode of an action to be accomplished.
17. Jan Patočka, "La position de la philosophie dans et en dehors du monde," in *Liberté et Sacrifice*, op. cit., 21. For the original quote by Paul Valéry: "La vie toute nue, quand elle se regard clairement," "qui n'a d'autre substance que la vie elle-même et d'autre cause seconde que la clair-voyance du vivant," see Paul Valéry, "L'âme et la danse," in *Oeuvres* (Paris: Gallimard, La Pléiade, vol II, 1960), 167.

ment in which the relation between man and Being, human existence and the totality of life, human movements in the moving of the appearing as such appears in its "nudity" insofar as here, both movement and its grounds are shaken. In this shaking, both movement and ground appear as groundlessness. What becomes evident here is that neither the objective nor the subjective meanings of movement can ground the groundlessness of moving as such, the gerundive event of moving. It is the third movement that shows how the two other movements are not "stages" in self-development but dimensions of this gerundiveness – so to speak – of the is-moving.

In *Notes on the Pre-history of the Science of Movement: World, Earth, Heaven and the Movement of Human Life,*[18] Patočka describes how objective determinations of movement pre-suppose – without acknowledging – ontological movement, that is, appearing as moving. Instead of opposing objective accounts of movement to a phenomenological first person, embodied-perspective experience of movement, Patočka shows the point in which both descriptions encounter and disengage. What gathers both positions together is the fact that both share the evidence of movement as bodily experience. But what both seem to forget is how movement is bodily not by being "self-motional," auto-kinetic but by being movement on a ground, and therefore a relation to an archi-point of reference, the earth. However, in contrast to Husserl's discussions of the archi-earth that "does not move,"[19]

---

18. Jan Patočka, "Notes sur la pré-histoire de la science du mouvement: le monde., la terre, le ciel et le mouvement de la vie humaine," trans. Erika Abrams in *Le monde naturel et le mouvement de l'existence humaine* (Dordrecht: Kluwer Academic Publishers, 1988), 3-13.

19. Edmund Husserl, "Grundlegende Untersuchungen zum phänomenologischen ursprung der Räumlichekti der Natur." First published in Marvin Farber, ed., *Philosophical Essays in Memory of Edmund Husserl* (New York: Praeger, 1968). This manuscript was written between 7th and 9th May 1934. At the envelope where the manuscript was kept by Husserl, the following comment was written: "*Umsturz der kopernikanischen Lehre in der gewöhnlichen weltanschaulichen Interpretation. Die Ur-Arche Erde bewegt sich nicht. Grundlegende Untersuchungen zum phänomenologischen Ursprung der Körperlichkeit der Räumlichkeit der Natur im ersten naturwissenschaftlichen Sinne, Alles notwendige Anfangsuntersuchungen.*"

the ground of all grounds, the archi-ground of earth *is* moving. For Patočka, the earth does move and moves all the time. It moves insofar as it nourishes, cares for and protects life. The earth moves because it is generative, gerundive and therefore a moving ground. In this sense, "earth's horizontal reigns over the vertical of life;"[20] and therefore "we are modifications and parts of earth."[21] However, Patočka also shows that the earth is not the only point of reference; it is the nearest and most accessible point of reference but not the only one. Thus, there is still heaven and the realm of light and obscurity, stars and constellations. Indeed, it is *in-between* earth and heaven that the movements of human existence discover their ground and reference. We feel, here, the resonance of Kant's words in the *Grundlegung zur Metaphysik der Sitten*, which Patočka referes to in *Negative Platonism*, saying that the "critical situation" of philosophical life is that of a life "having no point of reference or attachment, neither in heaven nor in the earth."[22] For Patočka this does not mean however that the only point of reference and attachment would be reason itself, as Kant's argument suggests. It means, quite differently, that the in-between of earth and heaven emerges here as the groundless ground of every movement. In-between earth and heaven, human existence is oscillation not between places but "in itself." The "self" is in itself "oscillation," a *seism*.

As the movement in which the "self" loses itself and not merely as a state of *self-lessness,* the third movement makes evident not only human existence as existing, but also discovers that earth and heaven are moving firmaments and hence that they themselves have a "*trans,*" for they are a moving beyond. As Patočka observes: "there is nothing that could propitiate for existence a definitive reference and rootedness, a final goal, an

---

20. Patočka, "Notes sur la pré-histoire de la science du mouvement: le monde, la terre, le ciel et le mouvement de la vie humaine," op. cit.
21. Ibid.
22. Patočka, "Le Platonisme négatif," in *Liberté et Sacrifice*, op. cit., 97.

always valuable "because."[23] The third moment is the avalanche of earth and heaven within existence, the avalanche in which the existing of existence becomes transparent, apparent throughout every plan of existence.[24] Here the "nudity" of existence emerges in its own nudity as much as earth appears as the "giver of every "where" and heaven as the "giver of every when."[25] This trembling, shaking or seismic upheaval of earth and heaven shakes not only existence but what renders different ways of existing separated existences. Shaken, here, is the strangeness of the concept of otherness, the absoluteness of this impression of otherness as something constituted in itself in confrontation with a selfhood in itself. This impression of absolute strangeness, at the basis of Husserl's concept of intersubjectivity can only be left behind, according to Patočka, through a trembling of earth and heaven in which the movement of existence that separated common existing in separated existences receives another orientation, the orientation from and towards a listening to the gerundive form of existing, to the *without grounds for existing as the only ground of existence.* In this experience, existence discovers itself as dis-oriented, unstable – a vertigo of uprootedness.[26]

If the entire project of Husserl's phenomenology is grounded on the idea of "self- responsibility," as referred to before, and if "responsibility" is pronounced in the whole history of Western philosophy as another expression for self-reflection grounded

23. Patočka, "Notes sur la pré-histoire de la science du mouvement: le monde., la terre, le ciel et le mouvement de la vie humaine," op. cit.
24. Patočka gives some literary examples of this, so to speak, cosmic avalanche in a text called "What is existence?." Here he discusses, if only briefly, Faulkner's novel *Wild Palms*, Thomas Mann's *Doktor Faust* and Dostoievskji's *The Idiot*. See "Qu'est'ce que l'existence?," in *Le monde naturel et le mouvement de l'existence humaine*, op. cit., 243-265.
25. Patočka, "Notes sur la pré-histoire de la science du mouvement: le monde, la terre, le ciel et le mouvement de la vie humaine," op. cit., 7.
26. See Patočka's fragment published as Annexe to "L'espace et sa problematique," in *Qu'est'ce que la phenomenologie?*, op. cit., 303-316. Here Patočka shows quite clearly that as ontological movement, human existence is not spatial for it is always situated in the own body and the body in places, but for it is rather than situated oriented resp. disoriented. The main determination of space is discussed here in terms of orientation rather than of positions.

on self-relation, either in the sense of subjective or inter-subjective existence, what can be said of "responsibility" from out of an a-subjective existing? In other words: what to say about responsibility when the ground of human existence appears as nothing but existing in its gerundive event, that is, as moving ground, as un-grounding and loss of grounds? And furthermore, how is it possible to conceive philosophical life when the ground of existence appears as existing as such, that is, existing without grounds?

Spiritual life, "life in amplitude" and "life in problematicity," e.g. philosophical life, is life capable of *finding* unity without having stable and solid ground: this is Patočka's claim. It is not defined as life in the search for harmony and for solid grounds. It is life capable of finding unity in existing as such, that is, in the groundlessness of its gerundive way of being: "life (in its) possible unity without firm grounds is nevertheless capable of overcoming absolute negativity, nihilism, and negative skepticism."[27] Philosophical life as life in amplitude and not in harmony – spiritual life and not merely intellectual life – is life capable of *finding* unity in the absence of solid grounds and not life grounded on solidity. Patočka does not say life as it is capable of grounding unity but rather as it is a *finding* of unity *in* groundlessness. A first meaning of a-subjective responsibility can be formulated, then, as responsibility for the possibility of finding unity in the gerundive groundlessness of existing. This responsibility can no longer be described as affirmative responsibility in the sense of a responsibility that affirms a firm ground for the autonomy of a theoretical and a practical subject. It is a negative responsibility, not in the sense that the subject denies or withdraws from responsibility in letting the self-movement of reality be. It is negative responsibility in the sense that it is responsibility for the possibility of finding unity in groundlessness. *It is responsibility for the possibility of responsibility and in this sense a responsibility for the negative.*

27. *Le monde naturel et le mouvement de l'existence humaine*, op. cit., 253.

Patočka connected this responsibility of the possibility of re-sponsibility with the experience of sacrifice, which in its Czech and German expressions says the offering gesture rather than the victimization. The offering is related to an opening, an opening for receiving the avalanche of heaven and the shaking of earth within existence, for receiving the presence of the night and of the orgiastic, as the naked presence of a generating loss. This is what is at stake in concrete experiences of exile, which *Patocka* not really discusses but opens up for a further meditation when he deals with the question of *dissidence*. The sacrifice described in dissident existence should be understood from out of the possibility of finding unity in groundlessness. The third move-ment shows the gerundive and groundless existing as a dissident movement, in the very etymological sense of the word, namely as *dis-sidere*, which means to un-settle not merely positions and situations but orientations and feelings, in so far as they are also a dissenting. Patočka discusses the birth of the "consciousness of responsibility" recalling Socrates' famous phrase: "it is better to suffer injustice than to commit injustice.[28] He equates the "con-sciousness of responsibility" with a "refusal of privileges"[29] and "the interior signification of extreme sacrifice." Extreme sacri-fice means sacrificing for no-thing, breaking down the logic of the use and abuse of sacrifice – in this question he is very close to Georges Bataille. Dis-sidence describes the possibility of finding unity in disorientation and uprootedness. A dis-sident is one who is settled in a hyphen, insofar as he/she is no longer settled in a former orientation but is not yet settled in a new one. A dis-sident is a life that is re-moved from a place before, yet never arriving at a place that lies before. It is a life moved otherwise, emotionally transformed, moved in another orientation rather than in a new orientation. It is life in exile discovering life as ex-ile. A-subjective responsibility is responsibility for the negative, in the sense that it is *responsive* and *corresponsive* to this possibil-

28. Plato. *Gorgias. eipon egó pou en tois émprosthen to adikéin tou adikeisthai kákion einai* (473a- 475e).
29. Patočka, "L'idéologie et la vie dans l'idée," in *Liberté et sacrifice*, op. cit., 47.

ity of finding unity in groundlessness. In this sense, responsability is a kind of re-conducting oneself to the nudity of existence, to its "without reason" in order to be oriented by ontological dis-orientation. This becomes very concrete in experiences of exile, both dissident and dissenting, where the subjective is attuned untimely to the gerundive existing, with the "as such" rather than with the "in itself." Indeed, the despair and quest for "subjectivity," so acute in experiences of exile – who I am? I am no longer the same, I will never become another – does not show the evidence of the self but exactly the contrary, namely, the groundless of the self. Patočka left some notes for a phenomenology of life after death,[30] where we can find some inspiring fragments for an understanding of what I am proposing to call "a-subjective negative responsibility" as a way to think with Patočka the question of responsibility. Showing that living being is indeed always a life after the death of others, living existence is not only co-existent with other living beings but also with no longer living beings; if living existence is co-existence in that there is always possibility of reciprocity, of being-with, co-existentiality with beings that are no longer living – that is, with the dead – is co-existentiality without reciprocity; a-subjective and negative responsibility is responsibility for being with and for being without; indeed, it is responsibility for being with the without and for being without a with. A-subjective negative responsibility is responsive and co-respondence to the being-with- the without and without the with.

Considering a-subjective existence as shaken existence, attuned to the gerundive existing – with the "as such" of existing and not with "in itself" – an existence experienced on the edge in dissident and exilic situations, and in the awareness of living existence as life after the death of others, philosophical existence is existence existing from out the negative force of the idea. The negative force of the idea is a force of "dis-objectivation" and of

---

30. Patočka, "Phenomenologie de la vie après la mort," in *Papiers phénoménologiques*.

"dis-realization," from which "all our capacities to fight against subjugation to "reality tout court" arise.[31] Idea is negative in the sense that it dis-realizes reality, dis-objectifies objectivity, opening a tear or a rip, a *chorismos* within, reality, within existence. The negative force of the idea is *chorismatic* and not charismatic. What it opens, what it tears apart, is the "tacit presence," as Patočka says, of the non-being of being, of the non-sensible of the sensible, of the unapparent way the appearing appears. In its negative, chorismatic force, the idea evidenciates the "mystery of evidence." Dis-realizing and dis-objectifying reality, the idea transcends the real. The idea is not transcendent in relation to reality, but it makes evident the non-being of the movement of being, that is, that the movement of being cannot be grasped as beings are grasped. Understood in this sense, the idea is neither object nor concept, overcoming every being, whether objective or subjective. It is the modus in which totality is given; totality is given *in* not being given as either objective or subjective. The negative and *chorismatic* force of the idea in human existence is the "mirror" of the unapparent modus of the appearing as such. In his notes towards a phenomenology of the appearing as such, Patočka will prefer to describe the human movement of existence as a "mirror" rather than as an image of the negative modus in which the appearing appears as such, withdrawing itself in what appears.[32] In the mirror of the gerundive groundless existing coming to the edge in human existence, the a-subjective structure of the appearing as such "appears." Experienced as the freedom of negativity, philosophical life is responsive correspondence to the appearing as such, to the modus of the appearing as appearing unapparently and hence negatively in everything that appears. As responsive correspondence to the negative modus of the appearing, philosophy is negative responsibility. It is responsibility for negativity. In "What is phenomenology?,"

---

31. See Patočka, "L'ideologie et la vie dans l'idée" and "Platonisme négatif," in *Liberté et sacrifice*, op. cit.
32. Jan Patočka, *Vom Erscheinen als solchen. Texte aus dem Nachlaß* (Frieburg: Karl Alber, 2000).

where philosophical life is described as a "force of negativity," the force of the *epokhé*, e.g. of detaching from thingness towards non-thingness, Patočka will rephrase responsibility as Über-Antwortung, literally "over-responsibility" (instead of over-determination), "*remise*" in Erika Abrams' French translation, a giving back. Über-Antwortung, over-responsibility means here a saying back towards, a response to gerundive existing that is already its own echo – something like a listening to the ground-less ground of existing. Formed in analogy to Über-setzung, translation, Über-antwortung could be understood as the translation of responsibility into listening response and correspondence to gerundive existence.

Association in Husserl and Freud – Passivity and the Unconscious

Nicholas Smith

> Psychoanalytic research [...] seeks merely to uncover connections by tracing that which is manifest back to that which is hidden.
> *Freud*

> Psychology is constantly involved in this great process of development, involved, as we have seen, in different ways; indeed, psychology is the truly decisive field. It is this precisely because, though it has a different attitude and is under the guidance of a different task, its subject matter is universal subjectivity, which in its actualities and possibilities is one.
> *Husserl*

1. Introduction

The meeting between phenomenology and psychoanalysis may well, at first sight, represent something of an odd encounter between a clinical practice and a theory of the constitution of the world.[1] But as soon as one takes a closer look, it becomes clear that it instead makes up something of a hidden nexus of central parts of post war philosophy. Thus the philosophies of Lacan, Merleau-Ponty, Lyotard, Fanon, Derrida, Irigaray, Kristeva and Butler, for instance, are inconceivable without taking this dual optics – dispersed over many different registers – into account. This is not to say that these are thinkers that subscribe to a general program (of, say "the unconscious" and "intentionality")

---

1. This text is a revised version of a chapter in my book *Towards a Phenomenology of Repression: A Husserlian Reply to the Freudian Challenge* (Stockholm: Acta Universitatis Stockholmiensis, 2010).

since it is often as much a critique of these concepts that is at stake as an acceptance of them. It is probably more appropriate to see it as a sign of the inherent potential of these traditions that these later thinkers have found so many different approaches and contexts in which to put these concepts to work.

But if that is so, then a question arises: where do psychoanalysis and phenomenology really meet? That is to say, what is the philosophical connection between these two traditions that from the outset could make their meeting into something more than external contingency? Is there a deeper link between them that goes beyond the level of a piecemeal sharing of concepts (consciousness, the unconscious, affection, repression, inhibition, etc.) and that reaches into their inner, functioning movements? I will try to respond to these questions by looking at the phenomenon of *association* as it functions in Freud's psychoanalytical method and Husserl's genetic phenomenology. Additionally, as a secondary aim, this will provide a clearer picture of what lies behind the contemporary situation, even though the concept of association may not necessarily play a central role for the thinkers previously mentioned. Freud, it will be recalled, advised his patients "to refrain from any conscious reflection and to abandon themselves, in a state of quiet concentration, to following the ideas which occurred to them spontaneously (involuntarily) – 'to skim off the surface of their consciousness'."[2] Given that Freudian psychoanalysis is a philosophy of the unconscious, of what happens beyond the reach of the active I, such a link between psychoanalysis and phenomenology must be sought in the domain of what Husserl calls the "passive I."[3]

2. "Short account of psychoanalysis [1923]," trans. James Strachey, in *Historical and Expository Works on Psychoanalysis*, Penguin Freud Library vol. 15, ed. James Strachey and Albert Dickson (Hammondsworth: Penguin Books, 1986), 166. Henceforth cited as PFL 15.

3. See *Ideen zu einer reinen Phänomenologie und phänomenologischen Philosophie. / Zweites Buch, Phänomenologische Untersuchungen zur Konstitution*, Hua IV, ed. Marly Biemel (Den Haag: Nijhoff, 1952), §54, 213 (henceforth cited as Hua IV, *Ideas II*) and *Späte Texte über Zeitkonstitution (1929-1934): die C-Manuskripte*, Husserliana Materialien 8, ed. Dieter Lohmar (Dordrecht:

'Passivity' can mean a lot of things – organic bodily processes such as the movement of blood in my arteries and veins,
mere sensible affection as opposed to active understanding, involuntary bodily movement, sleep, actions based on habit etc.
– but the sense that is primarily discussed here is another one.
In order to outline what passivity means in this context, I will
take my cue from Husserl's genetic phenomenology, which can
be said to be "explanatory" in contradistinction to static analyses which are "descriptive."[4] Genetic phenomenology discloses
the intentional processes that are operative without our being
aware of them, processes that necessarily lie behind every active process (perception, judgment etc.). Instead of focusing on
the static act-object correlation (as in *Logical Investigations* or
Ideas I), genetic analysis opens up the inner temporality of the
constitutive process, showing that here one finds not a chaos of
sense impressions but instead 'eidetic laws' or rules.[5] All activity
of consciousness is based on and presupposes a passivity which
"gives" or "pre-constitutes" that which is later taken up in consciousness:

> Passivity is what is in itself first because all activity es-
> sentially presupposes a foundation of passivity as well as
> an objectlike formation that is already pre-constituted in

Springer, 2006), nr. 21, 98 (henceforth cited as HuMat 8). The english
translation of Hua IV(*Ideas Pertaining to a Pure Phenomenology and to a
Phenomenological Philosophy, Second Book: Studies in the Phenomenology of Constitution*, trans. Richard Rojcewicz and André Schuwer, Collected Works,
vol. 3 [The Hague: Kluwer Academic Publishers, 1989] is henceforth cited
as CW 3.

4. See *Analysen zur passiven Synthesis: Aus Vorlesungs- und Forschungsmanuskrip-
ten (1918-1926)*, Hua XI, ed. Margot Fleischer (Den Haag: Nijhoff, 1966),
340. Henceforth cited as Hua XI. In english: *Analysis Concerning Passive
and Active Syntheses. Lectures on transcendental logic*, Collected Works, Vol. 9,
trans. Anthony Steinbock (Dordrecht: Kluwer Academic Publishers, 2001),
henceforth cited as CW 9.

5. See *Cartesianische Meditationen und Pariser Vorträge*, Hua I, ed. Stephan
Strasser (Den Haag: Nijhoff, 1963), 38f (henceforth cited as Hua I) and
HuMat 8, nr. 13, 41f. The english translation of Hua I cited is *Cartesian
Meditations: An Introduction to Phenomenology*, trans. Dorion Cairns (The
Hague: Nijhoff, 1969).

it. Thus, this also holds for the spontaneous accomplish-
ments of genuine *logos*.[6]

It is in a philosophy of passivity that Husserl and Freud really
meet, sketching out different parts of it from their divergent
perspectives. Whereas Husserl started out trying to explain the
constitution of logical and mathematical objects, and from there
on expanded his project to a general theory of sense perception
and then the constitution of the world, all from the point of
view of consciousness, Freud worked from the opposite direction and sought almost one-sidedly to explain the workings of
the unconscious as the source behind psychic and bodily suffering. Although Husserl in later texts (from the 1920's onwards)
moved in the direction of a "phenomenology of the so-called
unconscious," and Freud more and more came to emphasize the
necessary "communication" between the unconscious and the
conscious systems, neither of them reach sufficiently far into
passivity by themselves.[7] It is only when the results of the two
are combined that the contours of a new philosophy of passivity
begins to take shape, as one of the most important contributions to 20th century philosophy.[8]

6. Edmund Husserl, *Aktive Synthesen: Aus der Vorlesung "Transszendentale
Logik" 1920/21. Ergänzungsband zu "Analysen zur passiven Synthesis,"* Hua
XXXI, ed. Roland von Breeur (Dordrecht: Kluwer Academic Publishers,
2000), 3f (henceforth cited as Hua XXXI) and *Analysis Concerning Passive
and Active Syntheses. Lectures on transcendental logic*, Collected Works, Vol. 9,
trans. Anthony Steinbock (Dordrecht: Kluwer Academic Publishers, 2001),
276 (henceforth cited as CW 9).
7. See Hua XI, § 33, 154 / CW 9, 201 and "The Unconscious" in *On metapsychology*, Penguin Freud Library vol. 11, trans. and ed. James Strachey and
Angela Richards (Harmondsworth: Penguin, 1984), 194 (henceforth cited
as PFL 11).
8. For Aristotle, the relation between activity and passivity (or *poïein* and
paschein) is often described as one where the former is the ideal: "for always the active is superior to the passive factor" (*De Anima*, tr. J.A. Smith,
430a). This hierarchy has remained unquestioned in much of the tradition since then. With Spinoza and Schelling, however, this changed. The
philosophical connections between Freud, Husserl and Spinoza on this
are as far as I know unexplored. The relation between Freud and Schelling
is discussed in Marquard, O. *Transzendentaler Idealismus, romantische
Naturphilosophie, Psychoanalyse*. Verlag für Philosophie Jürgen Dinter: Köln,
1987; the relation between Husserl and Schelling (unlike that of Husserl

What is at stake is a new way of conceptualizing distinctions that are fundamental to Husserl and Freud, and that have been labelled as 'metaphysical' by deconstructionist modes of thinking before the wager is known. 'Consciousness' and 'the unconscious', 'activity' and 'passivity' – these have often been construed as sterile oppositions, deadlocked by a critique that was ultimately insufficient to decide the matter at hand.⁹ What promises to change this is simply the bulk of new, relevant material being released from the Husserl-archives ("new" in the sense that it was not published at the time of the innovative and highly influential interpretations by Derrida, Merleau-Ponty and others).¹⁰ These texts lay the ground for a new interpretation of conscious, unconscious, and related concepts. Thereby a path is also opened for a new interpretation of Freud, from which standpoint the philosophical impact of his thinking can be reassessed.¹¹

If the strength of Freud's investigations lies above all in the case histories, where the minutiae of individual life are shown

and Fichte which, despite appearances, is probably less important) seems to be virtually unexplored. Neither Husserl nor Freud wants to reinstall the hierarchy in the opposite register, but instead to work out new ways of articulating the relation.

9. This is a common theme from many of Derrida's early works, but in all of the thinkers mentioned initially similar remarks are to be found.

10. Crucial for the theme discussed here are Hua XI; *Zur Phänomenologie der Intersubjektivität: Texte aus dem Nachlass*, Hua XIII-XV, ed. Iso Kern. (Den Haag: Nijhoff, 1973), henceforth cited as Hua XIII-XV; *Phantasie, Bildbewusstsein, Erinnerung: Zur Phänomenologie der anschaulichen Vergegenwärtigungen. Texte aus dem Nachlass (1898-1925)*, Hua XXIII, ed. Eduard Marbach (Den Haag: Nijhoff, 1980), henceforth cited as Hua XXIII; *Die Krisis der europäischen Wissenschaften und die transzendentale Phänomenologie: Ergänzungsband. Texte aus dem Nachlass 1934-1937*, Hua XXIX, ed. Reinhold N. Smid (Dordrecht: Kluwer Academic Publishers, 1993), henceforth cited as Hua XXIX; *Zur phänomenologischen Reduktion. Texte aus dem Nachlass (1926-1935)*, Hua XXXIV, ed. Sebastian Luft (Dordrecht: Kluwer Academic Publishers, 2002), henceforth cited as Hua XXXIV; *Einleitung in die Philosophie: Vorlesungen 1922/23*, Hua XXXV, ed. Berndt Goossens (Dordrecht: Kluwer Academic Publishers, 2003), henceforth cited as Hua XXXV; *Die Lebenswelt : Auslegungen der vorgegebenen Welt und ihrer Konstitution: Texte aus dem Nachlass (1916-1937)*, Hua XXXIX, ed. Rochus Sowa (Dordrecht: Springer, 2008), henceforth cited as Hua XXXIX; and HuMat 8.

11. In another text I hope to be able to present also an interpretation of Freud from this point of view. My approach here is admittedly one-sided.

to reflect repressed and unconscious conflicts, then it also be-comes clear that there is no strong theory of consciousness in these analyses that could help us understand *how* the uncon-scious is able to manifest itself for us. Freud accepted a prin-ciple (his 'phenomenological' principle) in his discussions of the unconscious that is essential in this context: that we can only come to know of the unconscious after it has been 'transposed' or 'translated' into something conscious.[12] But his metapsychol-ogy, which is essentially his philosophy of mind, does not con-tain a theory of consciousness that is on a par with his thinking of the unconscious. The result of this is a certain imbalance in Freud's texts conceived as a philosophy of mind.[13]

This text will investigate Freud's concept of "free associa-tion" from the perspective of Husserl's analysis of association, as it was developed in his transcendental genetic phenomenol-ogy. For Husserl, association is intimately connected to both in-ner time-consciousness and originary affection, since it has the specific function of bringing unity to the living present (*leben-dige Gegenwart*). I will try to show that Husserl's transcendental analysis of association in the ordinary sense (where it occurs between already constituted objects) can provide a clarification of Freud's theory of "free association," which is the "basic rule" of psychoanalysis.

The most prominent feature of association, essential for the purpose of clarifying the Freudian basic rule, concerns the ques-tion of freedom of association: how can a Husserlian analysis account for that? The operative force of association, according to Husserl, lies in its capacity for (ideally) unrestrained binding, and it's being completely indifferent as to the nature of what it combines. It can bring anything into connection with anything, and this is the reason why Husserl calls it the most universal

12. "The unconscious," PFL 11, 167.
13. It is not a critique of the clinical aspect of Freud's psychoanalysis that is presented here, but of its implicit philosophy. I call it 'philosophy of mind' here in a preliminary, non-committal sense since it is clearly not a phe-nomenology but posits its concepts according to other principles.

type of synthesis. Since association is essentially an expression of the fundamental openness of consciousness for the ever new, for the arrival of an event that it cannot foresee, it may justly be called synthesis in general:

> The universal principle of passive genesis, for the constitution of all objectivities given completely prior to the products of activity, bears the title association. Association, it should be clearly noted, is a matter of intentionality, descriptively demonstrable as that [...]. Association is a fundamental concept belonging to transcendental phenomenology [*ein transzendental-phänomenologischer Grundbegriff*] (and, in the psychological parallel, a fundamental concept belonging to a purely intentional psychology) (Hua I, CM § 39, p. 113f/Engl. p. 80).

Husserl's account of association undergoes considerable change from the early conception to his mature position where it becomes the most basic process in the phenomenology of passivity (as will be shown in the sections two and four), a change that is intimately connected with the expansion from static to genetic phenomenology. The analysis of temporality provides the phenomenology of the extended concept of consciousness with its "general form," but it also becomes clear that this only represents a first, non-independent part.[14] For the full constitution of time actually requires a phenomenology of originary *association*, in order to bring impressional-kinaesthetic consciousness in contact with inner time-consciousness, as Husserl repeatedly emphasizes in the 1920's.[15] As Holenstein puts it, the investiga-

14. *Erfahrung und Urteil: Untersuchungen zur Genealogie der Logik*, ed. Ludwig. Landgrebe (Hamburg: Meiner, 1989), 75f; english translation in *Experience and Judgment: Investigations in a Genealogy of Logic*, trans. James S. Churchill and Karl Ameriks (Evanston: Northwestern University Press, 1973), 73.
15. See the lectures on passive synthesis, Hua XI § 27, "The Presuppositions of Associative Synthesis. The Syntheses of Original Time-Consciousness" (and Beilage XII), and *Experience and Judgment*, § 16 "The field of passive pregivennesses and its associative structure." But as Landgrebe has pointed out, Husserl's earlier analysis of time-consciousness in the 1905 lectures

tion of inner time-consciousness comes to its "consummation only within a phenomenology of association."[16]

By founding association in inner time-consciousness and sensuous affectivity, it becomes possible to sketch out a plausible philosophical connection between two problematic poles of Freud's metapsychology: the 'shallowness' of free association and the 'depth' of the repressed unconscious.[17] This is something that Freud's account of free association presupposes but cannot explain, since there is no clear account of the relation between the unconscious (which is the repressed "source" of the associations), and the consciousness where the associations manifest themselves. The role of free association as indicating unconscious depths means that the investigation here encounters a decisive question: either it accepts the psychoanalytical unconscious as something that is essentially out of reach for phenomenology, or it argues that Husserl's extended concept of consciousness can actually accommodate and ultimately clarify the basic processes of the Freudian unconscious. There is actually a strong consensus that the dynamic, repressed unconscious is something inherently different from phenomenology. Derrida for instance argues in a programmatic text that the "language of presence or absence, i.e. the metaphysical discourse of phenomenology is inadequate" to grasp the "radical alterity" of the Freudian unconscious.[18] A proper understanding of association

was not integrated with the impressional-kinaesthetic syntheses: "Die passiven Synthesen des Zeitbewußtseins sind dort noch nicht mit den kinästhetischen Synthesen zusammengebracht. Versucht man dies aber, so ergibt sich: ohne Impressionen gibt es keine zeitkonstituierenden Leistungen und ohne Kinästhesen gibt es keine Impressionen"; see "Das Problem der passiven Konstitution" (1982), 81. See also Claesges's discussion of this in "Zeit und kinästhetisches Bewusstsein. Bemerkungen zu einer These Ludwig Landgrebes" (1983).

16. Elmar Holenstein, *Phänomenologie der Assoziation: Zu Struktur und Funktion eines Grundprinzips der passiven Genesis bei Edmund Husserl* (Den Haag: Nijhoff, 1972), 64.

17. For a discussion of the temporality of the unconscious, see my "The Temporality of Sexual Life in Husserl and Freud," in *Phenomenology of Eros,* ed. Jonna Bornemark and Marcia Sá Cavalcante Schuback (Stockholm: Södertörn University, 2012), 171-192.

18. See Jacques Derrida, "La différance," in *Marges de la philosophie* (Paris: Mi-

will therefore also be an important part in arguing against the "radical alterity" thesis, which I think is, fundamentally, just plain wrong.

In the second section (§ 2) I will present a brief outline of Husserl's theory of association. I will discuss the position of Holenstein's *Husserls Phänomenologie der Assoziation*, which is still the main work that engages psychoanalysis and phenomenology in a confrontation from the point of view of association.[19] In section three (§ 3) the basic outline of Freud's concept of free association, in its relation to unfreedom (which is a key here), will be presented, with a particular focus on the mediating function that association plays for him in the relation between consciousness and the unconscious. In the next section (§ 4), I will briefly trace the background of Husserl's phenomenology of association, before approaching the main theme, which concerns the reinterpretation of association as a properly transcendental phenomenon. Here it is the relation between association and the phenomenological reduction that is at stake, since it must be shown that we can gain access to association in its relation to the fundamental investigation of inner time-consciousness from within a methodologically clarified position. This theme will therefore connect with discussions in previous chapters of the living present. The final section (§ 5) will examine a problem that surfaced in Freud's theory concerning the relation between free associations occurring in the present and an unconscious order which determines them. What is the intentional relation between, on the one hand, present-day associative chains in

nuit, 1972), 21f; cf. *Glas* (Paris: Galilée, 1974), 215. According to Ricoeur's famous verdict, Husserl's phenomenology can only reach the level of the psychoanalytical preconscious, and it is therefore unable to thematize the dynamic unconscious; see *De l'interprétation: Essai sur Freud* (Paris: Seuil, 1965), 381f. This point has been repeated so often that it has become a dogma, but it is no longer valid.

19. Also the outstanding book by Bruce Bégout, *La généalogie de la logique: Husserl, l'antéprédicatif et le catégorial* (Paris: Vrin, 2000, which has one of the best discussions of association in Husserl, relies on Holenstein's (now outdated) account when it comes to the relation between phenomenology and psychoanalysis.

which "one calls attention to the other," as Husserl describes it in *Experience and Judgment*, and on the other hand the presence of a hidden nucleus around which this chain circles? This problem will be approached by means of Husserl's theory of sedimentation, which shows how a past lived experience that is now "dead," "unconscious" and no longer exerts an affective force, can still be awakened by means of association.

2. Association in Husserl

Beginning with Husserl, one may start by asking where association in the most fundamental sense takes place: is it at the higher level which we most commonly think of, such as the bringing back of a previous event, or is it in the first gathering of the affective-hyletic material into the sense fields, which then taken together make up the "perceptual field"? Or does the genuine associability of the psyche lie at an even more remote level of consciousness? There are two major but fundamentally different processes in conscious life that Husserl distinguishes here: first we have associations in the ordinary sense, that is to say reproductive and inductive association that lead to the awakening of memories and to expectations in the future (association here occurs between two or more already constituted objects).

But Husserl also operates with another concept of association, the so called "originary association" (*Urassoziation*), which accounts for the most basic organization of the impressional sphere within the living present. An important aspect of this is the fusing (*Verschmelzung*) of affective and preaffective unities within the living present, and originary association thus brings about a unification of sensuous affective life. In the lectures on transcendental logic, Husserl describes the process of "transition" of the awakened empty presentations which turns them into rememberings, and there presents the first level of this transition as that of the *Urassoziation*. Originary association, Husserl claims, is

that systematizing affective awakening that makes possible the object-like structure of the living present, all kinds of original syntheses proper to the formation of unity of manifolds (Hua XI, §38, 180/CW 9, 230).

If taken by itself, outside of its insoluble connection with originary association, originary affection would be a "pure chaos," a "maelstrom of data."[20] Originary association is thus something that is presupposed by all kinds of constitution of objects, and it can only be separated from originary affection by means of abstraction. Association for Husserl thus gradually gains a novel meaning and finally becomes a name for the "universal principle" which guides passive consciousness as such.[21] This means that it comes to stand in an "immediate connection with the teaching of original time-consciousness," and association can therefore be seen as that which at the lowermost level of genetic constitution "gives unity to our lives."[22] Due to this extension of the concept of association whereby "originary association" has come to cover the most important aspect of the phenomenon, Husserl often refers to this without the prefix "Ur-."[23]

Both of these paths will be employed in order to try to clarify

20. *Erfahrung und Urteil*, §16, 75/ *Experience and Judgment*, 72: "*Chaos, ein blosses 'Gewühl' von 'Daten'.*" Since Kant, the thought of sensuality as a pure chaos that must be schematized by means of the concepts of reason, has threatened the philosophical world like an attack by aliens from Mars: "so würde es möglich sein, daß ein Gewühle von Erscheinungen unsere Seele anfüllte, ohne daß doch daraus jemals Erfahrung werden könnte [...] mithin würde sie zwar gedankenlose Anschauung, aber niemals Erkenntnis, also für uns soviel als gar nichts sein" (KrV, A 111).

21. Hua I, CM, § 39.

22. See *Experience and Judgment*, § 16 where the link between inner time-consciousness as the formal framework and passive association as that which provides this structure with sensuous material is clearly established. For the first quotation, see Husserl's letter to Mahnke from 1926 in *Briefwechsel* Vol. I-X, Husserliana Dokumente 3, ed. Elisabeth Schuhmann and Karl Schuhmann (Dordrecht: Kluwer Academic Publishers, 1994), 453f (henceforth cited as HuDo 3; and for the second quotation see the manuscript D 14/12b: "Die ganze Einheit des Lebens ist Einheit aus universaler Verschmelzung, also aus Assoziation." Cf. also Hua XI, 405: "Synthesis in ihren verschiedenen Gestalten als universale Einigung des Lebens eines Ich = Assoziation im weitesten Sinn."

23. Whether it is association in the ordinary sense or "originary association" that is referred to is almost always discernible from the context.

Freud's account of free association. Husserl's transcendental account of association in the ordinary sense is able to do so by virtue of its being based on a thorough examination of the relations that hold between inner time-consciousness and sensuous affectivity. Thereby it makes it clear how that which Freud calls the surface-phenomenon of free association can be founded in an extended concept of consciousness, instead of bypassing the latter in favour of jumping directly from a "skimming of the surface" of consciousness to the deepest, most inaccessible repressed unconscious. For Freud's "free association" always presupposes precisely such an account of the relation between various levels of consciousness (or between consciousness and the unconscious). Here the investigation of Husserl's extended concept of consciousness will be put to the test, since his analysis of association does not acknowledge anything unconscious in the strong sense that many align with Freud. But Husserl's analysis of "originary association" will also be examined, since it shows how association in an extended sense also functions at the most fundamental level of conscious life. Thereby the phenomenological analysis of consciousness throws light on processes and structures that precede and make possible that which stands in focus for Freud, for whom free association is tantamount to "skim[ming] off the surface of consciousness."[24]

The analysis of originary associations is approached in the lectures on passive synthesis (in Hua XI), where they account for the unification of the temporal sequence, thereby making possible "the object like structure of the living present."[25] In other texts, there is an attempt to begin to account for this genetically deeper level of passive constitution by means of an analysis of association as an "intentionality of drives":

The association as association of drives. We not only have

---

24. See Freud's "Short Account of Psychoanalysis," PFL 15, 166.
25. Hua XI, §38, 180. For a recent, good discussion of association as it occurs mainly in these lectures, see Victor Biceaga, *The Concept of Passivity in Husserl's Phenomenology* (Dordrecht: Springer, 2010).

to do with a mere association of "ideas," but with an association of acquired drives and processes of drives that have a direction, of passive processes of striving and their immanent effects. It is not the mere "idea" of such a process that is awakened, but the I as a subject of drives and its drive itself that is awakened (A VII 13/20a).[26]

But it is above all in later texts, notably in the C-manuscripts, that a more precise account of this process is given as it occurs at the level of "temporalization" (*Zeitigung, Urzeitigung*).[27]

3. Association in Freud

It was only gradually that Freud came to see that free association was more than one way amongst others for the disclosure of the unconscious.[28] But by and large, Freud came to regard it as the "fundamental rule" (*Grundregel*) of the psychoanalytical praxis.[29] This method attempts a step beyond the associationist psychology of Wundt's school, in that Freud does not regard it as sufficient to account for the stream of associations merely by recourse to the concepts of contiguity and similarity, understood in a narrow sense.[30] For these theories do not take into

26. "Die Assoziation als Assoziation von Trieben. Wir haben es nicht mit einer bloßen Assoziation von 'Ideas' zu tun, sondern mit einer Assoziation erworbener Triebe und gerichteter Triebverläufe, von passiven Strebensverläufen und ihren immanenten Auswirkungen. Nicht die bloße 'Idee' eines solchen Verlaufs wird geweckt, sondern das Ich als Subjekt des Triebes und sein Trieb selbst wird geweckt" (A VII 13/20a [St. Märgen, Oktober 1921]).
27. See for instance HuMat 8, nr. 13, 29, 66, 79, 96.
28. In a text from 1910 ("Five Lectures On Psychoanalysis," § 3), Freud presents three ways of reaching the unconscious that are regarded as being of equal rank: free association, the interpretation of dreams and of parapraxes (in *Five lectures on psycho-analysis*, The standard edition of the complete psychological works of Sigmund Freud / Vol. 11, ed. and trans. James Strachey and Anna [Freud London : Hogarth Press 1957], henceforth cited as SE 11).
29. See "Two Encyclopaedia Articles," PFL 15, 134f.
30. Freud discusses and criticizes Wundt's theory of association repeatedly; see for instance *The Interpretation of Dreams*, Penguin Freud Library Vol. 4, trans. and ed. James Strachey, Anna Freud et al (London: Penguin, 1991), Ch. 1 (henceforth cited as PFL 4) and *The Psychopathology of Everyday Life*, Penguin Freud Library Vol. 5 (Harmondsworth: Penguin, 1991), Ch. 5 (henceforth cited as PFL 5).

account the givenness of resistance between different agencies in the psyche, which has its source in processes that are beyond the reach of the conscious I.[31] Specific attention is given by the analyst to precisely those associations which awaken resistance in the analysand:

> We may assume that whatever associations, thoughts and memories the patient is unable to communicate to us without internal struggles are in some way connected with the repressed material or are its derivatives. ("The Question of Lay Analysis" [1927] PFL 15, 305).

Here Freud on the one hand establishes the highly important connection between the free associations occurring in the present, and that which is repressed, i.e. the personal history of the subject; while at the same time noting that what indicates the presence of such a connection is the resistance to the analysis.

Several things must be taken into account when it comes to "free association" in psychoanalysis, and particularly two common and related misunderstandings must be discarded. First it should be noted that free association is by no means a magical carpet flying us directly into the promised land of the Unconscious. As Freud clearly states, when the subject initiates the process of free association by modifying her ordinary self-perception and thus turning herself into "an attentive and dispassionate self-observer," what she is asked to do is "merely to read off all the time the surface of her consciousness."[32] From the material thus provided the analyst will then begin to find the path leading to what

---

31. Thus he states in *The Interpretation of Dreams*: "Whenever one psychical element is linked with another by an objectionable or superficial association, there is also a legitimate and deeper link between them which is subjected to the resistance of the censorship" (PFL 4, 677).
32. "Two Encyclopaedia Articles," PFL 15, 134. See also "Short Account of Psychoanalysis" PFL 15, 166, where Freud says that he would ask his patients "to refrain from any conscious reflection and to abandon themselves, in a state of quiet concentration, to follow the ideas which occurred to them spontaneously (involuntarily) – "to skim off the surface of their consciousness."

had been forgotten or avoided, since "everything that occurred to a patient setting out from a particular starting point must also stand in an internal connection with that starting-point."[33]

This discovery is by and large what puts genetic phenomenology in a position where it can be called upon for clarification, for it is clear that Freud's theory of free association corresponds to Husserl's theory of intentional implications, in that it allows the analyst to trace the meaning-connections that hold between various lived experiences and representations backwards as it were. Second point: it is not the case that Freud regarded the free associations as being "free" in the strong sense of being beyond the influence of the conscious I – that is to say, as something given "straight" from its unconscious source (whatever that could mean). Instead, Freud stresses that the "free" association is upon closer examination actually unfree and that that which restrains it is precisely the "unconscious" material which – in ways to be determined – helps to organize the paths that the associations will follow.[34] So the "inner connections" between a lived experience (what Freud called the "starting point" above) and the associations that arise, are also bound to yet another starting point, more distant, that will gradually begin to disclose itself as the hidden, unconscious centre of associations, dreams etc. Thus Freud said that he was led to the expectation that...

> ... the so-called "free" association would prove in fact to be unfree, since, when all conscious intellectual purposes had been suppressed, the representations that emerged would be seen to be determined by the unconscious material. This expectation was justified by experience ("Short Account of Psychoanalysis," PFL 15,166; tr. mod.).

It is thus not the practical impossibility of giving a full report of the processes in the mind that places restrictions on the "free-

33. "Two Encyclopaedia Articles," PFL 15, 134f.
34. "Short Account of Psychoanalysis," PFL 15, 166; see already *The Interpretation of Dreams*, PFL 4, 675, 679.

dom" of associations. It is the philosophically more important fact that with the "increased attention" and the "elimination of criticism," the representations that emerge are in fact shown to be determined by an unconscious order.[35] This point was suggested as one of the two "basic pillars" of the psychoanalytical technique in *The Interpretation of Dreams*:

> In the psychoanalysis of neuroses the fullest use is made of these two propositions [*Sätze*][36] – that, when conscious purposive representations are abandoned, concealed purposive representations assume control of the sequence of representations, and that superficial associations are only substitutes by displacement for suppressed deeper ones. Indeed, these propositions have become basic pillars of psychoanalytic technique (PFL 4, 679; tr. mod.).

This implies that the method of free association is in a fundamental way correlated to the unconscious, such that by repeatedly following an indefinite series of such associations, we gradually acquire the material necessary for the analyst to construct interpretations for the analysand to either reject or take up as part of a growing acquisition of her unknown life. There is accordingly a basic scheme which underlies the whole psychoanalytical investigation, but which is never really articulated in Freud's writings: free association is an inverted mirroring of an unconscious order. By following this inverted mirroring it becomes clear that the involuntary representations that occur in free association are determined by a hidden *telos*, rather than representing the sheer immanence of surface phenomena:

> For it is demonstrably untrue that we are being car-

---

35. See already *The Interpretation of Dreams*, PFL 4 675, 679.
36. And not "theorems" as PFL suggest for *Sätze* (in mathematical and logical contexts, a theorem is a *Satz*, a proposition which follows from the axioms whereas for Freud here *Satz* is used as a presupposition in a more lax sense).

ried along a purposeless stream of representations [*ziellosen Vorstellungsablauf*] when, in the process of interpreting a dream, we abandon reflection and allow involuntary representations to emerge. It can be shown that all that we can ever get rid of are purposive representations [*Zielvorstellungen*] that are known to us; as soon as we have done this, unknown – or, as we inaccurately say, "unconscious" – purposive representations take charge and thereafter determine the course of the involuntary representations (*The Interpretation of Dreams*, PFL 4, 675; tr. mod.).

But this talk of free association as being a kind of reflection of unconscious processes is a simplification which covers the more radical hermeneutical principle at work, for it suggests that the hidden representations are there in a sufficiently clear and distinct manner already prior to the association being articulated. Before this articulation, they may have existed in a more oblique manner, as a non-objectified mood, a complex of feelings, phantasies or bodily comportments etc., which means that the manifestation in free association is often not a reflection of a previously existing representation, but (on the way to) its very first discursive articulation.[37]

It is this "purposiveness" which is unknown to us, this hidden teleology, that the further analysis will try to disclose for as long as it proceeds. In this sense, the method of free association has as

37. This hermeneutical principle is the basis of the whole analysis of dreams, in that Freud explicitly states that the memory of the dream necessarily brings about a distortion (*Entstellung*) of the dream as dreamt: the transformation which occurs when the latent content of the dream is interpreted as a manifest content is what makes up the essence of the dreamwork. See "Remarks on the Theory and Practice of Dream-Interpretation," in *The Ego and the Id and Other works*, The standard edition of the complete psychological works of Sigmund Freud. / Volume XIX, 1923-1925, ed. James Strachey et al. (London: The Hogarth Press/The Institute of Psycho-Analysis, 1961), henceforth cited as SE 19; see also *The Interpretation of Dreams*, PFL 4, 650n [1925 addition]. And Freud also emphasizes that this is essentially a matter of self-interpretation, although mediated by transference: "The technique which I describe in the pages that follow differs in one essential respect from the ancient method: *it imposes the task of interpretation upon the dreamer himself*" (PFL 4, 171fn2; my italics).

its main goal to gradually disclose the rationality of the seemingly "irrational," the bringing to light of the hidden order that determines the unconscious. Following up on Husserl's suggestion of a division of labour, we see that the Freudian method picks up just where Husserl's investigation came to a halt, namely in the further specification of motives characteristic of "irrational" acts that are infused with sensibility, "the driven in the sphere of passivity."[38] The investigation of rationality may indeed proceed to shed light also on these obscure preliminary stages of rational thought and action, as the motives that have their source there indeed also comply with rationality – they belong (as we saw previously) to what Husserl calls a "stratum of hidden reason."[39]

But it is not only the connection with what is unconscious that is important, for the analysis of free association must also show that it is connected with thoughts occurring in normal, awakened conscious life. When recounting a dream and making each of its separate images into a starting point for free associations, these function as a kind of communicative bridge between the borders of rational, discursive thought and "irrational" dream life, or between secondary and primary processes:

> By pursuing these associations further we obtain knowledge of thoughts which coincide entirely with the dream but which can be recognized – up to a certain point – as genuine and completely intelligible portions of waking mental activity ("Two Encyclopaedia Articles," PFL 15, 137f).[40]

38. Hua IV, *Ideas II*, § 56b, 222f.
39. Hua IV, *Ideas II*, § 61, 276. This connects with the issue of pre-propositional states in accounting for irrational phenomena and the unconscious; see Sebastian Gardner, *Irrationality and the Philosophy of Psychoanalysis* (Cambridge: Cambridge University Press, 1993), 104f, 116, 154ff, 189ff. Although wary of conceiving of the unconscious in terms of "pre-propositional content," Lear admits that it could nevertheless be seen as "the stuff from which a reason might develop," which brings his analysis close to Husserl's transcendental logic too; see his *Freud* (London: Routledge, 2005), 38 and "The Heterogeneity of the Mental," *Mind* vol. 104 (1995): 869f.
40. See also *An Autobiographical Study*, PFL 15, 227.

There is yet another factor in this intriguing unfreedom of the free association to take into account, in that each association occurring in the analysis will also be motivated by the relation of transference to the analyst.[41] Although this latter factor is in some sense "external," the method, which proffers neutrality on the part of the analyst, brings with it that the focus will be shifted to "inner" factors, that is to say to the intentional world of the analysand. In the case of the influence exerted upon the free associations that stem from the relation to the analyst, i.e. transference, this shift would be one from genuine, real life facts about the personality etc. of the analyst (which the analysand would know nothing or very little about), to the inner expectations, prejudices etc. of the analysand.

Eventually, and during the course of a psychoanalytical process, this may not only reveal expectations concerning a person in singular: a whole, preformed set of personae that so to speak inhabit the inner stage of the analysand may become visible that correspond to the most important characters with whom one peoples one's inner life. The analyst may come to represent one or several of these "inner" characters during the analysis, and by coming to realize the difference between these pre-formed "personae" and people in real life, outside of the analysis, the analysand will have achieved a greater freedom which may in turn enable a more genuine experience of the world.

However, when one takes a closer look at the philosophical foundation of these "basic pillars" or "basic rule" of the psychoanalytical technique, in particular as concerns how this correlation between present, conscious free associations and an order that is unknown ("unconscious") but which yet determines them is possible, then one has to conclude that Freud has very little to say. If the free associations are that which connects the irrational with the rational, then by means of what processes in consciousness (taken in an extended sense) is this made possible? How

41. "We shall be justified in assuming that nothing will occur to him that has not some reference to that situation [of transference]" (*An Autobiographical Study*, PFL 15, 224).

must subjectivity be structured in order for the free associations to be connected to that which was repressed a long time ago? What are the operations in the mind that bring about this "deeper link" between repressed occurrences and the present representations? In short, what is the relation between the unconscious and consciousness? To all these questions, which are ultimately of a philosophical character, Freud has no response.

4. The Transcendental Reinterpretation of Association in Genetic Phenomenology

In Husserl's early works the phenomenon of association was primarily seen as a psychological concept.[42] Thus in the analysis of the sign in the first *Logical Investigations*, genuine indication (as for instance in the phenomenon of empirically "pointing to" something) was said to have its origin in association. Association was therefore tied to the facticity of the here and now, and accordingly something that had to be excluded from the field of phenomenological investigations.[43] But despite this, the actual analysis of association in *Logical Investigations* is remarkably acute. Husserl says that the "continuous result of the associative function" is to fashion that which is merely together in an unconnected way into "intentional unities that appear as belonging-together."[44] And when Husserl in *Ideas II* began to analyze associations in relation to motivation as the "fundamental lawfulness" (*Grundgesetzlichkeit*) of all spiritual life, he

42. See *Philosophie der Arithmetik. Mit ergänzenden Texte (1890-1901)*, Hua XII, ed. Lothar Eley (Den Haag: Nijhoff, 1970), 199ff, 211f, 252f. This holds also for *Logical Investigations* and the 1905 lectures on inner time-consciousness. A more promising position is taken in the 1907 lectures on *Ding und Raum: Vorlesungen 1907* (Hua XVI, ed. Ulrich Claesges [Den Haag: Nijhoff, 1973], hencefort cited as Hua XVI) since association there is seen not as a "genetic-psychological fact" but instead, and perhaps for the first time, as a "phenomenological fact" expressing a law of the formation of succession; but that is still some way from acquiring a transcendentally-constitutive power though (XVI, § 51, 177f).

43. *Logische Untersuchungen, Zweiter Band: Untersuchungen zur Phänomenologie und Theorie der Erkenntnis*, Hua XIX/1-2, ed. Ursula Panzer (Den Haag: Nijhoff, 1984), § 4, 33ff. Henceforth cited as Hua XIX/1 and Hua XIX/2 respectively.

44. Hua XIX/1, § 4, 36.

already from the outset did so by insisting on its temporal horizon.[45] For associations always occur as "relations between earlier and later consciousness," but within the "stream of actual time-consciousness."[46]

Husserl from the outset calls upon the higher order reproductive associations for their ability to give an account of a certain creative aspect of consciousness, its spontaneous ability to bring us into contact with that which is not meant by us, with matters that we are bound to without knowing it beforehand, i.e. to account for our ability to step into new worlds, as it were.[47] This is what enables him to speak of association as "the apriori of passive subjectivity" as "the constantly hidden life, towards which the I is not directed."[48] Although at first absent, the coming into presence of that which is given by means of association is made possible by its being located within my field of horizontal intentionality: that which awakens and that which is awakened stand in a relation of intentional implication.

45. Hua IV, § 56 "Motivation as the fundamental lawfulness of spiritual life." The whole idea to treat association as a form of motivation was not self-evident; as late as in 1916 Husserl asked himself whether it was legitimate to "speak of association as motivation at all" (A VI 25/11; quoted in HuDo 1, 204).

46. Hua IV, § 56, 222. In the 1905 lectures on inner time-consciousness, the phenomenon of association is conspicuously absent (also from the Beilagen in Hua X); when it occurs it is almost without exception treated in a negative manner, as in the critique of Brentano in §§ 3ff (which was taken up again in Hua XI, 77); cf. however *Zur Phänomenologie des inneren Zeitbewusstseins (1893-1917)*, Hua X, ed. Rudolf von Boehm (Den Haag: Nijhoff, 1969), 106, 167, 304. In *Ideas I* association is actually conceptually absent, although the discussion of "noematical intentionality" in §§ 101 and 104 is clearly related to it. In *Ideas III* Husserl, on the way towards the discovery of a passive association, says that not everything pertaining to the soul has to be related to the I, since associations are formed "whether the I participates or not" (*Ideen zur einer reinen Phänomenologie und phänomenologischen Philosophie / Drittes Buch, Die Phänomenologie und die Fundamente der Wissenschaften*, Hua V, ed. Marly Biemel [Den Haag: Nijhoff, 1971], § 3, 9).

47. Husserl underlined this "genetic" function of association in the 6th of the *Logical Investigations* (§ 15), in connection with both ordinary "wordless recognition" of objects (such as when we see a specific kind of tool that we recognize but whose name we have forgotten), and in scientific thinking.

48. *Phänomenologische Psychologie: Vorlesungen Sommersemester 1925*, Hua IX (Den Haag: M. Nijhoff, 1962) 504.

Now, in order for association to leave its empiricist background behind and come forth as a transcendental (that is to say constitutive) concept, it must first of all find its place within a systematically undertaken theory of the phenomenological reduction. For thereby the associative bond between intentional objects – and thus no longer real, natural objects or "ideas" of them – can be investigated as it manifests itself immanently, without being regarded as a mechanist-causal bond as in the empiricist philosophies of Locke and Hume.[49] Further, association can only come forth in its own right once static phenomenology has been supplemented with a systematic investigation of its temporal substructure, which genetic phenomenology provides. For association, as the intentional awakening of one content by means of another, carries within it a temporal order of the genesis of sense, and this is something that static phenomenology cannot thematize.[50] But the "change of sense" that is implied with the shift from a static to a genetic understanding of association, leaves the phenomenon itself unaltered. This means that what was excluded in the early works (due to its closeness to psychology), is at a later stage not only incorporated into the sphere of phenomenological investigations, but also given a foundational position in the phenomenology of passivity:

That association can become a general theme of phenomenological description and not merely one of objective psychology is due to the fact that the phenomenon of

49. On this, see Husserl's analysis in *Erste Philosophie (1923/4), Erster Teil: Kritische Ideengeschichte,* Hua VII, ed. Rudolf Boehm (Den Haag: Nijhoff, 1956), 170ff.
50. This transcendental reformulation of the concept of association is clearly brought out in a passage from *Erfahrung und Urteil,* § 16, 77/*Experience and Judgment,* 74: "What in a purely static description appears to be likeness or similarity must therefore be considered in itself as being already the product of the one or the other kind of synthesis of coincidence, which we denote by the traditional term association, but with a change of sense [*aber unter Verwandlung seines Sinnes*]. It is the phenomenon of associative genesis which dominates this sphere of passive pregivenness, established on the basis of syntheses of internal time-consciousness."

indication [*Anzeige*] is something which can be exhibited from the point of view of phenomenology. (This insight, worked out as early as the *Logical Investigations*, already constitutes there the nucleus of genetic phenomenology.) Every interpretation of association and its laws which makes of it a kind of psychophysical natural law, attained by objective induction, must therefore be excluded here. Association comes into question in this context exclusively as the purely immanent connection of "this recalls that," "one calls attention to the other." [...] And this relationship is itself capable of being shown phenomenologically. It presents itself in itself as a genesis; one of the elements is characterized relative to consciousness as that which awakens, the other as that which is awakened (*Erfahrung und Urteil*, § 16, 78/*Experience and Judgment*, 74f).[51]

What lies behind this reinterpretation of association? This question will be investigated in the remainder of this section. Let us first see whether the connection between inner time-consciousness and sensuousness can be given a more precise determination which could serve as a starting point. Husserl's whole phenomenology of passivity is in fact founded upon the analysis of inner time-consciousness as it cooperates with impressional-kinaesthetic consciousness, although in the early texts this cooperation is not yet clearly present. One text in particular in Hua X suggests itself in this context, since it contains a tentative appeal to the experience of association as that which brings about the *Zusammenhang* of the past:

---

51. Shortly after the *Logical Investigations* Husserl discovered association to be a "constantly co-functioning lawlikeness in genetic processes," but the insight of the transcendental, i.e. the universally constitutive meaning of association was a much later insight. See ms. A VII 13/187 [1918]: "Die Art, wie Assoziation universale konstitutive Bedeutung hat, habe ich sehr spät durchschaut, obschon ich sie schon in der ersten Göttingen Jahren als einen Titel für eine universale und immer mitfungierende Gesetzlichkeit der Genesis erkannte."

We can say; the present is always born from the past, a determinate present from a determinate past, of course. Or better: A determinate flow runs its course again and again; the actually present now sinks away and passes over into a new now, and so on. Even if there may be a necessity of an apriori kind involved here, an "association" nevertheless conditions it; that is, the nexus of the past is determined by experience, and it is further determined by experience "that something or other will come" (Hua X, Beilage III, 106/CW 4, 111 [1909-10]; cf. Hua XXIII, 258).

This is one of few instances where Husserl speaks of association in relation to inner time in Hua X (apart from his critique of Brentano). In this text a genetic approach starts to announce itself in the midst of a purely static conception of time: the present is not a staccato-like sequence of nows, instead it is "born" from the past, it is a "flow" that "runs its course," thereby opening the possibility to see the constitution of meaning in *statu nascendi*. There are other passages from the early texts on time-consciousness where Husserl emphasizes this connection, passages that were first made famous by Merleau-Ponty, Derrida and Levinas and then again worked through by Michel Henry, Marc Richir and others.[52] These texts suggest a slightly different, more concrete approach in comparison to the abstract-formal unity of *Urimpression*-retention-protention that is the theoretical foundation of the 1905-lectures:

We regard sensing as the original consciousness of time [*Das Empfinden sehen wir an als das ursprüngliche Zeitbewusstsein*] [...]. Sensation is presentifying time-consciousness [*Empfindung ist gegenwärtigendes Zeitbewusstsein*]. Representification is also sensing, in the sense that it is

52. It is notably two texts in Hua X, Beilage I and III, that are relevant here; see also Hua XXIII, Nr. 7 p. 251. See for instance Michel Henry, *Phénoménologie matérielle* (Paris: PUF, 1990): "La phénoménologie du temps est une phénoménologie de l'impression [...]" (43).

present and becomes constituted as a unity in the presentifying time-consciousness (Hua X, Beilage III, 107/CW 4, 112; tr. mod.).

This determination of inner time as *Empfinden* is wider and in a sense more fruitful in that it leads directly to the temporality of Husserl's "transcendental aesthetics," as this theme is developed notably in the lectures on passive syntheses and *Experience and Judgment*.[53] With this connection between time and sensibility in mind, the analyses of "sensibility as the psychic basis of the spirit [*seelischen Untergrund des Geistes*]" from *Ideas II* take on a deeper significance that will gain in clarity in the many later texts that continue the discussion of primary passivity first opened up there.[54] For this "psychic basis" that is discussed in *Ideas II* is nothing other than inner time-consciousness considered in conjunction with impressional consciousness:

> Primal sensibility [*Ursinnlichkeit*] is composed of the sensuous data [...]. Likewise, the sensuous feelings are founded in these sensuous data, and so are the sensuous drive data [*sinnlichen Triebdaten*], the drives not as something supposedly transcendent to consciousness but as primal lived experiences [*Urerlebnisse*], always belonging to the content of the psychic basis. That is a primal content of sensibility [*ein Urbestand an Sinnlichkeit*] (Hua IV, Beilage XII, 334/CW 3, 346 [1917]; tr. mod.).

53. A problem for the general interpretation of this whole area is that Husserl never succeeded in presenting a systematic overview of a phenomenological transcendental aesthetics, one that spans over both static and genetic analyses and that connects the passive syntheses of inner time-consciousness with those of bodily-kinaesthetic syntheses and the constitution of space. On this, see Vincenzo Costa, "Transcendental Aesthetic and the Problem of Transcendentality," in *Alterity and Facticity*, ed. Natalie Depraz and Dan Zahavi (Dordrecht: Kluwer, 1998), 9-28.

54. Hua IV, Beilage XII, Part I, § 2, 334/CW 3, 346. Holenstein incorrectly dismisses the whole analysis of association from *Ideas II* on the grounds that it is "ein wenig einheitlich und straff geglückter Versuch" that hardly transgresses the status of "Hinweisen, Aperçus und Exkursen," and leaves it out of his account (see *Husserls Phänomenologie der Assoziation*, 10).

It is on the basis of the intentionality that is discovered in these originary processes which proceed passively, without the participation of the I, that the new concept of association takes form. However, it must be kept in mind that Husserl at first regarded the intentionality that is operative in the passive sphere as an "improper" intentionality, in for instance the important appendix XII to *Ideas II*.[55] This hesitancy concerning whether to ascribe intentionality to the originary processes in passivity is consistent with a static perspective on constitution, but with genetic phenomenology even the simple syntheses of perception in the field of the living present show that the basic forms of objectivation occurs passively.[56] Intentionality can therefore no longer be restricted to the awakened I, but must be extended to the passive I. The characterization of "primal sensibility" from the texts just prior to the genetic breakthrough in 1917-18 is important for understanding what "originary association" is about, since Husserl includes not only sense data, feelings and drives within it, but also primary modes of pre-predicative relations. Amongst these we find the temporal binding of one phase with the next, and also the pre-perceptive syntheses of noematical contents within these; both of which are early forms of genetic constitution.

The gradual development of a transcendental, genetic approach shows how the phenomenological interpretation of the principles of association also differs from Hume's account.[57] The genetic approach does not start out from an immediate adherence to the traditional "laws" (resemblance, contrast and contiguity as they were first suggested by Aristotle), in order then

55. Hua IV, 335. See also HuMat 8, nr. 24, 112f, where Husserl talks of the originary temporalizing consciousness as *"uneigentlich"* and says that it is not intentional; but this is only true from a static point of view. On this, see Anne Montavont, *De la passivité dans la phénoménologie de Husserl* (Paris: PUF, 1999), 86 and Bégout, *La généalogie de la logique*, 31.
56. "They are not syntheses that the ego has actively instituted; rather they are syntheses that are produced in pure passivity" (Hua XI, 76/CW 9, 118).
57. The relation between Husserl and Hume is the subject of Richard Murphy's book *Hume and Husserl: Towards Radical Subjectivism* (Den Haag: Nijhoff, 1983). Although Murphy exaggerates the influence that Hume had on Husserl's genetic turn.

to analyze the structural relations etc. between them.[58] Instead, Husserl starts to investigate whether there is not an inner unity somewhere that lays behind these somewhat incoherent laws. In the lectures on passive synthesis Husserl had come to see that the living present must be intimately connected to association as a principle of passive synthesis, i.e. as the "source" of all awakenings and memory.[59] It is this early analysis of the structure of the living present that enables the reinterpretation of the traditional laws of association, which prior to that for Husserl appeared to be a mere arbitrary coalition of empirical-psychological generalities. It has to be shown that the effectivity of the laws of association does not depend on the previous givenness of elements that are already constituted, but that these latter are only possible through the functioning of these very same laws. This is why the *Urassoziation* as the originary connection between elements given through affection, must be able to account for the very genesis of meaning in the impressional field. That which enables Husserl to make sense of the laws of reproductive association is precisely the fact that there is a connection between the now, the past and the future which makes it possible to intuitively see whether a particular phenomenon is associated as being "similar" to, "contiguous" to or as standing in "contrast" to a given datum.[60] Association is thus shown to be in the aesthetic-sensible sphere what the Kantian categories are for logical consciousness. As Bégout says, association thereby becomes "the mark of a transcendental legality."[61] The heart of this beginning transcendental reinterpretation is accordingly the analysis of the living present, since Husserl here tries to show how these laws stem from the bond that is upheld therein between what is present and what has passed out of the field of presencing.[62]

58. See Aristotle, *On Memory and Recollection*, 451 b.
59. Hua XI § 38, 181.
60. Hua XI, §§ 37f, 180f; cf. XI, 480.
61. Bégout, *La généalogie de la logique*, 138.
62. See James Hart, "Review Essay of Husserl, Collected Works vol. 9 (Analyses Concerning Passive and Active Synthesis. Lectures on Transcendental Logic)," *Husserl Studies* 20 (2004): 145.

The genetic approach to association provides an analysis of presence that is clearly richer than its static predecessor, since it now affirms its intimate engagement with factical life and also in a fundamental way brings absence into play: the now is open to anything that it connects with. But despite these advances, the understanding of the relations that bind affective-associative consciousness with inner time-consciousness is still held back in 1926 in a decisive sense, since it essentially remains within the boundaries of the extended now as presented in the 1905 lectures on inner time-consciousness. For the reduction in the lectures on passive synthesis leads to a noetic-noematic stream of experiences, whereas the "radicalized reduction" (thematized in C 3 from 1930) and which leads to the "streaming-living present," shows us that the representation of consciousness as such a stream is merely a necessary yet naïve pre-stage.[63] This stream is *itself* something constituted, and the proper transcendental reduction must now disclose the source of this constitution. This enables Husserl to investigate the constitution of time as pertaining to the I more thoroughly in the C-manuscripts, and from this "self-transcending" source as a living streaming presence, to further account for all the layers of constitution ending with communally constituted objective time. The *Rückfrage* into the genetic sources of our world-apperception thus gains

---

63. Hua XXXIV, nr. 11 "Radikale Reduktion auf die strömend-lebendige Gegenwart ist äquivalent mit transzendental-phänomenologischer Reduktion" [C 3/3a-4b], 186: "This streaming living present is not that which we previously and also transcendentally-phenomenologically designated as stream of consciousness or stream of experiences. It is not in any way a 'stream' as the imagery suggests, that is to say a properly temporal (or even spatiotemporal) whole, which in the unity of a temporal extension has a continuous successive individual existence [...]." For a general account of the radical reduction, see Klaus Held, *Lebendige Gegenwart; die Frage nach der Seinsweise des Transzendentalen ich bei Edmund Husserl, entwickelt am Leitfaden der Zeitproblematik* (Den Haag: Nijhoff, 1966), 61–140. For an interpretation of the most important of the late reductions – the radicalized, the universal and the intersubjective reductions – and their interconnections, see Ch. 2–3 in *Towards a Phenomenology of Repression*. See also my "Self-alteration and temporality: the radicalized and universal reductions in Husserl's late thinking (*au-delà de Derrida*)," in *Phenomenology 2010 / Vol. 4, Selected essays from Northern Europe: traditions, transitions and challenges*, ed. Dermot Moran and Hans Reiner Sepp (Bucharest: Zeta Books, 2011), 51–86.

a new focus by revealing yet another prejudgement that clouds our self-understanding. This leads to the sphere of *Urzeitigung*, of originary temporalization, which is but another name for the most fundamental process taking place in the living present:

> The reduction to the living present is the most radical-ized reduction to the subjectivity in which the process of all becoming-valid-for-me is originarily completed, in which all being-meaning is meaning for me and experien-tially given for me as consciously valid meaning. It is the reduction to the sphere of originary temporalization, in which the first and original-source-like meaning of time appears – time precisely as living streaming present. (Hua XXXIV, nr. 11 [C 3/1930], 187)

The genetic analysis of association brings a kind of intentional-ity into view that leads to a deeper understanding of the noesis-noema correlation central to static phenomenology, and which indicates a path out of this seemingly self-enclosed correlation. By being able to recuperate also the various intentional rela-tions that are excessive in relation to the constitution of a mere noematic correlate (such as indications, potential meanings that are unrelated to the constitution of an objective sense), associa-tion gains access to a whole new field of phenomenological ex-ploration. Through its capacity to gather the multiple meaning-overflowing that occurs in passivity, and to connect these ideally without restriction across the borders of the past and the future, the frozen moment of the act-object correlation (which makes static phenomenology forever an abstraction) is superseded.

5. Sedimentation and the Universality of Association

If the psychoanalytical work consists in a "tracing back" of what is manifest towards its hidden sources, then this implies that the opposite path where the covering over or "repression" of an event (trauma) takes place, must first have been trodden.[64] Therefore the progression by means of free associations against the resistance and thus towards the repressed centre of ill-being, must be one that proceeds in the opposite direction of a work that has already been performed, undoing it. In this section the hypothesis of whether there are not hidden intentional relations that govern Freud's notion of free association will be examined.

As shown in section three, it is actually the unfreedom of association that poses the real problem: the restraints upon the associative process indicate an unconscious resistance, and as Freud always repeated, this is where the real work starts, sometimes bordering on the impossible. One way to begin to respond to this problem is by means of Husserl's theory of sedimentation of past lived experiences. Every thought, phantasy or lived experience that occurs in the present is always in part determined by our previous thoughts etc., since everything that has been present, whether as actuality or as inactuality, whether as primary target of attention or in the unnoticed background-horizon, becomes sedimented in the I. And as the retentional intentionality that structures our past also allows for associative-intentional relations between its elements, the way is open for what is ideally an unlimited possibility of connections between the contents of consciousness. Phenomenology could here show that "free association" is a part of a scientifically understood transcendental aesthetics, by inscribing it in a larger and more coherent framework. Such a framework would consist of originary association at the lowermost level of constitution which accounts for the ever new structuration of the living present. This would also interact with what becomes sedimented, and

64. "... psychoanalytic research [...] seeks merely to uncover connections by tracing that which is manifest back to that which is hidden [*nichts anders als Zusammenhänge aufdecken, indem sie Offenkundiges auf Verborgenes zurückführt*]," "On the Universal Tendency to Debasement in the Sphere of Love (Contributions to the Psychology of Love II)," in *On sexuality: three essays on the theory of sexuality and other works*, PFL 7, ed. James Strachey and Angela Richards(Harmondsworth: Penguin, 1977), 256; *Sexualleben*, Studienausgabe [SA] 5, (Frankfurt am Main : Fischer, 1972), 206.

given that the psychoanalytical "repressed" could be interpreted as something that lives on in sedimentation, it would also be a part of unconscious motivations that associatively communicate with the living present.

If we picture the constitutive process as a living being, then at the head we have the temporalizing flow where the ceaseless renewal of the "world" takes place, while everything that has been pre-constituted sinks down towards the feet, where it settles down into secondary passivity:

> [...] every accomplishment of the living present, that is, every accomplishment of sense or of the object becomes sedimented in the realm of the dead, or rather, dormant horizonal sphere, precisely in the manner of a fixed order of sedimentation: while at the head the living process receives new, original life, at the feet everything that is as it were in the final acquisition of the retentional synthesis, becomes steadily sedimented (Hua XI, § 37, 178/CW 9, 227).

According to Husserl's dynamic conception of the psyche which holds that it is in a constant state of change – *das Seelenleben ist nach Wesensnotwendigkeit ein Fluss* – all previous lived experiences have an afterlife in that they partake in the continuous "new formation or re-formation of dispositions" in the form of habits, memory, and the orientation of convictions, feelings and will; all at the ready disposal of association.[65] All experiences are thus sedimented into practical possibilities, potentialities for further action, so that each action is always in part the result of our previous actions.[66] There can therefore never be a purely spontaneous action, it is always already a response from our own sedimented history just as it is a response to the passive pregivenness of the world. All these processes of sedimentation

---

65. Hua IV, § 32, 132, 135f.
66. "Die praktische Intention ist verwirklichung einer bleibenden praktischen 'Überzeugung'" (A VII 13/18 [1921]. Cf. *Experience and Judgment*, § 19.

are only possible if association is constantly at work:

Constitution in all its forms is association in a sense which continuously expands itself. All association presupposes the originary association in the sphere of originary temporalization. Wherever this association does not do its work, there nothing can become sedimented, and when acts pertaining to the I and the I do not appear in this sphere of originary temporalization, then they cannot enter any associations (HuMat 8, nr. 79, 345 [C 16/1931]).

What is the relation between association at this level of passivity and the I? The "originary association" is clearly not related to the active, awakened I of normally functioning consciousness, and Husserl therefore speaks of the *Vor-Ich* or the "antechamber of the I" here.[67] After the event what has been present becomes a part of the living history of the I as habituality and practical possibility; though this is not in some "afterchamber" of the I, but precisely something that becomes a part of the pure I, as a motivational tendency.

Association as the condition of possibility of sedimentation is accordingly nothing without an established relation to the I as a centre of affection, to which both parts of an association in the ordinary sense relate, and as a unifying "pole of originary instincts" when it comes to the *Vor-Ich* as the genetic forerunner to the pure I.[68] The mode of being of an object that has passed into retentional sedimentation is that of a "has-been-conscious," and this does not change with the gradual loss of affec-

67. Nam-in Lee, has a good discussion about the status of the "I" at this level of originary association, and argues against the often voiced requirement that there be a fully active and awakened I ready at hand already at this level of genesis; see *Edmund Husserls Phänomenologie der Instinkte* (Dordrecht: Kluwer Academic Publishers, 1993), 165. For a clear distinction between the *Vor-Ich* and the genetically deeper *Ur-Ich*, see Shigeru Taguchi, *Das Problem des "Ur-Ich" bei Edmund Husserl: Die Frage nach der selbstverständlichen "Nähe" des Selbst* (Dordrecht: Springer, 2006).
68. E III 9/18 [1931]: "Der Ichpol [als] Pol von ursprünglichen Instinkten"; see also HuMat 8, nr. 57, 252f.

tive force.[69] So even when the constituted object reaches its limit of affective zero, and thus is no longer "alive," its meaning is still implicitly there in the shape of the "dead": it is only lacking in flowing life. It is important here to note that Husserl regards the whole problematic of how this "dead" but not meaningless object can come alive again, as pertaining to association.[70] This is how the associative awakening is described:

> A remote past suddenly dawns on me, the thought that just came to me comes into relief from the so-called unconscious in which the object given to consciousness, in the specific sense of a special prominence, is merely an island. Every present flows once more into this undifferentiated subsoil of the distant retention. The subsoil itself is without any prominence – though once in a while something does come into relief. It comes into relief: That is, a completely non-intuitive affection is there in entirely the same way that a chord that has just faded away emerges in a non-intuitive manner, possibly drawing my attention to it – albeit a chord that I (perhaps entirely in vain) want to make intuitive again (Hua XI, Beilage X, 385/CW 9, 476f [1920]).

Everything that is sedimented is therefore "still "alive," as it is expressed in a later text.[71]

Let me try to sum up the discussion by means of a question: in what way can this presentation of Husserl's theory of association coupled with sedimentation, help us with the main question concerning the clarification of the psychoanalytical *Grundregel*? First of all by showing the scope of Husserl's reflections: when originary association is taken into account, association becomes the general principle that accounts for the

69. Hua XI, § 37, 177.
70. "How it can become efficacious and even constitutively efficacious in a new shape is the problem of association" (Hua XI, § 37, 177).
71. Hua XXXIV, nr. 35, 472 [1934]: "Alles Sedimentierte ist noch 'lebendig'."

passivity of consciousness as that which precedes all conscious activity.[72] If the main hypothesis that is investigated here is correct, then this means that all of Freud's investigations of the unconscious and a large segment of the processes that he locates in the preconscious would be inscribed within the processes that Husserl ascribes to association. Would such a position not immediately entail a reduction of Freud's investigations, making (parts of) the unconscious into consciousness in one stroke?

That can only depend on whether there are processes presented by Freud that indeed fall out of the picture once they are subsumed under the transcendental-phenomenological concept of association. But since the widened concept of consciousness that followed from the genetic discovery of passive processes led Husserl to locate association as the most foundational type of movement within the psyche, it is, as I've tried to show, genetic phenomenology as such that must be taken into account in answering this question. The discovery that association has a "universally constitutive meaning" thus brought with it that not only the impressional sphere gained its inner unity by means of association; everything that pertains to the life of transcendental consciousness becomes united through association:

> Life is encompassed by a universally essential lawlikeness of passivity: that of the syntheses of association (HuMat 8, nr. 13, 42 [C 3/1931]).[73]

That association in the ordinary sense is a universal process in so far as nothing is alien to it, also means that it completely disregards any differences concerning the ontological status of

---

72. Hua I, CM, § 38, 112/engl., 78 (tr. mod.): "every construction on the part of activity necessarily presupposes, at the lowest level, a passivity that receives the object as pregiven, and, when we trace anything built actively, we run into constitution by passive genesis."
73. Cf. A VI 34/36 [1931]: "Nicht nur hyletische Daten konstituieren sich als Einheiten, auch das konstituierende Leben, auch die Kinästhese, die Akte des Ich, kurz alles und jedes, was zum Bewusstseinsleben gehört, konstituiert sich vermöge der immerfort wirkenden Assoziationen als Einheit."

what it combines. What is there in association is there as a given for consciousness, with its particular meaning-compound, totally indifferent to whether it crosses regions of being or time and thus essentially unfaithful to any schematizations of the world. Association is thus something of a ruthless, uninhibited procurer that will couple any given object with anything, and at a non-stop rate.

But this is also what accounts for its creative aspect, which constantly reopens our own past and brings back elements that would otherwise have remained sedimented. This also opens the future for us into something that can be lived, since we have already projected ourselves into it beforehand in phantasmatic "as if"-life; the anticipatory or "inductive" associations are intentions directed towards the future that fill out the empty horizon more or less concretely.[74] The constitution of meaning here takes on the form of mimetic projection of the past into the future by means of previous similar lived experiences, of course always checked and modified against what is encountered.

74. Hua XI, 119f, 184-191, 243ff.

Forms of Collectivity: Georg Simmel's Mass Theory and the Transformation of Social Philosophy in Weimar Germany[1]

Stefan Jonsson

Introduction

With the French Revolution and the advent of democracy, a new actor entered the political arena: the people. Almost a century later, with the consolidation of the organized labor movement, or the so-called fourth estate, this political force was successfully promoting universal suffrage, social justice, and establishment of democratic sovereignty.[2] Not everyone welcomed this social and political transformation. Many feared that the treasured voice of the people foretold the wicked rule of the mob. As ordinary people slowly worked their way into the political arena, the elite claimed

1. This text was part of a course on mass theories at the philosophy depart-
    ment of Pontifícia Universidade Católica do Rio de Janeiro (PUC), given
    in October–November 2010. I am indebted to the students at PUC who
    followed the course, and to professors Marcia sà Cavalcante Schuback and
    Luiz Carlos Pereira for having provided me with this opportunity within
    their exemplary program of academic, intellectual and collegial exchange.
    For a more elaborated version of this text and related topics, see my *Crowds
    and Democracy: The Idea and Image of the Masses from Revolution to Fascism*
    (New York: Columbia University Press, 2013).
2. For a comprehensive analysis of this development in Europe, see Geoff
    Eley, *Forging Democracy: The History of the Left in Europe 1850-2000.* (Oxford:
    Oxford University Press, 2002), 13-233.

that the stage of history was invaded by threatening masses.[3] The scholarly discourse of crowd psychology was an expression of this development and a reaction against democracy. From the outset, it exhibited an anti-liberal and anti-democratic tone. In his 1959 overview of theories of mass society, American sociologist William Kornhauser rightly called this an "aristocratic" theory, as it expressed "an intellectual defense of elite values against the rise of mass participation."[4] Along with this discourse came an array of terms and opinions that journalists, writers, and the educated classes appropriated and made part of their political worldview, especially their understanding of the lower classes.

Surveys of crowd psychology tend to dwell first on its French and Italian origins, usually establishing Gustave Le Bon's *La Psychologie des foules* (1895) as the doxa of the discourse, and often disregarding the more important research contributions of Scipio Sighele's *La folla criminale* and Gabriel Tarde's *L'Opinion et la foule* and *Les Lois de l'imitation*. The historical reviews then jump to Sigmund Freud's reinterpretation of Le Bon in *Massenpsychologie und Ich-Analyse* (1921). Freud's essay is typically seen both as a continuation of Le Bon's theory and as a new departure, out of which comes the various theories of the masses of the 1920s and onward.[5]

3. For an account of the discourse on the masses as a reaction against democracy, see my *A Brief History of the Masses: Three Revolutions* (New York: Columbia University Press, 2008), 5–117.

4. William Kornhauser, *The Politics of Mass Society* (London: Routledge and Kegan Paul, 1959), 21. Kornhauser distinguished the aristocratic criticism of mass society from the democratic one, which centered "in the intellectual defense of democratic values against the rise of elites bent on total domination" (21).

5. In addition to the numerous entries on "masses" and "mass psychology" in encyclopaedias of philosophy and the social sciences, which are all governed by this perspective, see Paul Reiwald *Vom Geist der Massen: Handbuch der Massenpsychologie* (Zürich: Pan Verlag, 1946); Serge Moscovici, *The Age of the Crowd: A Historical treatise on Mass Psychology*, trans. J. C. Whitehouse (Cambridge: Cambridge University Press, 1985); *Changing Conceptions of Crowd Mind and Behavior*, eds. Carl F. Graumann and Serge Moscovici (New York: Springer Verlag, 1986); Peter Sloterdijk, *Die Verachtung der Massen: Versuch über Kulturkämpfe in der modernen Gesellschaft* (Frankfurt am Main: Suhrkamp, 2000); Stanley J. Tambiah, *Leveling Crowds: Ethnonationalist Conflicts and Collective Violence in South Asia* (Berkeley and Los Angeles:

These surveys tell a continuous story where little changes between the understanding of the masses in late nineteenth-century Paris and the debate on the masses in interwar Germany and Austria. In fact, most analyses of crowds and crowd behavior in modernity still enroll Le Bon as their guide, as the discipline of crowd psychology continues to serve as *Leitmotif* for the analysis of crowd phenomena in no matter what society and historical period.[6] Of course, it is no falsification to construe crowd psychology as a continuous discipline with its specific genealogy of founders, traditions, branches, and intrinsic preoccupations. It is to be doubted, however, that this kind of history of ideas offers interesting approaches to interwar European history and culture. Nor is it certain that canonical crowd psychology serves us well as a master key to historical events of any kind. When Weimar ideas on "the masses" are analyzed in relation to this theory, the historical specificity and contextual references of the Weimar discussion is often occluded.

Late nineteenth-century crowd psychology was confined to clinical psychology, public policy, and history writing. The Weimar discourse on the masses, by contrast, concerns society in its totality. It addresses the future of humankind, often

University of California Press, 1996); Leon Bramson, *The Political Context of Sociology* (Princeton: Princeton University Press, 1961). For a rare exception to this body of work, see Roger Geiger, "Democracy and the Crowd: The Social History of an Idea in France and Italy, 1890-1914," in *Societas. A Review of Social History* vol. 7, no. 1 (1977): 47-71. As the title indicates, this essay deals not with Germany, and its historical frame is limited. Yet, it is exemplary in its contextualization of crowd psychology.

6.   There is thus a remarkable credulity even among critically-minded scholars as regards mass psychology. Many have used Le Bon as a theoretical authority on crowds, whereas those same critics would hardly apply similar late-nineteenth-century ideological paradigms as easily in their analyses of phenomena of stronger scholarly standing than crowds and masses. For cautionary cases, see Jonathan Crary, *Suspensions of Perception: Attention, Spectacle, and Modern Culture* (Cambridge, Mass.: The MIT Press, 1999), 241–247; Anton Kaes, *Shell Shock Cinema: Weimar Culture and the Wounds of War* (Princeton: Princeton University Press, 2009), 193–200; and Christine Poggi, "Mass, Pack, and Mob: Art in the Age of the Crowd," in *Crowds*, eds. Jeffrey T Schnapp and Matthew Tiews (Stanford: Stanford University Press, 2006), 159–202; and, above all, Serge Moscovici, *The Age of the Crowd*; and "The Discovery of the Masses," *Changing Conceptions of Crowd Mind and Behavior*.

unfolding entire metaphysical systems, as is the case with the theories of Sigmund Freud, Elias Canetti, Hermann Broch, and Oswald Spengler, or large-scale mappings of society as a whole, as in Weimar sociology before and after the First World War.

A crucial chapter is therefore missing in existing histories of the masses. Between the turn of the century and 1920 lie at least three events that shattered inherited assumptions about society and politics: first, the establishment of universal suffrage in most Western countries (in Germany in November 1918), brought about by the dual force of the workers' movement and the women's movement; second, World War One, with its patriotic frenzy; third, the Russian revolution, which many Europeans perceived as the ultimate "revolt of the masses," especially so in Germany which experienced its own wave of socialist revolutions in 1918-1919. A population fatigued by war, poverty, and unemployment now rejected their traditional political representatives, from the emperor to local officeholders, opting instead for a social organization in accord with principles of self-government and participatory democracy. Of course, all these processes had to have a tremendous impact on both the intellectual and the popular view of the masses.

What happened between Le Bon's 1890s and Freud's, Spengler's, and Canetti's 1920s was not just a transformation of the idea of the mass, but also a transformation of the idea of individuality in relation to which the mass had been viewed, analyzed, defined, and denounced. Intellectuals writing about the masses in the nineteenth century were lodged securely in a belief in individuality. When trying to define the masses they typically described them as a negation of their chosen mode of self-definition. Positing themselves as independent individuals defined by reason, ethical responsibility, and erudition, crowd psychologists asserted that the mass lacked such faculties. It was irrational and ruled by passions.

With the exception of Durkheim, however, French sociology of the 1890s failed to develop any properly sociological conception of collective life forms. Social phenomena were explained as the products of the psychological interactions of individuals. One such product was the mass, defined as a union of individuals governed by communal passions, and agitated by emotional suggestion to the extent that their individual identities were swept away. By affirming that members of a crowd lacked individuality – reason, identity, character, culture – crowd psychology usually served to dispute the lower classes' ability to function as responsible political agents, and hence to deny them the right to vote.[7]

But what if belief in individuality wavered? What if individuality could no longer credibly serve as the foundation of social order, decision-making, and moral behavior? In the 1890s, the jargon of mass psychology often served to exclude those who supposedly had not raised themselves to the civilized level of the cultured bourgeois and thus had no chance of becoming autonomous individuals. In the 1920s, by contrast, the jargon about the masses voiced a deeper anxiety about a future *without* individuals, and hence also without rationality, morality, responsibility, self-mastery and whatever depended on the principle of individuality. In his famous cultural diagnosis of 1931, *Die geistige Situation der Zeit*, Karl Jaspers identified "the mass" as a foundational feature of the contemporary world, in the sense that individual will was everywhere cancelled by the qualities of the majority. "The basic problem of our time," he concluded, "is whether an independent human being in his self-comprehended destiny is still possible."[8]

7. Thus, the antinomy between rational individuality and irrational masses, which marks the discourse on the crowd in the 1890s, may be interpreted as the result of the elite's effort to contain a social contradiction. By fabricating the lower classes as irrational crowds, the discourse protects the right of the upper classes to remain the representatives of society against working-class demands for universal suffrage and economic improvements. According to Michelle Perrot, in France between 1885 and 1898 there were on average almost one workers' strike per day, the number reaching its climax in 1893, when 634 strikes are reported. This is the very period when mass psychology was established as a scientific doctrine (*Les Ouvriers en grève*, 2 vols (Paris: Mouton, 1974), 2:568; quoted in: Susanna Barrows, *Distorting Mirrors: Visions of the Crowd in Late Nineteenth-Century France* (New Haven: Yale University Press, 1981), 19.

8. Karl Jaspers, *Man in the Modern Age*, trans. Eden Paul and Cedar Paul (London: George Routledge and Sons, 1933), 241; *Die geistige Situation der Zeit* (Berlin: Walter de Gruyter, 1931), 33, 189.

In this essay I will discuss some of the foundations and further developments of the European discourse on the masses, in particular the transformations that the notions of the mass and the individual underwent as they were incorporated into the early discipline of sociology in Germany during the first decades of the twentieth century. Before entering this discussion, however, it is crucial, especially in the context of a book such as this one, to recognize that what I will be discussing is just one – and in European history the most dominant – inflection of the crowd as a prototypical concern of the political philosophy of modernity. Needless to say, alternative theories of the role of collectives in politics and history were also formulated in this period, which we also associate with the emergence of modernity and democracy. For instance, Latin American history demonstrates specific ways of addressing the problems that I will focus on, and there have thus developed political and sociological theories of masses and crowd behavior that diverge from the European material that I will deal with here. Indeed, in Euclides da Cunha's classic *Os Sertões*, the author already in 1902 developed a theory of collective psychology and mass behavior to account for the Brazilian public's reaction on the Canudos uprising of 1896–97 and the public support for the ruthless violence deployed in the suppression of the rebel community.[9] By treating the Canudos crisis not as a revolt of the masses against an enlightened and educated political elite that represented the true interests of the young Brazilian republic, but rather as a conflict between two or more collectives, each claiming to speak in the name of the people in its own way, each demonstrating its own specific traits of what in mass psychology counted as

9. Significantly, Euclides da Cunha thus does not employ mass psychology mainly to explain the charisma of Antonio Conselheiro and his followers. Rather, it is when discussing the propaganda disseminated by the press and the political establishment *against* Canudos and the "Conselheiristas" that Euclides da Cunha explicitly turns to the "collective psychology" of Scipio Sighele and other European crowd theorists. Mass behavior is thus seen as an attribute not of the popular multitude, but of the Brazilian elites; Euclides da Cunha, *Rebellion in the Backlands [Os Sertões]*, trans. Samuel Putnam (Chicago: The University of Chicago Press, 1944), 225–234.

mass insanity and mass hysteria, Euclides da Cunha brought to the discourse of the masses a political prudency and theoretical refinement rarely seen in Europe at that time. Ultimately, the collective madness that European thinkers tended to ascribe to the lower classes, Euclides da Cunha ascribed to the nation as such.[10] In this context, however – and no doubt as a symptom of my Eurocentric bias – these reflections on Brazilian theorizations of crowd politics can only be developed indirectly, by implicit comparisons to the cruder European varieties that will take up the following pages.

Georg Simmel's Masses

How to describe the slow transformation of French mass psychology into the twilight discussion on mass society and cultural decline in Weimar Germany and Austria's first republic? Georg Simmel's career bridges the years between the codifications of mass psychology around 1890 and the end of World War One. Simmel was also the first one to introduce French and Italian mass psychology in Germany and Austria, presenting the two books that exerted the greatest influence on late-nineteenth century discussion on crowds and masses. Already in November 1895 he reviewed Le Bon's *La Psychologie des foules*, published in France the same year.[11] Two years later he also reviewed the German translation of Scipio Sighele's *La folla criminale*, originally published in 1892.[12]

10. Hence the very last words of Euclides da Cunha's report: "The trouble is that we do not have today [a theory of] acts of madness and crimes on the part of nations ..." (*Rebellion in the Backlands [Os Sertões]*, 476).
11. Georg Simmel, "Massenpsychologie," in *Die Zeit. Wiener Wochenschrift für Politik, Volkswirtschaft, Wissenschaft und Kunst* Vol. 5, no. 60 (23 November 1895): 119f. Reprinted in Georg Simmel, *Gesamtausgabe*, ed. Otthein Rammstedt (Frankfurt: Suhrkamp, 2000), 1: 248-251.
12. Georg Simmel, "Ueber Massenverbrechen," in *Die Zeit. Wiener Wochenschrift für Politik, Volkswirtschaft, Wissenschaft und Kunst* Vol. 13, no. 157 (2 October 1897): 4-6 in Simmel, *Gesamtausgabe*, 1: 353-361. The title of the German translation of *La folla criminale* is *Psychologie des Auflaufs und der Massenverbrechen*, trans. Hans Kurella (Dresden: Reissner, 1897). Notably, Simmel also introduced Gabriel Tarde and reviewed his *Les lois de l'imitation* in *Zeitschrift für Psychologie und Physiologie der Sinnesorgane*, vol. 2 (1891): 141f. Reprinted in Simmel, *Gesamtausgabe*, 1: 388-400.

Simmel is rarely mentioned in historical accounts of crowd theory. It is true that he never devoted a specific book or essay to the topic. In order to understand his theory of the masses we need to extract it from the general sociological writings in which it is embedded. In Simmel's work we see a German thinker approaching the category of "the masses" as it was elaborated in French crowd psychology, but only in order to open it up, extending its reference and finally applying it to the social field in its entirety. To be sure, Simmel's concept of the masses remains remarkably constant throughout this transformation, but he places it in a different theoretical and historical context. After an initial dialogue with the positivist crowd psychology of Tarde, Le Bon, and Sighele, Simmel's notion of the masses embeds itself in a different philosophical environment. The new landscape is shaped by influences from Bergson and Nietzsche, among others. Its name is vitalism, or *Lebensphilosophie* – both *lieu commun* and doxa of German thought at the beginning of the twentieth century.[13] In this way, Simmel adjusts the conceptual machinery of mass psychology to the tradition of German social philosophy, at the same time retooling it for durability in the political terrain that emerged after World War One.

In his article on Le Bon, Simmel immediately problematizes the notion of the individual as the foundation of society and knowledge. Is it not true, he asks, that the historical method of the *Geisteswissenchaften* and the heredity theory of the natural sciences (i.e. Darwinism) have demonstrated that the individual is a mere cross section (*Schnittpunkt*) of social tendencies? "Thus, society is everything, and what the individual can add to its properties is a *quantité négligeable*." Yet, this proposition, too, is problematized. For is it not also true, Simmel asks, that all things that we value in life, everything exceptional and elevated,

---

13. Donald N. Levine, "Introduction," in Georg Simmel, *On Individuality and Social Forms: Selected Writings*, ed. Donald N. Levine (Chicago: University of Chicago Press, 1971), xiv; Fredric Jameson, "The Theoretical Hesitation: Benjamin's Sociological Predecessor," in *Critical Inquiry* 25, no. 2 (winter 1999): 272f.

are "the products of individuals who have raised themselves above the social average?."[14]

It is impossible, Simmel concludes, to determine whether society is prior to the individual, or vice versa.[15] Intellectual paradigms have sometimes privileged the individualistic viewpoint, sometimes the social, Simmel observes. In contemporary France, most intellectuals lean toward the individualistic view, he argues, mentioning as evidence the enormous French interest in Nietzsche, as well as Le Bon's "ferocious charge against all kinds of democracy and socialism."[16]

Having thus refused to privilege either "individual" or "society," Simmel goes on to refute many of the assumptions of both Le Bon and Sighele. Both had defined the crowd as a single being governed by a "mass soul." Simmel objects that this definition stems from a confusion of cause and effect. Collective action often results in one massive effect – the destruction of a building, the roar emerging as if from one throat. This is where the confusion sets in, Simmel explains: "the unified external

14. Simmel, "Massenpsychologie," 119.
15. Simmel,"Massenpsychologie," 119. As Simmel later writes in *Soziologie*, the interpenetration of the social and the individual is so complete, that the question as to what is what and what comes first is merely a matter of perspective. Society is made up by individuals, but these individuals are made up by society (*Soziologie: Untersuchungen über die Formen der Vergesellschaftung* [Munich and Leipzig: Duncker and Humboldt, 1922 (1908)], 366). In his *Grundfragen der Soziologie* (1917), Simmel provides the following definition of the human: "Der Mensch als ganzer ist sozusagen ein noch ungeformter Komplex von Inhalten, Kräften, Möglichkeiten, und je nach den Motivierungen und Beziehungen des wechselnden Daseins gestaltet er sich daraus zu einem differentzierten, grenzbestimmten Gebilde. Als wirtschaftender und als politischer Mensch, als Familienmitglied und als Represäntant eines Berufes ist er sozusagen ein ad hoc konstruiertes Elaborat" ("Grundfragen der Soziologie [Individuum und Gesellschaft]," in *Gesamtausgabe* Vol. 16, eds. Gregor Fitzi and Otthein Rammstedt [Frankfurt am Main: Suhrkamp, 1999], 109). "Man in his totality is a dynamic complex of ideas, forces, and possibilities. According to the motivations and relations of life ans its changes, he makes of himself a differentiated and clearly defined phenomena. As an economic and political man, as a family member, and as a representative of an occupation, he is, as it were, an elaboration constructed ad hoc" ("Fundamental Problems of Sociology: Individual and Society," in *The Sociology of Georg Simmel*, trans. and. ed. Kurt H. Wolff [New York: Free Press, 1950, 1964], 46).
16. Simmel, "Massenpsychologie," 119.

event resulting from many subjective mental processes is interpreted as an event resulting from a unified mental process – a
process, namely, of the collective soul."[17]

Simmel also rejects the idea that the crowd can be defined by
suggestibility. In Simmel's view, the psychological processes of
an individual within a crowd is not different from those of an individual by himself. The emotional impact of a mountain view
is not qualitatively different from the impact of a surrounding
crowd.[18]

In refuting the idea of a mass soul and that of suggestibility,
Simmel in fact rejects two major criteria that until then had been
used to define the crowd, with the result that he dissolves the
foundation of French and Italian crowd psychology and removes
the frightening qualities that it attributes to "the masses." Yet, in
limiting the substance of the definition of the masses, Simmel at
the same time extends the concept's applicability. No longer an
entity following its own psychological laws, and no longer a simple ideological projection of the bourgeoisie, the mass is retained
as a category for a certain type of sociation, or *Vergesellschaftung*,
that encompasses modern society in its totality.

In one stroke, Simmel thus turns "the mass" into a sociological category. In his view, the aim of sociological inquiry
was precisely the examination of various forms of sociation
(or *Vergesellschaftung*). Sociology should not conceptualize the
contents of human activity, but the *social forms* under which this
activity is pursued. Basically, this entailed the formal study of
human interaction, including the ways in which this interaction
generates institutions, hierarchies, and structures of subjectivity, in a word, various forms of sociation. Like Max Weber and

17. Simmel, "Ueber Massenverbrechen," 5.
18. "Unser Seelenleben wird doch in jedem Augenblicke durch Menschen
und Dinge so beeinflusst, dass es in Isolierung davon überhaupt nicht zu
denken ist; die Aufgabe der Psychologie ist, zu beschreiben, wie es sich
unter diesen Umständen entwickelt. Innerhalb eben dieser kann Ich nun
zwischen dem Einfluss etwa einer Landschaft oder eines religiösen Ein-
druckes oder einer umgebenden Menge keinen principiellen Unterschied
entdecken" ("Über Massenverbrechen," 5).

Ferdinand Tönnies, the other two great founders of German sociology, Simmel inserted these forms of sociation in a historical
trajectory whose guiding thread is rationalization, differentiation, and individualization. These processes spell the doom of
one kind of society – Tönnies's *Gemeinschaft*, Weber's world of
enchantment and charisma, and Simmel's small-town life with
its homogeneous mindset and personalized exchange. In their
wake, a new society emerges. For the human subject, these processes appear to be liberating. Yet, the emancipatory thrust ends
in unprecedented forms of unfreedom, as the subject becomes
entangled in a network of functions and abstractions that de-
prives it of individuality. If we follow Tönnies' analysis, we encounter, at history's end, the instrumentalized aggregate that
he called *Gesellschaft*. If we follow Weber's analysis, we encounter a person locked inside the infamous iron cage. If we follow
Simmel, we are faced with the mass, now being posited as the
dominant form of sociation in modern society.

In my view, Simmel's definition of the mass may be summarized as follows: "the mass" is the concrete form in which the relation of human subject and society is made manifest in modern
society. This relation can be analyzed historically or formally.
Let me explain its historical meaning first.

On the very first page of his *Soziologie* (1908), Simmel states
that it was the emergence of the masses that made scholars discover the relation of individual and society.[19] As the lower classes
ascended during the nineteenth century, they also advanced into
the view of the upper classes, making these realize that the world
is not just made up by individuals situated by providence in different stations and ranks, but that there is a phenomenon called
society that conditions which class an individual will be part of.
Each human subject now appeared as socially conditioned, impossible to conceive of in abstraction from society. Historically
speaking, therefore, the presence of the masses for the first time
made manifest the relation of human subject to society.

19. Simmel, *Soziologie*, 1f.

It follows from this, Simmel argues, that the masses, in fact, are the historical origin of sociology itself, because the task of sociology is precisely to examine the relation between subject and society that the masses have exposed. Incidentally, and as evidence of Simmel's originality, this notion of the masses is very different from that of his colleague Ferdinand Tönnies. Whereas Simmel analyzed the masses as a historical formation typical of modernity, Tönnies subscribed to the more common idea that the mass was simply another name for the ordinary people, whom he regarded as the uneventful but timeless agency behind social change – the grass of history, on which society stood.[20]

Let me now turn to Simmel's formal analysis of the masses as a concrete representation of the relation between human subject and society. Simmel here repeats one crucial element of Le Bon's and Sighele's analyses, although he casts it in a theoretical frame that he developed already in *Über sociale Differenzierung* of 1890. This element concerns the leveling impact of the masses. A crowd, Simmel argues, must base its actions on desires and qualities that all its members have in common, and "what everyone have in common can only be the property of the one with the least property."[21] What Simmel argues, in short, is that the a crowd is never more intelligent than its least intelligent member, never better than its worst part, never richer in possibilities than its poorest member. "Because it is always possible for the one who is up to step down, since the one who has more also possesses what is less; but the one who is down cannot ever step up."[22]

Simmel founds this argument on a theory about the rela-

---

20. Ferdinand Tönnies, *Community and Society*, trans. Charles P. Loomis (East Lansing: The Michigan State University Press, 1957), 225: "The anonymous mass of the people is the original and dominating power which creates the houses, the villages, and the towns of the country. From it, too, spring the powerful and self-determined individuals of many different kinds: princes, feudal lords, knights, as well as priests, artists, scholars. As long as their economic condition is determined by the people as a whole, all their social control is conditioned by the will and power of the people."

21. Georg Simmel, *Über sociale Differenzierung* [1890], in *Gesamtausgabe* Vol. 2., ed. Otthein Rammstedt (Frankfurt am Main: Suhrkamp, 1989), 210.

22. Simmel, "Massenpsychologie," 119.

tion between "the individual level" and "the social level" that is central to his sociology.[23] He argues that the smaller and more homogeneous a society is, the smaller is the difference between the level of the individual and the level of the social group. As society grows larger and more heterogeneous, the individual has greater possibilities to differentiate himself. The diversification of labor allows anyone to perfect his or her mastery of a limited task. As a consequence, however, the common ground shared with others is greatly reduced; it can consist only of the simple needs and generic traits of the entire species. Whenever a human being wants to interact with others, or wants to influence them, he or she must descend to this level, for this is the only ground that he or she shares with those fellow humans. This form of sociation is further increased by a related process, which concerns not so much the relation of the individual and the social level as the relation between the individual level and the size of the social community: the smaller and more homogeneous the society is, the smaller is the freedom and differentiation of the individual within it, but the greater is also this individual's possibility to influence society. By contrast, the greater and more heterogeneous the society is, the greater also is the freedom and differentiation of the individual, yet the lesser is the individual's possibility to influence society and get social recognition. Thus, as the size of the social group increases, individual freedom increases, while individual agency decreases.[24] The form of sociation in modernity thus allows everyone to become a genius in his own *Gebiet*, but at the cost of becoming an idiot in everything else. Simmel calls it a "sociological tragedy."[25]

---

23. Simmel, *Über sociale Differenzierung*, 199-236. The analysis of mass behavior formulated here thus returns in his article on Le Bon, "Massenpsychologie" of 1895, in his majestic *Soziologie* of 1908, and in *Grundfragen der Soziologie (Individuum und Gesellschaft)* of 1917. The remarkable constancy of Simmel's analysis of the masses is signaled in that certain formulations are repeated in all four publications.

24. Georg Simmel, "Group Expansion and the Development of Individuality," in *On Individuality and Social Forms*, 251- 293; original in *Soziologie*, 527-573; cf. *Über sociale Differenzierung*, cf. 169-198.

25. "The more refined, highly developed, articulated the qualities of an

The consequences of the sociological tragedy are manifest-
ed in the mass, Simmel asserts. An individual who attempts to
assert his or her individuality socially finds that he or she can
effectively do this only by descending to the lowest common
denominator of the members of his society. It is in this context
that Simmel produces a clear definition of "the mass." He discusses the questionable virtue of journalists, actors, and dema-
gogues who "seek the favour of the masses." This would not be
so bad, he states, if these persons really served the mass as a sum
of individuals. Yet, the mass they serve is no such sum:

> It is a new phenomenon made up, not of the total indi-
> vidualities of its members, but only of those fragments of
> each of them in which he concides with all others. These
> fragments, therefore, can be nothing but the lowest and
> most primitive. It is this *mass*, and the level that must al-
> ways remain accessible to each of its members that these
> intellectually and morally endangered persons serve –
> and not each of its members in its entirety.[26]

The sociological tragedy is accentuated by a closely related dilemma, what Simmel calls "the tragedy of culture." For Simmel,
human life is an ongoing attempt to express one's inner being
in external forms, cultural products, identities, and institutions.
These forms constitute what Simmel calls "objective culture,"
in contradistinction to "subjective culture," the ineffable life
process itself, that Henri Bergson called *élan vital*, which con-

individual are, the more unlikely are they to make him similar to other
individuals and to form a unit with corresponding qualities in others.
Rather, they tend to become incomparable; and the elements in terms of
which the individual can count on adapting himself to others and forming
a homogeneous mass with them, are increasingly reduced to lower and
primitively more sensuous levels. This explains how it is possible for the
"folk" or "mass" to be spoken of with contempt, without there being any
need for the individual to feel himself referred to by this usage, which
actually does not refer to any individual." ("Fundamental Problems of
Sociology: Individual and Society," Wolff, *The Sociology of Georg Simmel*, 32;
Grundfragen der Soziologie, 94.)
26. Ibid., 33/96.

stantly urges for expression and for form.[27] As layer upon layer of objective culture accumulates, these petrified sediments will gradually prevent the life process from reaching full expression.[28] Modern culture is more tormented than any other era by the conflict between individuals urging to express their individuality more strongly than ever and a life world grown so dense, rigid, and intrusive that it effectively prevents everyone from expressing his or her individuality. In his famous essay "The Metropolis and Mental Life" (1903), Simmel contends that the growing division of labor reduces the individual "to a *quantité négligeable*, to a grain of dust as against the vast overwhelming organization of things and forces which gradually take out of his hands all progress, spirituality and value [. . .]."[29]

As we have seen, in his article on Le Bon's mass psychology Simmel stated that the mass reduces the individual to a "quantité négligeable," a negligible quantity. Here, using the same figure of speech, he claims that modern society as such reduces the individual to a negligible quantity. Evidently, the same form of sociation is at work in both cases. Simmel argues, in short, that in modern society, the mass constitutes the relation – the point of mediation – between the human subject and society. The mass is the objective culture, and the structure of sociation,

27. Georg Simmel, "Subjective Culture," in Levine, *On Individuality and Social Forms: Selected Writings*, 227-234. "Vom Wesen der Kultur," in *Brücke und Tür: Essays des Philosophen zur Geschichte, Religion, Kunst und Gesellschaft*, eds. Margarete Sussman and Michael Landmann (Stuttgart: Koehler, 1957), 86-94.
28. The contradiction between the immediacy of "subjective culture" and the mediated forms of "objective culture" is a chronic feature of history, Simmel states ("The Conflict in Modern Culture," in Levine, *On Individuality and Social Forms: Selected Writings*, 393). Yet, only in modern culture is the conflict so acute as to reveal itself as the driving force of history: As a result, "the typically problematic situation of modern man comes into being: his sense of being surrounded by an innumerable number of cultural elements which are neither meaningless to him nor, in the final analysis meaningful. In their mass, they depress him" ("Der Begriff und die Tragödie der Kultur," in *Philosophische Kultur: Gesammelte Essais* [Leipzig: Werner Klinkhardt, 1911], 273).
29. George Simmel, "The Metropolis and Mental Life," in *On Individuality and Social Forms*, 337. Translation modified. "Die Grossstädte und das Geistesleben," in Simmel, *Brücke und Tür*, 240f.

in opposition to which the subject tries to express his or her individuality. In Simmel's theory, everything external to the mass is also external to the social; it is individual. The mass is the social essence of the human subject.

Let's return to Simmel's historical examination of the forms of sociation that prevail in modern society. As I have mentioned, Simmel argues that it was the emergence of the masses that forced scholars to the discovery of "society." The truly dialectical moment in Simmel's analysis arrives when he explains that the emergence of the mass as a dominant form of sociation, is, in its turn, a result of individualism.[30] The individualism of equality and the rights of man emancipated individuals from those pre-modern social bonds that previously circumscribed their being, setting them free to realize their universal human essence. Yet, this emancipation of everybody's human qualities has tragically led to its opposite, Simmel claims. The human essence that someone can realize consists only of the primitive parts of his or her being that he or she shares with everyone else. In a word, universal human being is a mass being.

But there is also a different individualism, Simmel stresses. There is the individualism of Romanticism, according to which each subject strives to express not a universal essence but his or her particular essence, or individuality. This project also founders, however, but for different reasons. The weight of "objective culture" is in modern society so great that there is no room for anyone's expression of his or her "subjective culture."

Ultimately, then, what emerges in Simmel's analysis are two notions of individualism, which prevent each other's realization. There is an individualism of equality that levels everyone to the common level of the masses – the sociological tragedy. There is an individualism of difference that throws up such an excess of petrified objective culture that all efforts to express one's individuality are crushed – the tragedy of culture. In both cases, the

30. This analysis runs through Simmel's work, from *Über sociale Differenzierung* (1890), 181-190, over *Soziologie* (1908), 527-573, and "Die Grosstädte und das Geistesleben" (1903), to *Grundfragen der Soziologie* (1917), 122-149.

result is the same: a society of masses.

When Simmel speaks of the mass, he does not speak about a concrete social phenomenon, as the French crowd psychologists did. The crowd is for him a sociological structure, always construed in dialectical tension with another abstract structure, individuality. In Simmel's *Lebensphilosophie*, these structures are eventually assimilated into a metaphysics, as two forms of appearance of the eternal dialectic between life and form. Just as life seeks to appear in its naked immediacy, but can do so only by producing forms that betray this immediacy, so does individuality seek to realize itself by raising above the common level of the masses, only to find itself pulled down to the baseline from which the project of self-realization must begin anew. This is what Hegel would have called a bad dialectic, because it has no telos or synthesis. It is also related to what philosopher Max Scheler, in a famous address of 1927, defined as a process of equalization or evening out (Ausgleich).[31] Scheler saw this as the dominant tendency of modernity, and he argued that it could usher in an era of democracy and tolerance, erasing national boundaries and defusing the conflict between masses and elites, provided it received an adequate political response. However, Simmel does not recognize any possibilities of that kind. For him, the problem is not so much that the dialectic is infinite, because as long as it continues, the rejuvenating process of life is an end in itself. The problem is rather that in modernity, the dialectical process has reached a standstill, as the poles have been equalized. The institutional forms that once kept individuality elevated above the dull level of normality have been dismantled. Therefore, the dialectical tension between individuality and mass has collapsed. The two will henceforth ceaselessly pass over into each other.

Simmel devoted one of his most brilliant essays to a cultural phenomenon that epitomizes this rapid oscillation between

---

31. Max Scheler, "Der Mensch im Weltalter des Ausgleichs," in *Philosophische Weltanschauung* (Berlin: Francke Verlag, 1954), 89-118.

individual and mass, uniqueness and conformity: Fashion. Fashion satisfies the demand for social adaptation and makes the subject conform to the mass. At the same time, fashion allows everyone to feel like a unique individual. The human subject becomes unique by participating in a mass phenomenon, and he or she adapts to the mass by expressing his or her individuality.[32] Fashion allows the human subject to be a part of the mass and an individual at one and the same time. Fashion thus signifies the destruction of those embankments that once separated the dry ground of individuality from the fluid element of the masses.

I mentioned that Simmel saw the emergence of this form of sociation, the mass, as a result of individualism. If we place Simmel's major work, *The Philosophy of Money*, alongside his long chapter on power in *Soziologie*, we see that his work also provides a materialist foundation for this argument. In *Soziologie*, he describes the mechanisms of "Superordination and Subordination" that stabilize and stratify any given society. *The Philosophy of Money*, for its part, describes how the money economy, the great leveler, dissolves institutional arrangements and makes all personal values and individual identities fluid and interchangeable.[33] These processes thus erode those mechanisms of "Superordination and Subordination" that once stratified society by erecting a hierarchy of representatives and represented, individuals and masses. A society without a firm framework for the organization of power and the stratification of the social field is a society where individuals and masses are inseparable. Simmel's theory articulates the form of sociation that prevails in such a society, a society in which everybody moves from triumphant individuality to absolute anonymity in an instant. When distinguishing this form of sociation from others, Simmel always employed the notion of the mass.

---

32. Georg Simmel, "Fashion," in *On Individuality and Social Forms*, 296. "Die Mode," in *Philosophische Kultur*, 32.
33. georg Simmel, *Philosophy of Money*, trans. Tom Bottomore and David Frisby (London: Routledge, 2nd ed. 1990) 283-429.

Conclusion and Further Perspectives

"My legacy," Georg Simmel wrote shortly before his death, "will be like cash, distributed to many heirs, each transforming his part into use according to *his* nature."[34] I believe Simmel's theory provides such a supreme articulation of the ideological dilemmas in post-war Germany and Austria that it fuses with the general cultural discourse of the era. As Simmel himself predicted, the dilemmas that he examined were inherited by many and resolved in vastly different ways.

At one extreme, the traditional principle of individuality was reinforced and magnified as the only solution to the deplorable alienation and leveling of the human condition that, supposedly, characterized modernity, and post-war Germany and Austria in particular. By the 1920s, writes intellectual historian Fritz Ringer, "no German professor doubted that a profound 'crisis of culture' was at hand."[35] One result of this tendency was a constant rehashing of Simmel's antinomy of individuality and massification.[36] "Contempt for the masses is a typical characteristic of most intellectuals of the Weimar Republic," Helmuth Berking observes.[37] This contempt, he asserts, was a defensive reaction.[38] Werner Sombart, a colleague of Simmel and a highly influential figure in early German sociology, provides another illustration. Summarizing the state of the masses, to which he

---

34. Levine, "Introduction," xiii.
35. Fritz K. Ringer, *The Decline of the German Mandarins: The German Academic Community, 1890-1933* (Cambridge, Mass.: Harvard University Press, 1969), 254.
36. In addition to sociological works analyzed in this chapter, examples are provided by, for instance, Gerhard Lehmann, *Das Kollektivbewusstsein: Systematische und historisch/kritische Vorstudien zur Soziologie* (Berlin: Junker und Dünnhaupt Verlag, 1929); Georg Stieler, *Person und Masse: Untersuchungen zur Grundlegung einer Massenpsychologie* (Leipzig: Felix Meiner Verlag, 1929); Siegfried Sieber, *Die Massenseele: Ein Beitrag zur Psychologie des Krieges, der Kunst, und der Kultur* (Dresden and Leipzig: Globus Wissenschaftliche Verlagsanstalt, 1918); and Julius R. Rossbach, *Die Massenseele: Psychologische Betrachtungen über die Entstehung von Volks- (Massen-) Bewegungen Revolutionen* (Munich: Rudolph Müller & Steinicke, 1919).
37. Helmuth Berking, *Masse und Geist: Studien zur Soziologie in der Weimarer Republik* (Berlin: Wissenschaftlicher Autoren Verlag (WAV), 1984), 65.
38. Berking, *Masse und Geist*, 66-68.

counted the lower classes in general, Sombart found three distinguishing traits:

> 1. The masses are mentally limited, not just stupid; that is, they only have practical understanding: their intelligence measures up to the concrete and the technical, not to the abstract and general, to what is practical rather than theoretical. [...] 2. The masses do not let themselves be guided by rational grounds in their behavior, but either by custom or by compulsive impulses, feelings, moods: they have an "irrational," feminine predisposition. 3. The masses are in their emotional life at a very low level: the average of their scale of values is very low: values of pleasure and utility are predominant. Their sensations and feelings are primitive, "natural," crude, undifferentiated.[39]

Sombart was pained by a post-war situation in which the privileges of the intellectual elite were undermined by media technology, urban forms of life, and ideas of democracy. For German mandarins whose worldviews were organized in terms of "Bildung," "Geist," "Kultur," "Persönlichkeit," "Seele," "Innerlichkeit," and "Individualität," the masses could only appear as a symptom of decline. Hence the frequent appeals to the necessity of personal cultivation and aesthetic education of all citizens, hence the calls for *Führung*, and hence the reminders of the re-

---

39. Werner Sombart, *Der proletarische Sozialismus ("Marxismus")*, vol. 1: "Die Lehre," vol. 2: "Die Bewegung" (Jena: Verlag von Gustav Fischer, 1924), 2: 170. [1. Die großen Massen sind geistig beschränkt, nicht etwa'dumm'; das heißt: sie haben nur praktischen Verstand: ihre Intelligenz ist dem Konkreten, Werkhaften, nicht dem Abstrakten und Allgemeinen, dem 'Praktischen, nicht dem Theoretischen gewachsen. [...] 2. Die großen Massen lassen sich in ihrem Verhalten nicht von Gründen leiten, sondern entweder von der Überlieferung oder triebhaften Impulsen, Gefühlen, Stimmungen: sie ist 'irrational', femenin veranlagt. 3. Die großen Massen haben ein tiefes Niveau in ihrem Gefühls- und Empfindungsleben: der Durchschnittspunkt ihrer Werteskala liegt sehr niedrig: Annehmlichkeits- und Nützlichkeitswerte herrschen vor. Ihre Empfindungen und Gefühle sind primitiv, 'natürlich', grob, undifferentziert.]

sponsibility of the elite in the life of the nation. Another writer, having described the 1918 November Revolution in Germany as a product of "feminine, primitive, fickle, moody, barbaric, and monstrous" masses, ended a 1919 book on "Die Massenseele" (The Mass Soul) with an exhortation: "Let us hope that a German leader with brazen heart and ironclad chest will arise from our people"[40]. This is the Weimar discourse on the masses that is best known, an "aristocratic" criticism of mass society, and the one that has been the focus of scholarly studies[41]. It is also the one that was ultimately realized in the fascist enthronement of the *Führer* as the embodiment of society. Sombart is representative in this sense as well; in the early 1930s, he came to support the Nazis.[42]

Theoretically, this version is as sterile as it is simple: given the definition of the masses as opposed to individuality, and given the view of individuality as the support of culture and knowledge, the conclusion follows automatically: a representation of the masses as disorderly and destructive, as an agent of

40. Rossbach, *Die Massenseele*, 31, 33.
41. For important studies, yet limited in focus as they deal solely with the areas of sociology, mass psychology, and cultural philosophy, see Berking, *Masse und Geist*; Helmut König, *Zivilisation und Leidenschaften: Die Masse im bürgerlichen Zeitalter* (Reinbek bei Hamburg: Rowohlt 1992); Nori Möding, *Die Angst der Bürgers vor der Masse: Zur politischen Verführbarkeit des deutschen Geistes im Ausgang seiner bürgerlichen Epoche* (Berlin: Wissenschaftlicher Autoren-Verlag, 1984); Manfred Franke, *Der Begriff der Masse in der Sozialwissenschaft: Darstellung eines Phänomens und seine Bedeutung in der Kulturkritik des 20. Jahrhunderts*, Diss. (Mainz: Johannes Gutenberg-Universität, 1985); see also the contributions by Volker Heins ("Demokratie als Nervensache: Zum Verhältnis von Politik und Emotion bei Max Weber"), Thomas Noetzel ("Max Webers 'Neue Menschen' – Das Leben als Bewährungsaufstieg"), Timm Genett ("Vom Zivilisierungsagenten zur Gefolgschaft: Die Masse im politischen Denkens Robert Michaels'"), and Alex Demirovic ("Kritische Theorie bürgerlicher Herrschaft und die Widersprüchlichkeit der Massen") to the anthology *Masse – Macht – Emotionen: Zu einer politischen Soziologie der Emotionen*, ed. Ansgar Klein and Frank Nullmeier (Opladen/Wiesbaden: Westdeutscher Verlag, 1999); also to be included in this category is Alexander Mitscherlich's classic: *Massenpsychologie ohne Ressentiment: Sozialpsychologische Betrachtungen* (Frankfurt am Main: Suhrkamp, 1972).
42. For an analysis of Werner Sombart's later thought and career, see Jeffrey Herf, *Reactionary Modernism: Technology, Culture, and Politics in Weimar and the Third Reich* (Cambridge: Cambridge University Press, 1984), 130-151.

leveling passions that must either be raised by education, struck down by suppression, or cleansed by fascist doctrines.

However, even this seemingly simple discourse was articulated in a variety of contexts and genres and with various degrees of originality. Georg Simmel's disciples and colleagues in sociology no doubt provided the most serious treatment of the topic, albeit never really challenging the binary framework that posited the mass as a deviation from a norm. Here I have no space to pursue this analysis, and will instead conclude by demonstrating how the analysis of the masses that I have traced through Georg Simmel's work was played out as an ideology and cultural stereotype in the general culture of Germany in the 1920s.

If we were to choose one cultural document to embody the spirit of Weimar culture, Fritz Lang's *Metropolis* from 1927 would surely be a predictable candidate. Not only because of its dystopian narrative about a future civilization where the companionship of machine and capital has reduced humanity to a toiling herd. And not only because of its experimental form in which futurism and science fiction were fused with social commentary and gothic expressionism into a vexing imagery of special effects and stage craft that surpassed everything else in its era. And also not only because it was the biggest and most expensive motion picture made in the period, a true mass mobilization of the productive capacity of Weimar's cultural industry. But also because of its archetypal portrayal of the crowd, which in Lang's film is a character in its own right, and the one most deeply affected by the cultural and political fantasies of its time.

The masses in *Metropolis* are anonymous and dressed in uniform. They are placed at the lowest level of the capital city, working in underground power plants and factories and holding meetings in the catacombs. Lang's masses are not only untouched by civilization and light. They also lack cognitive ability and individuality. Two forces control them: either the hard discipline that impels them to show up every day for their shift in the various plants where they work themselves to death; or the ideological manipulation that excites their passions to the point where they erupt in rebellions in which they destroy the machinery and cause the lower levels of Metropolis to be flooded, almost killing their own wives and children.

If the masses thus signify body and instincts, Joh Fredersen, the individual that rules Metropolis, signifies mind and intelligence. The film thus posits masses and individual as opposites, and it lets this opposition unfold in any number of related binaries: body against brain, hand against mind, depth against surface, earth against sky, darkness against and light, passion against reason, ignorance against science, primitivity against civilization, femininity against masculinity. The spectacular visual scenery as well as the filmic action is driven by these tensions and the attempt to mediate between them.

Interestingly, the main mediator and catalyst of these tensions is a woman, Maria. At the beginning, she soothes the hapless masses, encouraging their righteous instincts to help them endure. In the science-fiction scenario of the film, Maria is then cloned. Her double is identical in looks to the authentic Maria, but opposite in terms of character. The artificial Maria usurps her position as spiritual leader of the workers, and agitates them to revolt. The rivaling Marias – one virgin, one vamp – illustrate not only the ambiguously deceptive nature of femininity, which was another cultural stereotype of the era, but also display the alleged fickleness of the masses, as they impulsively react on any stimuli they receive. According to Lang's scenario, the masses must be guided by somebody capable of directing their passions toward constructive aims, as the real Maria strives to do. Otherwise, the masses become a force of destruction, as the artificial Maria is there to show.

The happy ending of Lang's film consists not in undoing any of the oppositions generated by its social fantasy, but in mending the social divide. This is accomplished through the ritual purging of the female desire embodied by Maria, whose destructive aspect is displayed by the robot-vamp that arouses the workers' lust to revolt; and at the same time through the symbolic castration of the workers, whose inability to maintain the high-tech infrastructure of Metropolis serves to justify their being held in servitude by their capitalist master. Sexual and political passions are thus thoroughly vilified and eliminated, as female desire is visually translated into self-defeating mass violence. As Andreas Huyssen has pointed out, the seductive character of the film stems from its capacity to ignite a sexual and political desire, which is then trimmed and adapted to the technological and economic demands of the existing order.[43] Anton Kaes is also on the mark, showing how the film systematically associates collective political organization with feminine hysteria and mad violence: "the very idea of a revolt is delegitimized."[44]

Instead of challenging the idea that most people are masses and live in the dark, *Metropolis* teaches that the majority needs firm and fair supervision by rational individuals. And instead of challenging the idea that only some are rational individuals, it teaches those happy few that they depend on the services of the masses. *Metropolis* is thus a film that opted for social compromise, at the same time calling for compassion for those who were suffering the consequences of status quo. The film rushed to endorse the crumbling compact between capital and labor, codified in the Stinnes-Legien agreement of November 1918 in which the employers offered social policy in exchange for the workers' renouncing of socialization, at the very time when support for the agreement had started to erode.[45]

For my purposes, what is most important is the film's function as a "sponge," to use an expression of Thomas Elsaesser, which sucks up all the ingredients in the dominant social and political imaginary of Weimar Germany.[46] In this imaginary, the

43. Andreas Huyssen, "The Vamp and the Machine: Fritz Lang's *Metropolis*," in *After the Great Divide: Modernism, Mass Culture, Postmodernism* (Bloomington: Indiana University Press, 1986), 65–81.
44. Kaes, *Shell Shock Cinema*, 196.
45. Heinrich A. Winkler, *Von der Revolution zur Stabilisierung: Arbeiter und Arbeiterbewegung in der Weimarer Republik 1918 bis 1924* (Berlin: Verlag J. H. W. Dietz, 1985), 75–84.
46. Thomas Elsaesser, *Metropolis* (London: British Film Institute Publishing, 2000), 20.

masses loomed large as an unstable and potentially dangerous agent at the depth of the social world. It is as though Fritz Lang tapped all the period's fears and fantasies of the masses and invented the visuals that matched them. The fame of *Metropolis* is due in no small part to its innovative experiments with the moving pictures' ability to render masses in motion. It set the standard for cinematographic depictions of crowds, showing how the rhythms and physiognomies of the collective vary depending on its location in street, church, factory, dance hall, political meeting, or the like. According to many commentators, however, Lang's experiments with perspective, superimposition, projection speed, editing, and special effects only tended to confirm established ideas of the masses as the underbelly of humanity.[47] Spanish filmmaker Luis Buñuel remarked in his review of the film that Lang had in fact forgotten one actor, "full of novelty and possibilities: the crowd." For despite the omnipresence of crowd scenes in *Metropolis*, the mass seemed present not for its own sake, nor to demonstrate some more specific social condition, but as a vindication of an authoritarian perspective according to which reason and agency were wholly on the side of the individual mastermind. As Buñuel stated, the multitudes of *Metropolis* "seem to fill a decorative role, that of a huge ballet; they aim to impress us by their beautifully choreographed and balanced movement rather than allow us to see their soul, their subordination to more human, more objective agencies."[48] The same point was later elaborated by Siegfried Kracauer, who regarded *Metropolis* as a dress rehearsal for fascism, in which the masses were patterned into ornaments according to the directions of the leader. The workers' "rebellion results in the es-

47. For a discussion of the reception of *Metropolis*, see Huyssen, "The Wamp and the Machine," 65–68; Elsaesser, *Metropolis*, 42-56; as well as Holger Bachman, "The Production and Contemporary Reception of *Metropolis*," and Michael Minden, "The Critical Recption of *Metropolis*," both in *Fritz Lang's* Metropolis: *Cinematic Visions of Technology and Fear*, ed. Michael Minden and Holger Bachmann (Rochester, N. Y.: Camden House, 2000), 3-56.
48. Luis Buñuel, "Metropolis," trans. Carol O'Sullivan, in *Fritz Lang's* Metropolis, 107. Originally published in *Gazeta Literaría de Madrid*, 1927.

tablishment of totalitarian authority, and [the rebels] consider this result a victory."[49] In this way, *Metropolis* illustrates how the main ideological problem in Weimar culture was most typically resolved. The masses were everywhere. And wherever they were, authority was called for.

---

49. Siegfried Kracauer, *From Caligari to Hitler: A Psychological History of the German Film*, (1947; revised edition, Princeton: Princeton University Press, 2004), 164.

Multitude and Democracy

Fredrika Spindler

What is a multitude? In the political-philosophical landscape of the past decade, this somewhat antiquated notion has established itself in various languages, from Toni Negri and Michael Hardt's influential and much-debated works *Empire* and *Multitude*,[1] to the work of other theoreticians like Etienne Balibar, Ernesto Laclau, and Paolo Virno, to name just a few. For Hardt and Negri, the multitude designates a new political subject, characterized by a collective, multiform, differentiated and most of all moving being; a border-transgressing, loose but essentially dynamic assemblage of individuals whose movements are determined by common desires. The multitude is a collective political subject, constituted in that global age that in theoretical terms should rightly be called post-sovereign: our own age, in a world in which a ubiquitous, all-engulfing capitalism has transcended all national borders and particular regimes, but where, also, a global proletariat can take shape in new compositions, constellations of power and communities of production. Born out of the suffocating powerlessness that is the effect of capitalism's hydra-like despotism, it constitutes a bastard, a monster opening up for a democracy that is ontological rather than a parliamentary regime.

Hardt's and Negri's thesis has, not surprisingly, met with as much enthusiasm as criticism: political activists all over the world claim it as the expression of the possibility not only of rethinking but also of realizing a politics of the future; others – philosophers certainly but also political actors question not only its optimism, unyielding to any compromise whatsoever,

1. Michael Hardt and Antonio Negri, *Empire* (Cambridge, Mass.: Harvard University Press, 2000). Michael Hardt and Antonio Negri, *Multitude: War and Democracy in the Age of Empire* (London: Hamish Hamilton, 2005).

and point to the undeniable odors of radical Marxism that ema-
nate from it – a Marxism from which many have, for several
decades, sworn themselves free, speaking of it as an unfortunate
youth-related disease from which they have happily long since
recovered. Whether the theories of Hardt and Negri are valid,
and their understanding of history, their analysis and diagnos-
tic of the contemporary are correct can and must, of course be
discussed. But in order to do so, the concept constituting the
central point of the thesis, and constituting also both the point
of departure, understood as condition, and the object, understood as the aim of the analysis, must be submitted to a closer
examination. What is a multitude, the collective multiplicity
that in this instance appears as both constituting and acting, but
which is also, at the same time, characterized by its looseness,
namelessness, diversity, and disparity? What does this far from
new concept, brought in from the Latin *multitudo* – thereby easily understood in both English and Latin, but far more foreign,
strange and even perhaps clumsy in Swedish – a philosophical
multitude that in its specifically defined conceptuality claims to
be something else than any given manifold or multiplicity, and
which, in its essential collectivity, differs from the most obviously closely related terms such as mass, mob, crowd, just as much
as from the more positively connoting political term *people*? In
other words, in what way can we understand the multitude as
the specific political subject it claims to be, and how are we to
understand it in its proper conceptuality?

As is well known, the use of the term multitude in Hardt's
and Negri's works constitutes a direct reconnection to Spinoza's
political analysis. The 17th-century philosophical context that
Spinoza addressed in his *Theologico-Political Treatise* and the
Political Treatise – the former, as is well-known, published anon-
ymously during Spinoza's lifetime and the latter posthumously
and incomplete – had no reason not to be familiar with the notion of multitude: the term occurs frequently in early Modern
and Modern political philosophers that, occupied, as they are,
with examining and establishing the conditions for a sustain-

able and well-functioning political state and regime, invariably found themselves confronted with the question concerning how a large number of people – the mass – can and should be governed by an absolute sovereign, obliged by the power that he wields to guarantee the largest possible amount of freedom and rights for those that he governs. Hence, the multitude in Hobbes' *On the Citizen*, (*De Cive*) and *Leviathan* is the very concept of the unspecified, menacing gathering of lawless individuals who, through the institution of civil right, move from a savage and chaotic state of nature – where all are at war against all – to a stable civil state, thereby transforming from a multitude into citizens, having both rights and duties. And when Spinoza, in the *Theologico-Political Treatise* – composed in haste in the middle of a political crisis that placed the relatively tolerant Dutch society of the time in danger of becoming the battlefield of different political and ecclesiastic parties, analyses precisely how a too tight-woven connection between different structures of power constituted by political and religious authorities not only results in a population that is enslaved, insecure and superstitious, but furthermore, entails putting the state in danger in a fundamental way, it might, from a political perspective, be seen as an analysis that comes very close to that of Hobbes. Just like his predecessor, to whose texts he indeed refers, Spinoza speaks of the necessity of establishing a strong state grounded on a sovereign power; like Hobbes, he also talks of a social pact through which the population is to be transformed into citizens, by transferring their natural right to the civil right that founds and sustains the society shared by all and guaranteed by the sovereign. However, contrary to Hobbes, and to most of the Modern political-philosophical tradition, Spinoza will claim the necessity of, firstly, a radical separation between political and religious power. This is because religiosity, in the general sense, is founded in superstition, wishful thinking and non-reasonable thinking, thereby constituting a much too powerful vector of abuse of power, abuse of hopes and fears, and, generally speaking, all sorts of sad passions. Secondly, Spinoza claims that civil right, in order to be real and efficient, in fact must be founded on what for him is natural right – the *conatus*, or persevering in an actual existence, that characterizes every living organism.

Thus, the political and ethical analysis undertaken by Spinoza in his political writings, perfectly in coherence with what he has formerly established in the *Ethics*, in fact turns the modern political problematic or question somewhat upside down. If the question was and remains how it will be possible to ascertain a durable and peaceful society – of which the purpose, in Spinoza's words, can and must be nothing but the making real and guaranteeing of each and every one of its citizen's freedom – the key to Spinoza's reasoning is not the question of how to ensure that the menacing and irrational mass submit itself to the sovereign's conditions. On the contrary, the question will be that of understanding how the human being's functioning on both an individual and a collective level leads to the possibility of a society that – fundamentally and ontologically – is always already democratic, empowering rather than enslaving, open rather than closed – but that also always, at its core, bears the risk or possibility of its own subversion, destruction and ruin. The main difference between not only Spinoza and Hobbes, but between Spinoza and modern contractual theoreticians, resides in the understanding of the human being that is not an already constituted individual, a whole and full subject, that more or less voluntarily will engage in a pact with other human beings in order, together with them, to constitute a collective existence: instead, the human being is understood as being always already, in her individuality (that is, as an indivisible unity made up of a specific, actual and living body with its mental correspondence called ideas) constituted by an existing-together, determined by it and indissolubly connected with it. This collective existing-together is for Spinoza both a condition and an inescapable ground or foundation, both on the local and on the infinitely extensive, global plane.

To the readers of the *Ethics*, this appears in no way as strange or mysterious: every singularly existing mode is formed by the relation between its own degree of power – that is, its conatus – and the powers of the whole that surrounds it. The more compatible these other powers are with the power of the singular mode, the more it will develop and gain strength. Inversely, the more incompatible the surrounding powers are with those of the singular mode's power, the more weakened, threatened and dissolved it becomes. The condition of a mode's continued existence is thus to have surroundings as compatible with itself as possible. In Spinoza's words, it becomes a matter of surrounding oneself with modes whose composition is congenial to one's own to the highest possible extent, since analogous compositions imply analogous powers that can be united to each other in a constructive way. This is the reason why Spinoza, right from the start, claims that human being on a modal or ontological level can only be understood through a human co-existence that determines her the most, since the affective similarities in individual human compositions imply a complex tissue of mutual, multiple determinations. But this also implies a radical seamlessness between the individual and the collective existence: just as the human body is composed of a large number of parts, that all relate to one another by certain measures or degrees of movement and rest, and are held together by a communicating dynamic in a state of tension and mutual causality, so the individual human bodies, each defined by its degree of conatus, are parts of compositions far more extended than the single body. From this perspective, nature as a whole constitutes one single body: so, too, does every society, federation, group – in fact, every different (and not only) human constellation that is held together by common affective ties. If the individual is formed and determined by its context, the whole is just as formed and determined by the individuals that compose it: this is the reason why we, when it comes to understanding both an individual and a collectivity, are dealing with a continuously shifting, moving, multiform figure that continuously exhibits change in its composition. Thereby, we also understand the fundamental instability that characterizes all compositions – an instability evident to a higher extent the more they are composite, and thus contain more possibilities of affecting and being affected in turn.

Spinoza's work highlights this relation from two different perspectives. In the *Ethics*, the focus is on the movements and affective connections that structure the relation between the singular mode itself and the world, in order to show how external determination can be matched by an increasing inner determination, that is to say, an increasing degree of power of *conatus* through joyous passions that render possible adequate knowledge. In the *Theologico-Political Treatise* and the *Political Treatise*, the question remains the same, but from the obverse perspective: here, it is about how the collective composition is determined by the whole of the individual passions, thereby shaping the context in which individuals are affected again in turn. The analysis of these movements constitutes the ground for a political thinking that wants to enable the same increase of *conatus* on a collective level that the *Ethics* stages on a local level. The difficulty of this, unsurprisingly, is very proportional and fully logical: the passions that structure the singular individual are limited to a singular body and its thus *relatively* limited affectivity, while the passions of the collectivity are at play in a body infinitely more extended and composed. Consequently, the movements between joyous and sad passions are infinitely more variable and violent, with consequences that, in an exponential way, influence all the parts of the whole. Seen from this double perspective, it becomes clear, justly pointed out in the analyses of both Alexandre Matheron[2] and Etienne Balibar,[3] why Spinoza's political analysis, in a way very different both from his predecessors and his successors, is not primarily about the relation between the state and the individual and vice versa, but about the relation between the individual and the collectivity,

2. Alexandre Matheron, *Individu et communauté chez Spinoza* (Paris: Éditions de Minuit, 1988).
3. Étienne Balibar, *Spinoza et la politique* (Paris: PUF, 1985) and "Spinoza l'Anti-Orwell. La crainte des masses," *Les temps modernes* vol. 41, no 470 (1985): 353-398.

which, in turn, can be expressed in various manners of political regime. The political question thus takes shape in attempting to understand the movements between individual and collectivity, singularities and pluralities, since it is these movements and their inner logic that are at the basis for the possibilities of instituting a sustainable state.

The problematic concerning the relation between individual and collectivity leads us back to the question of what the multitude is, and the part it plays in Spinoza's political ontology. To the reader of Hobbes, it would be logical to conclude that the term has a general sense: the multitude (in Hobbes) is the mass, the multiplicity of individuals that are to be united in order not to pose a threat, either to one another or to the constituted state – or, of course, to the sovereign. But for Spinoza, collective existence not only has many faces, but also many names. The detailed analysis of Étienne Balibar[4] shows that the concept of multitude occurs in fact rather sparsely: in the *Ethics*, it hardly figures in the political sense, and only rarely, on a limited number of occasions, in the *Theologico-Political Treatise*. Collective existence, in both these works, goes under other denominations, all of which signal the problematic power of this existence: *ignari* (the ignorant), *plebs* (the mob without education), *vulgus* (the man on the street), and even *turba* (swarm). In a few contexts, we find more positive, albeit rather hypothetical terms: *populus* (the people) and *cives* (the citizens). All these notions are, for Spinoza (as for Hobbes and many other political philosophers) negatively charged: through a combination of quantity, affectivity and ignorance – that is, ignorance of what passions determines its ideas and actions – the mass constitutes something explosive, hardly compatible with the stability that every state regime, without exception, must necessarily strive for since no state wants to abolish itself. Parenthetically, however, it is important that we note that the ignorance in question here is not, for Spinoza, the unfortunate privilege of a certain kind of col-

4. Ibid.

lectivity, but the result of an ontological, fundamental state for every human being, as long as she is determined to a high extent by external circumstances that she can't influence, rather than being determined by rational knowledge that manages to enlighten the ways in which external events imply an increase or a weakening of her own power: this, as we know, is the main subject of the *Ethics*. In the *Theologico-Political Treatise*, this analysis is further developed to show how ignorance is forcefully used by political and/or religious structures of power in order to govern the mass or the people by means of its own (sad) passions – that is, by fear, superstition and hatred. So, notions of mass, mob and so on are just as negative and potentially dangerous in Spinoza's eyes as in Hobbes', and many others. But in Spinoza's view, there are two major points that are absolutely decisive for the political analysis and for the development of the theoretical, political subject which remains to be formulated. In the first place, this collective explosiveness cannot be domesticated or tamed by means of violence for more than a very limited timespan, which explains why a repressive regime abolishes itself more rapidly than any other, and by no means solves the problem at hand. The question of how, from a governing position, to "deal" with the mass, can thus not be a matter of restricting the collectivity's forms of expression. In the second place, the presentation of a dichotomy of, on the one hand, state, and on the other, an unbridled mass, is a misrepresentation from the very start since, for Spinoza, collective existence constitutes the state, is the grounding locus of its formation and at every moment constitutes its immediate mirror image. This is why Spinoza claims that democracy is an ontological state, a principle within every kind of government – democracy thus here understood as the power of the mass constituting every society and resulting in one or another form of government, as analyzed in detail in the *Political Treatise*. In a paradoxical way, this analysis shows that democracy, understood in the ontological sense, is always already at play whenever a collective existence is formalized – in other words, even the forms of government that

Spinoza considers most catastrophic – such as despotism and totalitarianism – have, in fact, a democratic foundation since they have been made possible and have been realized by collective passions that, rather than being at work in a constructive way, have led to a diminishing of the power of thinking as well as the power of acting.

However, Spinoza's choice of words in the analysis, more politically refined and expressed, of the *Political Treatise*, shows that collective existence, understood in terms of the mass, swarm, ignorant people in general – in short, all the negatively charged terms that designate those that have to be governed at any cost – always already carries a political and historical over-determination: the many, the mass and the mob in fact are no acceptable terms for a political collective subject, precisely because these terms do not acknowledge the constituting role that collectivity not only ought to have but in fact *always already does have*. Instead, collectivity is situated, by these terms, as an unspecified quantity in relation to an already governing élite, regardless of whether its form of government is monarchic or aristocratic in manner. In other words, the mass, the swarm and even the people – *populus* – has, in these denominations, always already been bereft of its essentially constituting role, and thereby rather constitute political objects rather than political subjects. This is the reason why it is necessary to employ a new term – both from a theoretical point of view, since the political analysis needs an acceptable and adequate conceptual apparatus, but also practically, since Spinoza's analysis in fact aims at establishing a better, more just, more liberating and more reasonable society where collectivity and its double-edged but nonetheless real power is made visible and becomes explicit. Different from the "mass," the "mob" or the "people," the "multitude" stands for this constituting political subject whose internal relations and affectivity create our societies, regardless of whatever shape they take. And it is only in taking as a point of departure the understanding of how this highly real political subject functions – that is to say, how it is formed and shaped by movements of affectivity – that a functioning politics can be shaped. This is what Spinoza always returns to throughout the investigations in the *Political Treatise*: the power of a state is and can only be that of the multitude constituting it, and this power, regardless of whether we speak of an individual or a state, must in turn always be understood as a *conatus* that varies according to the joyous or sad passions to which it is subjected. In a literal sense, we see here how the connection between ethics and politics – between the *Ethics* and the *Political Treatise*, and the *Theologico-Political Treatise*, is constantly re-actualized, as variations on one and the same theme. What is recurrent is the analysis of an affectivity, not only as a point of departure but also as a never achieved process. This also makes clear Spinoza's strong stand against any idealistic political philosophy, as stated in the first chapter of the *Political Treatise*.

Yet it is also this realism – that is the understanding of the fundamental role played by affectivity – that creates difficulties: precisely because Spinoza's multitude must be understood in terms of an ever-moving affectivity, the analysis shows the impossibility of situating it as a *stable* and *constituted* political subject. The multitude is thereby, from Spinoza's own point of view, a concept of double sense: on the one hand, it is the given, necessary and unavoidable for any political reflection since it is indeed what makes possible (and necessary) the political as such. On the other hand, it is a power that disables and resists the political inasmuch as we understand "the political" to mean a perennial construction or solution. Establishing the conceptuality of the multitude – that is, rendering visible its reality – is thereby only one aspect of a problem far more complicated, that in the end always asks the question of how a society is to function in the best possible way.

If contemporary philosophy wants to embrace the multitude, it then has to be willing to deal with a concept of significant complexity. Beyond – and given – the necessary and resolutely affirmative value of re-formulating a concept that in a forceful way gives reality to the collective political subject that continuously shapes our civil existence, there is the question of what the multitude does in relation to the idea of absolute and real, efficient democracy that is desired as much by Spinoza as by, for instance, Hardt and Negri. I will not develop this question further here, but will nevertheless try to outline some points for continued discussion.

The first point concerns the relation between the multitude and the different manners of governing. Spinoza's analysis in the *Political Treatise* shows two things: one, that the multitude constitutes the immanent and continuously acting power of every political society: two, that at the base of every political regime or government there is, in fact, an ontological democracy – a democracy that, from an etymological point of view, we should rather call a "multitudocracy"; since its *kratos* or power does not stem from a constituted people in the classical political sense. From this it follows that the idea of the multitude certainly must be linked to a democracy, but only in the ontological sense and not in terms of a specific, effective, political regime. In practice, the multitude is thus established as the political subject that taken *per se* does not constitute a counter-concept either to monarchy or to aristocracy, these terms being the two general ones used by Spinoza to define different manners of government. Rather, both of them are just as much the effects of the affectivity of the multitude, as an absolute democracy would be.

The second point, which is in fact a consequence of the first one, turns around the very real difficulty of thinking – and even more of realizing, in the strong sense, the passage between ontological and real democracy, that is, a democracy that could be constituted in a specific historic moment. That Spinoza himself left this passage unwritten might indeed be seen as emblematic – and perhaps not only because his untimely death made impossible the achievement of the previously announced last part of the *Political Treatise*, but also, as Balibar rightly notes, because there appears to be a close to insoluble difficulty imbedded in the very definition of democracy. For, if the multitude is democratic by nature, it is also nonetheless passional – that is, determined and formed by its own affectivity. As is made clear by the analysis in *Ethics*, knowledge – that is the path to a life determined by one's own force and the exponential increase of this force by ways of joyous affects – has to do with increasing our rational (adequate) ideas and diminishing our irrational or inadequate ideas. However, we are *affected* by our rational ideas just as we are affected by the inadequate ones: the condition that renders the rational, adequate ideas determinative is thus that they must affect us on a more forceful way than the irrational ones. Hence, to Spinoza, reason or rationality is not the absolute and regulative measure postulated by the idealistic theories of enlightenment philosophy, but an affection that, given the particular circumstances, can have more or less power. And here is the core of the problem: the more parts the affected body is constituted of, in the more ways in which it can be affected; the larger the assemblage is, the more affective power the circumstances have that influence it will also have. That affects can have a negative charge; that they can, so to speak, go the wrong way, is indeed something that Spinoza both fears and knows. At the same time, though, there are continuous possibilities and openings for an increasing and positive force: the intelligence of the multitude, the power of the common, is not utopian but a living reality, just as much as is the contrary. The strength of Spinoza's analysis, which is also what makes it challenging, is precisely that there is no teleology: the theory of affection is exponential, but because of this it is also always moving – continuous change is its condition of reality, which runs counter to the demand for stability and normativity that is always necessarily implied in the political idea of democracy. And perhaps it is precisely this predicament that Jacques Rancière touches upon when, in *The Hatred of Democracy*,[5] he shows the internal paradox of democracy, its radical groundlessness, which makes it less of a solution or salvation and more of a continuous action – a movement and a will, more than a constituted form of regime. This

---

5. Jacques Rancière, *La haine de la démocratie* (Paris: La fabrique, 2005).

is of importance, not least in that it highlights how democracies of our own time would at the most qualify, for Spinoza, as sophisticated aristocracies, or, in Rancière's words, oligarchic states of right. It is this fundamental uncertainty, versatility and groundlessness that a coming theory of the multitude must take as its point of departure, confront and incorporate.

What Art Can Do? Politics, Experimentation and Museums

Luiz Camillo Osorio

> Politics is not the exercise of power or struggle for power. It is
> first of all the configuration of a space as political, the framing
> of a specific sphere of experience, the setting of objects posed as
> common and of subjects to whom the capacity is recognized to
> designate the objects and discuss them.
> *Jacques Rancière*

> It may sound naïve, but I think that for all its failings, the world
> of art and culture is still the only one where something like that
> can be done...the media can't do it anymore; they've become a
> vulgar business like any other. The world of culture – museums
> and universities – is the last place where you are still free to
> dream of a better world....
> *Alfredo Jaar*

I

The relationship between art and politics has been the subject
of an ongoing debate, whether in terms of new theoretical approaches or insofar as it concerns curatorial projects.[1] Thus, what
follows does not exactly lay claims to originality. I shall refer to
the ideas of Jacques Rancière, seeking only to deal with possible
articulations of the relation between aesthetics and politics and
focusing upon contemporary art's modes of reception as based on
its apparently inevitable and certainly risk-filled reception on the

---

1. As immediate examples, I would include authors such as Jacques Rancière,
   Giorgio Agamben, and Claire Bishop, as well as the São Paulo biennial of
   2010, the Berlin biennial of 2012 and the mounting of the Museo Reina
   Sofia's permanent collection, among so many others.

part of museums. What are the effects of this insertion upon contemporary art practices? How does this reception re-signify this space which has heretofore been the province of norm and canon?

What interests me about Rancière's work is the way politics is considered from the perspective of the space of appearance, redistributing roles, voices, narratives and redefining forms of subjectification and sociability. On the other hand, art is presumed to be art because of its ability to bring about displacements, surprises and friction within modes of perception, thus stimulating the imagination – and opening up spaces of action – beyond that which is given. According to Rancière, such displacements produced by art are a result of the very specificity of the aesthetic. "It was in keeping with the idea, spelled out by Kant and Schiller, according to which aesthetic experience is a specific sphere of experience which invalidates the ordinary hierarchies incorporated in everyday sensory experience."[2] By producing intervals in the sensible surface of the world, art deconstructs convention, confounding expectations, disseminating questions, disconnecting words and things, concentrating and dilating our experience of time and of space.

Within this interval art is political; it mobilizes new distributions of the sensible. It is precisely where Kant deals with the singular judgment of beauty, of disinterest and endless finality, that we are able to see, following Rancière's trail, a possibility of approaching the political phenomenon in terms of its contingency and, simultaneously, of universal opening. Responsibility for action and judgment occur before (and within) the circumstances of the moment, alluding to a network of shared and conflicting meaning which nonetheless maintains itself on the horizon of shared everyday life. Confronted with aesthetic experience, we simultaneously exercise that which is proper to us, aligning it with a sense of belonging in the world. In the act of judgment we perceive ourselves simultaneously as individuals

2. Jacques Rancière, "From Politics to Aesthetics?," *Paragraph*. Vol. 28 (2005): 15.

and as members of a community-to-be.

This political appropriation of the Kantian aesthetic is of particular interest to us insofar as it makes us realize, within what is considered to be the origin of a formalist tradition within the philosophy of art, an ability to intervene and reconfigure a reality the tone of which is clearly political. How to displace/unfold formal experimentation in the direction of a force capable of actualizing itself in the world? To what extent does the focus upon the spectator contained within the aesthetic judgment of Kantian origin – and not its rejection – obliges us to separate spectator and passivity, enhancing a call to participation which permeates the perceptive act of the spectator himself? To what degree can art and its metaphorical dimension – to be art and to appear to be reality – take on political pretensions? What should be the politics of art in a world tamed by museum and market? All of these questions may be telescoped into one: can it be expected of art today that it continue to bewilder us and perhaps even to transform reality? I should like to use the verb "to bewilder" in terms of its aesthetic suspension and political mobilization.

Many of the aforementioned questions have run parallel with the history of art in the twentieth century, most specifically with the history of artistic vanguards. In a way, it may be said that the history of engagement in art is indistinguishable from the very history of the modernist avant gardes. It is no coincidence that the Marx and Engels' *Communist Manifesto* of 1848 is contemporary with Gustave Courbet's *Realist Manifesto* of 1855, which he presented in Paris at the opening of his own independent art shows during the Universal Exhibition as a form of protest against the letter salon.

To analyze aspects of this programmatic orientation of the avant-gardes, keeping in mind their desires, expectations and frustrations, is interesting to define its current relevance. It was this moment in the mid-nineteenth century that engendered the constitution of a modern poetics from Manet to Duchamp (and including Cézanne, Van Gogh, Seurat, Picasso and their inadequacies in terms of established pictorial convention). This movement within artistic practices was accompanied by a confrontation with institutions, resulting in the creation of the Salons des Réfusés and societies of independent artists. From the Communist Manifesto of 1848 to the Russian Revolution of 1917, a sequence of political events spreads everywhere, preparing the terrain for the emergence of revolutionary rupture. Concomitantly, an equation is established between (the artist's) engagement, (society's) awareness and purification (of expressive media). In this process, the role of art and the status of works were redefined in terms of their greatest possible political effectiveness. Ultimately, more than being a wager of sorts on the expressive power of a type of painting purified of literal illustration, Malevich's "white square" exemplifies a sensibility uprooted from fossilized conventions of representation, all of which would be available to a revolutionary future that would create a new man and a new society. The flat surface of the canvas is the place of experimentation for new life forms which conflated art, publicity, and design with mixtures of painting, posters and utilitarian objects.

Concomitantly with the engagement of that constructivist avant-garde, intent on the post-revolutionary process and its internal conflicts, I should like to highlight the political dimension of Dadaist non-engagement and, in particular, of the one constituted by the derisory poetics of Marcel Duchamp. Constructivism and Dadaism are complementary pairs in this history of the avant-garde. To both – and for diverse reasons and contexts – art is more of an attitude than a finished object. The two movements associate this stance with a rejection of the past and the creation of a new individual and a new society. In fact, the difference between these movements may be associated with the relationship between the individual and society as well as the distinct contexts within which it was being considered. Not by chance, Dadaism was born in Zurich (which was neutral during the First World War) – where non-conformity came mixed with an active nihilism. Constructivism, on the contrary, was born in revolutionary Russia, where nonconformity was shot through with an unshakable faith in the possibility of transformation, not only political and social but above all spiritual.

This is what must be highlighted in each movement. Dadaism is a revolution of the individual, of individual creative potential, and it denies an immediate link with society. It is a dysfunctionalizing practice. In Constructivism – as underscored by its very name – revolution is a social construct and art must assume itself as a collective production which is a determinant part of a new social functioning. It is not by chance that – to the Dadaist artist – art must go to the cabaret, resistance comes through enjoyment whereas, to the constructivist, art must go to the factory, where resistance will be transformed into new forms of production. As stated, different contexts produce different promises. What they have in common is art's need to engage with life, to move beyond its own condition as art.

Nevertheless, we know that both the Russian Revolution and Dadaist derision were eventually defeated or incorporated – one by the very consequences of the revolutionary future in a revolutionary state and the other by the institutional co-optation of anti-art's negative will. In other words, looking back from the present, Constructivism and Dadaism survive as "art" alone, without having fulfilled their desires for social construction or dissemination of creative rebellion. Both survive in museums and in art history books. What can we learn from these defeats? What remains in those places undesired by the revolutionary vein – the museum and history – of the poetic strength and political nonconformity of those movements? How to preserve an inadequacy? How to deal with art's political efficaciousness and its capacity for social transformation? How to deal with these experimental attitude-works in the neutralized space of museums? How can part of the aborted dreams that nourished these works continue to reverberate? The challenge, therefore, is to sustain in those works some of the latent transformative power which was originally a part of them and that would be able to bring about new forms of subjectification, new principles of individuation, other possibilities of life within society.

In light of these questions regarding the legacy of the avant-gardes and their institutional absorption, it is our role to inquire about the political relevance of contemporary art. This political unrest and its reverberation in contemporary poetics may be analyzed from several perspectives ranging from deliberate activism to the new artists' collectives, and including the various strategies for public insertion of works of art. The possibility of experiencing new meanings that are subjacent to the modern experience of art is the foundation for a political (and poetic) freedom that assumes itself as an opening to the new. In dealing with this claim to a consideration of art's political reverberations, a recent observation made by Rancière in an interview published in Art Forum should be recalled: "An art is emancipated and emancipating when it renounces the authority of the imposed message, the target audience, and the univocal mode of explicating the world, when, in other words, it stops wanting to emancipate us."[3]

What is of interest is making the political permeate the aesthetic without rejecting it in the name of an ideological program. The aesthetic regime emerges in the late eighteenth century as a rejection of poetics which had normative pretensions with regard to artistic practices. This indetermination of the aesthetic led to the emergence of criticism as an exercise for disseminating the meanings formalized by the works.

It is within the aesthetic regime of art that its identification ceases to be verifiable "via a division between ways of doing and making" and becomes "based on distinguishing a sensible mode of being specific to artistic products."[4] A notion of aesthetic experience was [being] constituted. Always problematic and differentiating, in which the subject saw himself confronted by the unknown and enhanced his opening up to the world, expanding

3. Jacques Rancière, "Art of the Possible: Fulvia Carnevale and John Kelsey in conversation with Jacques Rancière," *Artforum* March (2007).
4. Jacques Rancière, "The Distribution of the Sensible," in *The Politics of Aesthetics,* trans. Gabriel Rockhill (London: Continuum, 2004), 22-23.

its horizons of meaning. Once a technical view of art had been surpassed, the experience of the works would produce meaning concomitant with the disturbing possibility that it might not become art. It is in this aspect that Rancière characterizes the aesthetic regime as the moment in which "artistic phenomena are identified by their adherence to a specific regime of the sensible, which is extricated from its ordinary connections and is inhabited by a heterogeneous power, the power of a form of thought that has become foreign to itself: a product identical with something not produced, knowledge transformed into non-knowledge, *logos* identical with pathos, the intention of the unintentional, etc."[5] The uniqueness of the artistic phenomenon is to the aesthetic event as dissent is to political action. Is art still capable of producing dissent in today's world?

II

Given that we live in an age dominated by the institutionalization of art, by the vertiginous growth of biennials and art fairs and by the inflationary acceleration of the market, the question of how to replicate the potency of the heterogeneous remains; how is the dissenting spark of the sensible to be kept burning? The risks of co-optation are immense, but to refuse conflict and contradiction, remaining on the margins of the circuit, does not appear to be a viable alternative. The purity of isolation and its rational convictions do not bring with them the conflict of difference that is able to expand horizons to new forms of art. "To ask how can one escape the market is one of those questions whose principal virtue is one's pleasure in declaring it insoluble...for artists as for everyone else there's the problem of knowing where one plant one's feet, of knowing what one is doing in a particular place, in a particular system of Exchange. One must find ways to create other places, or other uses for places."[6]

To consider the possibility of creating other uses for old plac-

5. Rancière, "The Distribution of the Sensible," 22-23.
6. Rancière, "Art of the Possible," 262.

es seems important to me in order that the entry of works into the museum is not reduced to a canonization which produces distancing or – in the case of less conventional and more experimental works – a co-optation that reiterates any possibility of criticism or conflict. The question to be posed pertains to the manner by which the institution receives the works without rendering them merely adequate and docile objects. How to liberate heterogeneity and aesthetic suspension – potencies inherent to art – in a situation dominated by the coldness of norm and market? What is intended is the very precariousness of the normative and heterogeneous quality of institutionalization, rendering the museum an open and indeterminate space in which to negotiate unpredictable possibilities of art, exhibition and education – ultimately, of non-canonized forms of life.

In order to rethink the uses of museums – which, with no loss to their legitimizing role – might constitute themselves as spaces simultaneously dedicated to artistic experimentation *and* political discussion, I should like to report on two recent experiments which took place at the Museu de Arte Moderna do Rio de Janeiro. I am referring to exhibitions by the artists Elisa Bracher and Nan Goldin. The former was on view from October 2011 to March, 2012, and the latter from February to April, 2012. Bracher's work exemplifies the experimental process and its unfinished quality functioning within the museum. It highlights the possibility of displacing the hesitations of the creative process into the exhibition space itself, thereby taking on risks of indeterminacy and failure – without, of course, any loss to the work's poetic or formal power. As for Nan Goldin, what *she* brings to the museum is the conflict-ridden relationship between the production of images and moral norms; in other words, the way in which fiction produces the world by manipulating the possibilities of what is seen and what is felt, displacing established conventions of subjectivity and sociability. They were two very different exhibitions which juxtaposed silence and noise, formal concentration and the excitement of images. Nonetheless what they had in common was an ability

148

to surprise and disorient the public.

From its very beginnings, Elisa Bracher's work has been characterized by its public and monumental scale. It is no mere coincidence that the museum room in which her work was presented is called "the monumental space," with its verticality, its immense concrete wall, natural lighting, its suspended mezzanine, its sheer scope and silence. The artist's works were heavy, extremely so. They were made of solid lead – in all, over twenty tons of it – and none of it touched the floor. Gray and opaque, the sheets and the sphere were fastened to suspended beams and hovered over the space. It was an equilibrium of forces which was supported by the structure of this powerful building designed by Brazilian architect Affonso Eduardo Reidy. Her pieces filled the void, working in between sculpture and installation, between the physical presence of the materials and the tensioned energy of the space. They created a place that was the enhancement of a malleable atmosphere which physically affected us. To circulate near the work within that monumental space was to experience one's own body in contact with what was outside it, with an imposing exteriority. Nonetheless, it is important not to mistake stateliness and monumentality for the excesses of spectacle. In its silence, in its gravity, the work was, above all else, anti-spectacular. It rejected all sense of affectation. Its weight weighed; its tension tensioned. In turn the grey was light and opaqueness, containment and expansion. The boldness of the scale drew strength and support from the lead's austerity.

Yet it took more than a month to set up this installation. The sphere – which in the initial project weighed a ton and a half – had already grown to eight tons even before it began to be mounted. Made of solid lead, it was suspended by two steel cables weighing five hundred kilos apiece. Engineers, architects and specialized workmen entered the museum and took on the risks. Three sheets of lead hung from beams and surrounded one of its sides, occupying a space of approximately fifteen meters. Each one of them weighed five tons. The scaffolding which held up the sphere was supposed to have been removed prior

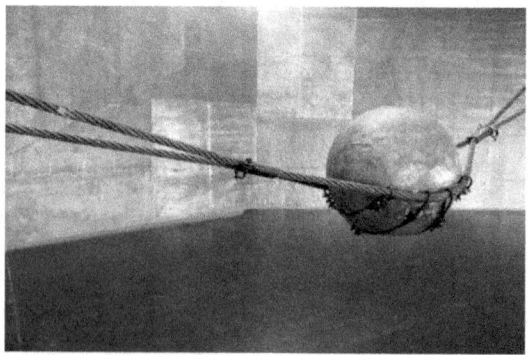

Installation views of Elisa Bracher, *Ponto final sem pausas* (2012).

to the show's opening. However, some days before that, one of the sheets slowly began to collapse. What to do? Postpone the opening? Cancel the exhibition? Various sectors of the museum felt – rightly so, to a certain degree – threatened and the most prudent measure would have been postponement. Nonetheless, given that setting up the installation was so clearly a part of the work itself and that the public was following the entire process in a state of bewilderment, there seemed to be no reason why the exhibition should not (should not) proceed as scheduled without the work being duly finished, exposing the flaws, the failure, the mistakes and the fragility inherent to the creative process.

In this unstable equilibrium between process and work, between the finished and the unfinished, the sharpness and the fragility, the institutional space assumed its responsibility as an experimental space, moving beyond its normative nature without neglecting its own normative nature. The museum continues to be a museum, but what was merely a space to legitimize finished works became a tricky territory of trial and error, hesitation, displacement, doubt and decision – all constituted as act. In a way, the museum might be a repository for the most exemplary aspect of the creative experience: the courage of the founding gesture, in all of its constituent power and fragility. The setting up continued for more than three weeks, during which the exhibition was quite normally visited by the public.

Before analyzing the Goldin exhibition, and by way of analyzing the similarities between these two experiences in terms of their relationships to the museum, let me once again quote Rancière: "The main enemy of artistic creativity as well as of political creativity is consensus – that is, inscription within given roles, possibilities, competences."[7] Believing that consensus is the enemy of creativity, the MAM decided to house an exhibition by Nan Goldin which had been rejected by another institution in the same city one month prior to its opening, arguing

7.   Rancière, "Art of the Possible," 263.

that some of the scenes in its slideshows were incompatible with its educational mission statement. In the name of dissent and of its pedagogical function in particular, given that the exhibition had been offered to it, it was up to the MAM, to take on the risks and face the possibility of legal action.[8]

Without going into detail with regard to Brazilian legislation and its endless interpretations, what presented itself as the possible legal complication was, in fact, an apparent contradiction to be assumed and debated between the Brazilian Constitution's provisions regarding freedom of artistic creation and certain paragraphs of Brazil's Estatuto da Criança e do Adolescente [Child and Adolescent Statute] which touch upon the use of images of children, all of which left room for moralist interpretation. An intense debate raged in the Brazilian press and the exhibition arrived at the MAM with loud controversy in attendance.

The exhibition contained an utterly lyrical group of landscape photographs and three slide-shows: The Other Side, Heartbeat and The Ballad of Sexual Dependency. How could images focused on affection and intimacy be accused of pornography? In order to attempt to transform controversy into debate, the curators and the MAM's Núcleo Experimental de Educação e Arte [Experimental Center for Education and Art] programmed a forum of public debates to which lawyers, sociologists, anthropologists, psychoanalysts, social workers, critics, curators and so forth were invited.[9] In order to fuel the debate and the multiple perspectives for interpretation two very

8. When another institution vetoed the show in November, 2011, curator Ligia Canongia asked me whether MAM might be willing to house it. Although it was impossible to do so at that moment, three months later a change in MAM's schedule made it possible for the show to be added to its roster of exhibitions. It should be noted that the institution which had originally rejected the exhibition honored its commitment to financially support of the show.

9. The idea for this forum was suggested by educational center coordinators Jessica Gogan and Luiz Guilherme Vergara and based on a similar experiment undertaken by the Andy Warhol Museum in Pittsburgh when that institution dealt with issues of racial conflict.

simple and direct questions were initially proposed: what does exhibiting mean? What does it mean to exhibit the work of Nan Goldin? Our intention was to make use of the exhibition as a moment in which to experience heterogeneous ways of seeing and thinking.

As previously emphasized, what may be immediately highlighted was the discrepancy between what the slide show images revealed and the controversial tone which they produced. It is not that they are incapable of generating discomfort or unease; first and foremost, though, these images contain a series of more interesting questions that deal with a complex contemporary subjectivity, with the ties of affection which we build, with ways of dealing with fatherhood, motherhood, masculinity, femininity, sexuality, love, affection, pain, loneliness, joy, encounters and, ultimately, with life as it is: plural, unpredictable, tragic and lyrical. What is impressive about her work is its ability to bring together different people, to attract a diverse and plural public to the museum, seducing them through the power of her images, the potency of the musical element and the atmosphere created by her installations in which austerity and emotion are enhanced.

To return to the controversy and the conflict-ridden territory which the museum incurred by housing the exhibition at the precise moment of an institutional conflict, we should also add the notification received from the Ministério Público Federal [Federal Prosecution Office],[10] accusing the museum of incitement to pedophilia and violence against women. A federal public prosecutor [Procurador da República] thus made his way to the MAM in order to check out the content of the images and the consistency of the accusations. When he arrived at the museum, he visited the exhibition carefully, returning on another day to attend one of the forum debates. Ultimately, his legal decision was completely favorable to the museum's initiative

10. It is important to know that in Brasil a Federal Prosecutor, besides criminal actions, also deals with class or collective actions.

of putting on the exhibition, regardless of any personal evaluation of the images and leading to the dismissal of the suit. In the conclusion to his detailed and careful explanations in the trial documents, he made one particular observation of considerable pertinence to what I have been discussing here, to wit: "Undoubtedly, the most important demonstration of institutional maturity in a democratic and pluralistic society is its ability to accommodate divergence within a framework of tolerance towards – and recognition of – diversity, for dissent depends as much upon freedom as it does upon agreement [concordance]." I would take this last sentence a bit further and go so far as to say that freedom relies more heavily upon dissent than concordance [or agreement].

It is in managing this conflict between norm and transgression, determination and indetermination, potential and risk, that museum spaces have been questioning themselves, attempting to come to terms with art's possibilities and impotence in an institutionalized world, shot through by disquieting interests, but called upon to deal with the disconnect between past and future. Confronting it allows for an exploration of new possibilities of meaning that suggest themselves in the interval – the residue of power which is the province of art. It is up to the museums to live up to the residue, nourishing the public with the ability to be surprised, to question, to be able to see things independently and to imagine worlds that are different from those already constituted and established.

Aristotle's Logical Analysis of Motion in *Physics I*

Charlotta Weigelt

Aristotle's *Physics* is, as far as we know, the first work to attempt a systematic and unified philosophy of nature, *phusis*. It is often emphasized that the kind of theory of nature that Aristotle aims at in the *Physics* (and elsewhere) differs significantly from natural science in the modern sense, but it is equally important to realize that Aristotle is not immediately concerned with natural science in the ancient sense either. In the *Physics* he not only develops his predecessors' inquiries into the world of nature, but also introduces a new conception of the very pursuit of natural science.

Before Aristotle, the philosophical exploration of nature had centered on the attempt to discern the basic elements of nature, like water, air, and so on, as well as on finding something like a basic principle or order that could make intelligible how these elements are combined and arranged into various natural processes. We find one of the first attempts to provide such an explanation in Anaximenes' idea that the elements change their outward features and also turn into other elements due to a process of rarefaction and condensation.[1] Following his predecessors, Aristotle too picks out motion, *kinēsis*, as the basic phenomenon of nature, but he is dissatisfied with all previous attempts to explain this phenomenon. In particular, he is convinced that the earlier natural philosophers have failed to give an accurate ac-

1. Hermann Diels and Walther Kranz, *Die Fragmente der Vorsokratiker* Vol. I. (Zürich: Weidmann, 1951), Fragment B1. All references to the Pre-Socratic fragments are to this edition.

count of the possibility of motion: in fact, they have not even raised this is as a problem. But as the pupil of Plato, whose work to such a great extent was provoked by Parmenides' denial of the possibility of motion, it is impossible for Aristotle to take the existence of motion and change for granted. Plato had certainly taken a decisive step towards undermining Parmenides' position, perhaps most notably in the *Sophist*, where he had attacked his predecessor's sharp division between being and not-being, but he was not prepared to give up the contrast between being and becoming. Accordingly, to demonstrate the reality of motion is for Plato to argue for the necessity of admitting the presence of not-being within being.[2]

Against Parmenides and his followers, however, Aristotle wants to show that motion should not be put on a par with mere appearance or not-being to begin with, as it constitutes a mode of being or reality in its own right. He sees, in other words, the need for a different kind of ontology, in which motion is recognized as the mode of being peculiar to nature or, rather, to natural objects. The challenge is to achieve this without finding oneself forced to sacrifice the idea that there is a fundamental, stable order in nature, which can form the object of scientific knowledge – which was precisely what Parmenides and Plato were seeking but could not find in nature, since nature seems to be in a state of constant flux. So if knowledge is about what exists and is real, as Parmenides and Plato had argued, then if there is to be a science of nature as the realm of motion and change, these phenomena must be shown to have their place in reality.

This is not to suggest that Aristotle intends to provide some kind of proof of the existence of nature and its processes: on the contrary, he takes such an attempt to be ridiculous (193a3 ff.).[3] Nature is intelligible in itself: it is everywhere a cause of order (252a12), and the natural philosopher must therefore find a way to explicate it from within, namely by pointing out those among

2. In the *Sophist*, the confrontation with Parmenides begins at 237a3 and continues almost to the end of the dialogue.
3. Unless otherwise indicated, all references are to the *Physics*.

its aspects or features that render it comprehensible. Throughout the *Physics* Aristotle approaches the phenomenon of motion from a variety of perspectives and questions, combining empirical investigations with ontological as well as logical considerations: he discerns its causes, defines it in teleological terms (that is, as the fulfillment of the potential as such), explains how it is related to time and place, shows it to be a continuous and as such infinitely divisible phenomenon, and argues for its eternal existence and ultimate dependence upon an unmoved mover. But this series of investigations begins with, and is made possible by, the question concerning the principles or foundations, the *archai*, of motion, which Aristotle launches in Book I, where he introduces and develops a logical perspective on motion, thus focusing on its conceptual and formal, rather than on its empirical aspects. In particular, he eventually takes as his guiding clue that *archē* which in his view is the most basic and intelligible of all principles: the law of non-contradiction.[4] The underlying idea seems to be that, before natural science can begin, its framework has to be established and made transparent, in such a way, namely, that the formal possibility of motion is secured.

As we shall see, when elaborating his logical analysis of motion, Aristotle explicitly raises anew the question that had preoccupied Parmenides and Plato: the question concerning the relation between being and not-being. Just like Plato, Aristotle considers it necessary to dissolve the absolute opposition between being and not-being that had formed the basis of Parmenides' thought. But in comparison to Plato, Aristotle is less interested in the metaphysical dimension of the interrelation of being and not-being. Rather, he treats of being and not-being as contradictory *terms*, by means of which motion can (and should) be analyzed. It is this 'demythologization' of not-being, I think, that will enable Aristotle to eventually give a truly positive account of motion, namely as the fulfillment of potentiality.

---

4. For Aristotle's defense of the law of non-contradiction as the first principle of science, see *Metaphysics* V.3-8.

The Critique of the Eleatics

The question concerning the possibility of motion is, as we have just seen, initially posed as a question concerning the principles or foundations, the *archai*, of motion. That this is the concern of natural philosophy is asserted at the very outset of the *Physics*:

> In view of the fact that knowledge and understanding in all disciplines, which are concerned with principles, causes, or elements, is attained through an acquaintance with these (for we think we know a particular thing when we are acquainted with its primary causes and first principles, all the way down to its elements), then, clearly, also in the science of nature our first task must be to try to settle questions about principles (184a10-16).[5]

The question concerning the principles of nature is from the outset taken to concern the principles of *motion*, not the material components of natural things – that is a question belonging to natural philosophy in a more narrow sense than the kind of inquiry into nature that is the objective of the *Physics*.[6] Moreover, Aristotle does not confine himself to providing an answer to the question about the *archai* of nature, but also makes the question itself into a problem, as he engages in a discussion of what is implied or presupposed in this kind of question, as well as of what it takes for this question to make sense at all.

The first, and as it will turn out, decisive thing to note is that the question itself implies a distinction between the principle itself and that of which it is a principle (185a4-5). It seems, in other words, that the question points to a manifold within reality, which is not necessarily ontical, that is to say, it does not presuppose that there actually exists a plurality of things in

---

5. All translations are mine, unless otherwise indicated.
6. In *De generatione et corruptione*, which proposes to treat of generation and destruction, as well as of alteration, in a quite general way, Aristotle nonetheless pays more attention to the material constituents of natural beings (see Book I), as compared with his discussion of change in the *Physics*, which centers on the principles or grounds of change.

the world. Rather, the manifold is ontological: it indicates that there is a difference between being a principle and being something that has a principle.

But this difference in being is precisely what Parmenides refuses to accept, or so at least Aristotle interprets his saying that reality is single and one. Parmenides is introduced, together with his disciple Melissus, as a proponent of the thesis that there is only one, immutable *archē* of nature, which almost immediately is reinterpreted as the idea that being (*to on*) is one and immutable (184b15 ff.).[7] This apparently means that everything is supposed to be in the same way, or in Aristotle's words, that 'being' has but one sense (e.g. 186a24-25). One might wonder how Aristotle can make Parmenides' claim that being is one and immutable into a statement on the number and nature of the *archai* of nature. His idea is probably that, if we read Parmenides as a natural philosopher concerned with exploring the grounds of nature, then, apparently, according to Parmenides there is only one ground: being itself. In Aristotle's view, however, that simply does not make any sense. In other words, Eleatic monism does not even allow for the question of grounds to be posed, which conclusion Aristotle draws already at the outset of his confrontation with the Eleatics: "For if being is one, and one in the way they think, then there cannot be any ground: a ground is of some thing or things" (185a3-5).

The background to the Eleatic claim, which Parmenides and Melissus actually share with the early natural philosophers, though they draw a radically different conclusion from it, is that, on the one hand, nothing can be generated out of nothing, for in that case there is no basis or substrate from which generation could take its start, but that, on the other hand, it is just as incomprehensible how something could be generated

---

7. *To on* may be interpreted either as 'that which is' or as 'being' (in the sense of 'beingness') or, for that matter, as referring to the very expression *on*, 'being' (rather than to the phenomenon). In his critique of Parmenides, Aristotle draws on all these possible meanings of *to on*, as his point is precisely that Parmenides is unable to distinguish between them.

out of being, because then that something seems to be already.[8] Empedocles therefore states that: "There is no birth [*phusis*] of any mortal being, nor is there any end in destructive death; there is only mixture and separation of what has been mixed. Birth [*phusis*] is only a name given to that by men" (Fragment B8).[9]

The Eleatic thesis is, however, that change as such is nothing but an illusion, that is, granted that change must be conceived in terms of a transition between being and not-being. If nothing can be generated either from being or from not-being, all you can say is that being itself is, which is precisely what Parmenides had claimed: *esti gar einai* (Fragment B6, line 1). This statement gives Aristotle the support he needs for his claim that Parmenides holds that 'being' only has one sense. The aim of Book I is by and large to refute this view, and, more precisely, to show that generation in a sense proceeds both from being and from not-being, though not in the same way.

Note that both the Eleatics' and the natural philosophers' doubts about the possibility of generation presuppose the principle of non-contradiction, and more precisely a very strong interpretation of it: everything either is or is not without qualification.[10] On this interpretation the principle of non-contradiction is turned into a principle of non-contrariety: being and not-being are regarded as absolute opposites, so that not-

---

8. Aristotle reviews this assumption at the beginning of chapter 8 (book I). *De generatione et corruptione* opens with a discussion that aims to show how the assumption made it impossible for the early philosophers to distinguish accurately between generation and alteration; book I.1.

9. I have followed Diels-Kranz' suggestion as to how *phusis* should be interpreted in this fragment (they translate it as *Geburt*).

10. This is of course not to say that either the natural philosophers or the Eleatics had explicitly stated something like the law of non-contradiction. Plato comes close to formulating it at a number of places in his works; the closest he ever comes to a definition of the law of non-contradiction is perhaps in the *Republic* 436b8-9: "It is obvious that the same thing will not be willing to do or undergo opposites in the same part of itself, in relation to the same thing, at the same time." Translation by G. M. A. Grube, rev. C. D. C. Reeve, in *Plato – Complete works* (Indianapolis/Cambridge: Hackett, 1997). "In the same part of itself" translates *kata tauton*, which could also, and perhaps more accurately, be translated as 'in the same respect'.

being is identified with nothingness. Moreover, according to Parmenides, that being is absolutely divorced from not-being is a necessity. In his poem, the road of conviction is described as one leading to the insight "that it is and that it cannot not be" (Fragment B2, line 3). Thereby, the possibility to understand "not-being" as "not being this or that," that is, as not-being in a specific sense, is blocked from the start, since what is cannot stand in any relation to not-being.[11]

By contrast, Aristotle's own formulation of the law of non-contradiction reads as follows: "It is impossible for one and the same attribute to both belong and not belong to the same subject at the same time and in the same respect."[12] In order to be able to interpret the law of non-contradiction in this way one has, first, to make a distinction between different categories of being, and in particular single out the category of substance over against the other categories. This division will provide the basis for Aristotle's critique of the Eleatics, and of Parmenides in particular.

When proposing that reality is one and that the apparent manifold of natural processes is in fact an illusion, the Eleatics are not only denying the basic assumptions of natural science, that there is a natural, changing world, but, as we have already seen, they are also making it impossible to speak about a foundation or *archē* of nature, since that kind of talk only makes sense if we admit that there are different senses of being. If not, not only natural science but also ontology or metaphysics becomes a meaningless pursuit, since ontology is founded upon the distinction between beings on the one hand and the categories of being on the other. Simply put, it does not make any sense to ascribe different attributes to objects if we do not allow for any ontological difference between the objects and their at-

11. In his excellent commentary on Plato's *Parmenides*, S. Scolnicov labels Parmenides' principle 'the absolute principle of non-contradiction'; *Plato's Parmenides* (Ewing, NJ: University of California Press, 2001), 13.
12. *Metaphysics* 1005b19–20. Strictly speaking, what Aristotle says is that "it is impossible for the same [*to auto*] to both belong and not belong to the same [*tō autōi*] at the same time and in the same respect."

tributes. Plurality is thus not a threat to the possibility of science but, on the contrary, a necessary requirement.

The critique of the Eleatics cannot be scientific, in the sense of appealing to one or another argument intrinsic to the science of nature, since the Eleatics are rejecting not this or that thesis about nature, but the very possibility of natural science (not to say nature itself). It will therefore not do simply to establish empirically, and in a 'positive' way, the principles governing motion, for that will not convince the Eleatics, since they know perfectly well that their denial of motion is at odds with empirical evidence, but we have to show that their own position is inconsistent for logical and maybe also for metaphysical reasons. Consequently, Aristotle remarks, to provide the means for this kind of critique must be the business of "a different science or of one common to all" (185a2-3). This observation of Aristotle's has been taken to refer either to metaphysics (as the supreme and as such all-encompassing science) or to dialectic (since dialectic is a way of reasoning that can be used within any kind of scientific or philosophical discipline).[13] If we look at the line of argumentation that Aristotle actually directs against the Eleatics, it is not difficult to see why one has come up with these two alternatives, for Aristotle is rather obviously both making use of some basic ideas common to his logic and his metaphysics (notably the distinction between substance and attribute and its ontological interpretation) and proceeding in the manner proper to dialectic, whereby he spells out the presuppositions as well as the (absurd) consequences of the Eleatic position.

Terence Irwin, who takes the above-mentioned common science to refer to dialectics, regards Aristotle's critique of

---

13. W. D. Ross notes that the Greek commentators thought that the science referred to is dialectic, but argues himself that it must be metaphysics, since dialectics is to Aristotle not a science, *epistēmē*, at all; *Aristotle's Physics: A Revised Text with Commentary* (Oxford: Clarendon Press, 1998; orig. publ. 1936), 461. W. Charlton takes the science in question to be dialectics, *Aristotle's Physics: Books I and II* (Oxford: Clarendon Press, 1992; orig. publ. 1970), 53, and so does also T. Irwin, *Aristotle's First Principles* (Oxford: Clarendon Press, 1988), chapter 3.35.

Parmenides as mainly a matter of exercise in the art of arguing, which is valuable "for gymnastic purposes,"[14] since dialectics cannot, as Aristotle sees it, have as its aim the proof of the existence of motion. In fact, dialectics does not prove anything at all: it just scrutinizes common opinions, *endoxa*, with respect to their assumptions and consequences.[15] And as long as no kind of demonstration of the reality of motion has been delivered, Parmenides and his followers will not give in. But it seems unlikely that Aristotle would interrupt his search for the foundations of nature just to give his audience a bit of training in argumentation. The critique of the Eleatics is an important part of the attempt to secure the possibility of natural science. Indeed, the sought-for *archai* of nature are equally the *archai* of the *science* of nature, and if these can be shown to be not empirical but logico-metaphysical principles, then we may safely conclude that the science of nature is firmly based upon formal ontology.

To begin with, the distinction between things on the one hand and their different possible attributes on the other hand has to be established and defended. Let us begin by just taking a look at the different categories of being which language itself conveys, Aristotle suggests. What can the Eleatics possibly mean, Aristotle asks himself, when they say that all things *are* one, in view of the fact that 'being' is said in many ways, which diversity we express with categories like substance, quality, quantity, and so on? It is simply absurd to say that everything is the same, for example that everything is a substance, or a quality, etc. "If there will be both substance, quantity and quality, then, irrespective of whether or not they are separated from each other, there is a plurality of beings" (185a27-29). Again, the point is that we do not have to assume a plurality of things existing separately: it is enough to analyze the concepts of substance, quality, etc. to realize that it makes no sense to say that all things are one. But it does not work to say that everything

---

14. *Aristotle's First Principles*, op. cit., 68.
15. Cf. *Metaphysics* 1004b25-26: "dialectics can only examine what philosophy is capable of knowing."

is one in essence either, for that would make all our conceptual distinctions collapse, so that "the teaching will concern not how all beings are one but nothing" (185b23-25).

Thus far, Aristotle has argued against the Eleatics mainly by appealing to common sense: we are all familiar with the distinction between things and their properties. However, common sense is not referred to as to an infallible judge. On closer scrutiny, it points beyond itself, towards something more intelligible: the ontological distinction between substance and the categories of being, which requires philosophical reflection to become clear.

The main point that Aristotle makes in his critique of Parmenides is that the thesis on the unity of being makes being itself into a kind of substance, that is, in that it fails to recognize the distinction between beings and being. Parmenides has to say, Aristotle claims, that to be means to be 'truly' or 'essentially' and, secondly, that the only thing which truly is, is being itself.[16] The expression he uses in this connection is *hoper on*: 'that which really is', which to the best of my knowledge only occurs twice in Aristotle's work outside the context of the *Physics*.[17] On Aristotle's view, Parmenides is forced to say either that there is some entity or substance which is *hoper on*, that which essentially is, in which case its attributes are not (the attributes are not at all, because only that exists which is what essentially is), or that *hoper on* is a predicate, meaning 'is essentially', but in saying that something is essentially, that to which this predicate belongs cannot itself be said to be, because then you introduce a difference in being. Once again, Parmenides ends up in this dilemma because of his interpretation of the law of non-contradiction: as the absolute opposite of not-being, being can only have one sense, essential being, whereas all other, supposedly non-essen-

16. We see the traces of this notion of self-predication in Plato's early dialogues, where Socrates repeatedly stresses that, for example, beauty itself is much more beautiful than all beautiful things; e.g. *Symposium* 211-212, *Phaedo* 100b-c, *Protagoras* 330d-e.
17. At *Metaphysics* 1003b33 and 1045b1. Plato uses the expression *hoper hen* in the *Sophist* 244c1.

tial modes of being must be identified with nothingness.

Let us grant, Aristotle says, that there only are white objects and that 'white' only has one sense: there is still a difference between being the color white and being that object to which the color belongs. But Parmenides does not see this.

> It is necessary for him, then, to assume not only that 'being' has the same meaning, whatever it is predicated of, but also that it means 'essentially being' and 'essentially one'. For an attribute is predicated of some subject, so that the subject to which being is attributed will not be (for it is different from being). Something, therefore, which is not will be. Hence 'essentially being' will not belong to anything else. For the subject cannot be a being that is, unless 'being' means several things, in such a way that each thing is in some sense. But one has assumed that being has but one sense. (186a32-b4)

To Parmenides, then, being is essence, and the only thing which is in this eminent, essential sense of 'being' is being itself. As a consequence, not only is it impossible to make a distinction between different senses of being, but also the very distinction between being and not-being collapses: what sense can it possibly have to say that something is not, that is, to negate something, when the very presupposition for any statement whatsoever about reality is that only being itself is, and, moreover, that being itself only is (and nothing more)? Parmenides' being swallows everything up, as it were, so that all distinctions collapse.

The Legacy of the Earlier Natural Philosophers

The positive result of the critique of Parmenides is that it has been shown that the very question of the *archai* of nature implies an absolutely basic distinction between beings and the different categories of being. Natural science thus finds its foundation in ontology. This result is the starting-point for Aristotle's own positive account of the *archai*, which he now develops by means of a critical dialogue with the earlier natural philosophers: the *phusikoi* or *phusiologoi*, as he calls them (which expression refers to virtually all Pre-Socratic thinkers except the Eleatics and the Pythagoreans). If the possibility of motion is formally dependent upon the above-mentioned ontological distinction, then motion has to be described as the motion of a thing having first one attribute and then another: on the one hand, motion must involve some kind of difference between the initial and the final phase, and on the other hand, there must be some kind of thing that is subject to change in some respect. Accordingly, there is no such thing as motion in the abstract and, further, there are as many forms of motion as there are categories of being (200b32-201a3). Aristotle will later modify this statement, however, and confine motion to the categories of place, quality and quantity (225b5-9).

But if motion (*kinēsis*) involves a thing changing in some respect, then generation and destruction, where the thing itself is subject to change, are not cases of motion. Later, Aristotle will declare them to be instances of change (*metabolē*).[18] I will return to this distinction below.

When turning to the natural philosophers, Aristotle finds that they tend to conceive of the principles of nature in terms of opposites, and, more precisely, as contraries. The idea that the foundation of the natural world must be thought of in terms of opposites, is something that Aristotle preserves and develops, and he defends it by saying that:

> ... the principles cannot be generated either out of each other or out of anything else, but, on the contrary, everything must be generated out of them. And this property precisely belongs to the primary principles: partly because, as primary, they are not generated out of anything else, partly because, as opposites, they are not generated out of each other (188a27-30).

---

18. The distinction between motion and change is the topic of book V.

The principles or *archai* should explain the processes of nature, and as such they cannot be natural objects themselves, subject to generation and destruction, or so at least Aristotle appears to view things at this stage. We will see later that he modifies his view on this point. The opposites of which the predecessors have spoken are of different kinds: hot and cold, full and empty, love and strife, and so on, but they all have in common that they are contraries (*enantiai*), to be distinguished from contradiction (*antiphasis*), which Aristotle for his part regards as the most important form of opposition, and not just in the context of formal logic, but also with respect to motion and generation, as we shall soon see.

To return to the natural philosophers' account of the principles of nature: this account is not entirely satisfactory, Aristotle remarks, because these philosophers do not really give any reason for their choice of opposites. Besides, their pairs of opposites are of two different kinds:

> They differ from one another in that some assume contraries which are prior, others contraries which are posterior; and some are more readily known by concepts, others more readily known by perception[19] (for some posit hot and cold, or again moist and dry, as causes of generation, while others posit odd and even, or again strife and love; and these differ from each other in the way mentioned). Hence their principles are in one sense the same, in another different: different, certainly, as indeed most people think, but the same inasmuch as they are analogous. For all are taken from the same table of columns, some of the opposites including others, while others are included under them. In this way, then, they are expressing themselves both in the same way and differently, some better and some worse: some, as I have said, take as their contraries what is more readily known by concepts,

19. 'By concepts': *kata ton logon*; 'by perception': *kata tēn aisthēsin*.

others what is more readily known by perception (the universal is known by means of concepts, the particular by perception: for concepts concern the totality, whereas perception is of the part) (188b30-189a8).

That Aristotle favors those opposites that are better known in conceptual regard over against those that are familiar to sense, is hardly surprising, considering that scientific knowledge (about nature) requires that one move from the level of *aisthēsis* to that of *logos*. Aristotle indeed makes such a move here, though not by introducing some other, definitely 'logical' pair of opposites, in addition to those that have been suggested by his predecessors, in order to thus account for the processes of nature. Rather, he wants to stress the formal, conceptual relation itself: this is the lesson to be learned from the natural philosophers: that is to say, no matter what kind of opposites they have been talking about, they have shown that this is the form any account of motion must take.[20]

There is yet another difference to be noted: the opposites that Aristotle mentions in the passage just cited were regarded by the Pre-Socratics not merely, and perhaps not even primarily, as states between which change takes place. Rather, they express the order of the natural world. To take just one example, Empedocles' love and strife is a principle that explains why elements can be mixed so that a new thing is generated, and again separated so that something is disintegrated.[21] But it does not depict the structure of the process of motion itself, which is what Aristotle is after.

20. Aristotle is criticized for this move by D. Bostock, who thinks that, in the *Physics*, the early natural philosophers' inquiry into nature "has somehow got sidetracked into something altogether more general," that is, since Aristotle seems to be more interested in logical reflection than in empirical investigation; "Aristotle on the Principles of Change in *Physics* I," *Space, Time, Matter, and Form: Essays on Aristotle's Physics* (Oxford: Clarendon Press, 2006), 2. But on Aristotle's view, the inquiry into nature precisely requires a foregoing logical reflection, which alone can provide it with a truly scientific basis.
21. Cf. e.g. Fragment B26.

If motion is to be analyzed in terms of opposites, it hardly comes as a surprise that Aristotle declares that we must begin our exploration of motion from a logical perspective (188a30-31):

> First, then, one must assume that no being by nature is such as to act on, or to be acted on by, any other thing at random, nor may anything come from anything else, unless one takes it in an accidental sense. For how could white come from educated, unless educated happened to be an attribute of the not-white or black? But white comes from not-white, that is to say, not from any not-white, but from black or some intermediate color (188a31-b1).

What Aristotle says here is, evidently, that motion and generation are not chaotic or chance phenomena but do have a determinate structure. If an educated person becomes pale, then there is no intrinsic connection between being educated and being pale, that is to say, it is not *as* educated that the person becomes pale, but being educated is something that just happens to apply to the person becoming pale: it is an accidental property. Instead, what has to be the case is that the person who *becomes* pale earlier had a skin with a different kind of color, like dark: it is only with respect to the color that we can speak about change here. In other words, becoming white implies that one was not pale before. It is therefore clear that change must involve difference and not-being. One truth about motion that is accessible from a purely logical point of view is, thus, that the very concept of change requires that we have a difference between the initial and the final stage of the process, where the end, more precisely, must be a negation of the beginning. Another logical truth asserted by Aristotle in this context is that change is within definite ranges, that is, categories.[22]

22. This last point is also made by Charlton, *Aristotle's Physics: Books I and II*, 66.

When Aristotle says that "white comes from not-white, that is to say, not from any not-white, but from black or some intermediate color," one usually takes this as a confirmation to the effect that Aristotle thinks that motion is a transition between contrary, not contradictory states. For, so the argument goes, if we take contradiction as a model in our analysis of motion (so that motion is a process not from black to white, but from not-white to white), then we have a nonessential or accidental relation between the starting-point and the end-point of motion (since 'not-white' can mean anything, for example 'educated').[23] However, if Aristotle's interest is primarily logical at this stage of his analysis, to the extent that he is concerned with establishing the formal conditions of motion, then we should expect him to base his analysis upon contradiction and not upon contrariety, since the former is the most important opposition from a logical point of view. And this indeed seems to be the case: the concepts Aristotle introduces to capture the relation between the opposites are form and privation, *eidos* and *sterēsis* (cf. 191a3-14, 193b18-20). Accordingly, the possibility of motion requires that we have a transition from a particular state to the negation of that state (or the other way round) or, in other words, motion is, *in some sense*, a transition from not-being to being (or the other way round), for motion (*kinēsis*) is a form of change (*metabolē*), and contrariety is a kind of specification of contradiction (the former falls within the scope of the latter).

Further, the above quotation implies that Aristotle thinks that the scope of a negation must be the same as that of the affirmation, so that we have a determinate negation. Otherwise, the law of non-contradiction does not apply. For if 'not-pale' is taken to mean 'educated', for example, then it is possible to affirm both that a person is pale and that he is not pale.[24] What complicates

---

23. See Irwin, *Aristotle's First Principles*, chapter 3.37. Charlton simply takes for granted that the opposites are contraries; *Aristotle's Physics: Books I and II*, 65-67 ff.

24. This is exactly what it looks like in Plato's *Sophist*, 256-259, where the negation of attributes is totally unrestricted (cf. Charlton, W. *Aristotle's Physics: Books I and II*, 66): "So *that which is* [*to on*] indisputably is not mil-

things is that Aristotle here is contrasting properties, not states or statements: he says that "white comes from not-white" (*leukon men gignetai ex ou leukou*) the reason for which is that he has not yet introduced the subject (*hupokeimenon*) as the third principle of motion, but is focusing entirely on the relation between the opposites. But this relation can at bottom only be made sense of as a relation between statements involving a subject. In itself, 'not-white' is no positive attribute at all. So when speaking about 'not-white' as the opposite of 'white', Aristotle is probably counting on us to understand that what he means to say is that there is something which has the property of not being white.

In *De Interpretatione*, Aristotle labels expressions like 'not-man' as 'indefinite names' (16a32). He does, however, allow for sentences like 'a man is not-just', and seems to consider them as more or less equal to sentences like 'a man is not just', though the form of the latter kind of sentences is quite obviously more adequate than the former, with respect to both logic and grammar.[25] Aristotle's main interest in this connection is to show that we must not believe that the negation of a sentence like 'every man is wise' is 'every man is not-wise' (20a27-29), not that we cannot use expressions like 'not-wise' at all. Accordingly, there is no real problem in construing motion after the model of contradiction, so that we say, for example, that a man changes from not-just to just: this is simply a shortened and somewhat awkward way of saying that a man who once was not just eventually became just.

Why, then, should motion at all be formulated in terms of contrariety rather than in terms of contradiction? Maybe to avoid a problematic metaphysics of states, that is to say, if talking about things like 'not-white' gives the impression that it is

lions of things, and all of the others together, and also each of them, are in many ways and also are not in many ways" (259b4-7). Translation by N. P. White, in *Plato – Complete Works*.

25. See the classifications of sentences in chapter 10. There Aristotle says, among other things, that "'No man is just' follows from 'Every man is not-just'" (20a20-21). I want to thank Luiz Carlos Pereira for reminding me of this discussion in *De Interpretatione*.

possible to have the property not-white as a positive attribute (rather than just to not be white). If you are not white, then this means, metaphysically speaking, that your skin has some other color, because every surface must be colored – but from a logical perspective this metaphysical necessity (that you must have a determinate color and not just not be white) does not matter. So, whereas contradiction is the proper kind of opposition from a logical point of view, contrariety shows you what is metaphysically or factually possible.

In order to give a proper description of motion, however, it is not enough to provide a pair of opposites. We also need some kind of basis or ground for the opposites themselves. In one sense, Aristotle's point is clear: when something changes from being cold to being hot, there is an object, a 'something', which is what undergoes and in this sense 'underlies' (*hupokeisthai*) the motion in question, but which in itself, or with respect to its substance, remains the same – at least when we are speaking about *kinēsis*, that is, alteration (*alloiōsis*: change with respect to quality), change of place (*phora*) or change of quantity (increase or decrease: *auxēsis* and *phtisis* respectively). If I get well after having been ill, I just move between two different states, but I am still the same, that is, with respect to my essence or as regards what I am (a human being). This seems to be the point of the following remark:

> Granted, then, that they [the principles] are finite in number, there is a reason for not making them merely two. For one could wonder how either density should be of such a nature as to act in any way on rarity or rarity on density. The same is true of any other pair of contraries: for love does not gather strife together and make something out of it, nor does strife make anything out of love, but both act on a third thing different from both (189a21-26).

One could also take this as a point about language: when we

say that a person who was ill became well again, we are speaking about one and the same subject (which underlies the different attributes) but with the help of two predicates. This is of course precisely how Aristotle characterizes substance, *ousia*, in the *Categories*: "all the other things are either said of the primary substances as subjects or are in them as subjects" (2a34-35). This is possibly also the point of the following claim: "But the principle must not be said of any subject. In that case, there will be a principle of the principle: for the subject is a principle, and seems to be prior to what is said of it." (189a30-32). The subject, *to hupokeimenon*, literally 'that which underlies', can refer both to the substrate (here the concrete object) which is presupposed in every kind of change from a state to its contrary, and to the subject to which we ascribe different attributes.

However, if not only the subject but also the pair of opposites is a principle (or two principles), and as such foundations of motion, though at the same time presupposing a substrate that can be acted upon, then they do in a way have a ground in their turn. And this is precisely what Aristotle claims in a passage immediately preceding the one just quoted: "Besides, one would probably run into difficulties if one does not posit some other nature to underlie the contraries. For we never see the contraries constituting the substance of any being" (189a27-29). To be sure, this is not correct if applied to the case of generation of substances, that is to say, when something receives its form in the sense of its essence: here one of the opposites seems to be precisely the substance of the thing generated. Probably, however, Aristotle does not have this kind of generation in mind here, but rather wishes to confine himself to cases of motion such as the case of a man who becomes educated, but does not come into being as such – even though, throughout this discussion of the principles of motion he talks about *genesis*, generation, but this is because he has not yet drawn the distinction between becoming something and becoming in an absolute sense (see below!). Another way to understand this is that Aristotle wants to remind us here that the form is ontologically dependent upon the thing whose form it is.

The Difference Between Becoming and Becoming Something

In chapter 7, Aristotle emphasizes the difference between on the one hand the unchanging, self-subsistent substrate, and on the other hand its accidental attributes, which do not enjoy independent existence, such as for example in the combination 'a man becomes educated' (note that Aristotle now begins to articulate the structure of motion in terms of full sentences). Here we must thus distinguish between being a man (that remains, *hupomenei*, as Aristotle puts it) and being educated (that does not remain; 190a10-13). A man who is educated is certainly one in number, but not one in conceptual or formal regard. This distinction is a first, extremely important step towards a proper conception of motion, not least since it will allow us to affirm the reality of motion (as opposed to rejecting it as being more or less identical to not-being).

The distinction between generation in an unqualified sense (that is, of substance) and generation in accordance with one or other of the categories (qualitative change, quantitative change and change with respect to place) will be the basis for the distinction between change and motion, which, as we have seen, Aristotle explains in terms of the difference between contradiction and contrary opposition. Aristotle may thus conclude:

> Plainly, then, if natural beings have causes and principles, from which they primarily are and have come to be, not accidentally but what each thing is said to be in its substance, then everything comes to be from both the substrate and the shape. For the educated man is composed in a way of man and educated: you can analyze its concept into the concepts of its elements. It is clear then that what comes to be will come to be from these elements. Now the subject is one numerically, but two in form (on the one hand the man, the gold and, in general, the countable matter: it is more of a 'this', and what comes to be from it does not do so accidentally; for it is the privation

and the contrariety, on the other hand, that are accidental attributes of it). But the form is one, like order or education, or some other thing said of something in the same way (190b17-29).

Generation (here taken in a wide sense) may both be said to proceed from not-being as well as from being – *in a certain sense*, not absolutely. When we speak about unqualified generation, we have in mind change with respect to matter or to form, whereas alteration only involves change of affections, and that is to say, of accidental attributes.[26] But the earlier thinkers (not least Parmenides) were unable to realize this, which made them "turn so far aside from the road which leads to coming to be and passing away and change generally" (191b32-34). More precisely, they were blind to the phenomenon of nature, in the sense of that which underlies all change, including generation and destruction. In order for change to be possible, there always has to be such an underlying nature, but that does not mean that nothing can come to be out of not-being.

In order to show how this is to be understood, Aristotle gives the following illustration:

> We, on the other hand, say this: that something comes to be out of a being or a non-being, or that a being or some non-being acts on or is acted on by something, or that it comes to be any particular thing, is in a way not different from the case of a doctor who acts on or is acted on by something, or when something is or comes to be out of a doctor. By this last we may mean two things, so clearly it is the same when we say that something is out of a being, and that a being acts or is acted on. A doctor may thus build a house, though not as a doctor but as a builder, and he comes to be pale, though not as a doctor but as dark. But he doctors and becomes ignorant of the art of

26. Cf. *De generatione et corruptione* 317a23-27.

doctoring as a doctor. Now since we most properly say
that a doctor acts or is acted on, or that something comes
to be out of a doctor, only if it is as a doctor that he does
or undergoes or comes to be this, then, clearly, to say that
something comes to be out of a non-being, is to say that
it does so out of a non-being as non-being (191a34-b10).

This passage is certainly not immediately clear (not least because
Aristotle uses examples of alteration, not generation or destruction), but the point seems to be this: That which undergoes
change must always be taken in the right sense, which was what
the earlier thinkers failed to see. So when a doctor becomes pale,
this is not generation from a state of pure not-being, but from
not-being in an accidental sense (he who is a doctor happens to
be dark, that is, not pale). Similarly in the case of generation from
being: A thing comes into being accidentally from being, that is
to say, from some matter (or subject), which is a form of not-being only insofar as some privation belongs to it (compare it to the
case with the doctor being dark or not gray). Accordingly, what
is comes to be accidentally from not-being, namely from a privation, though it does not in itself or essentially come to be from
this privation but from some matter which has this privation.

The earlier philosophers thus made a mistake when they assumed that generation should be construed as generation either from being or from not-being. In fact, neither 'being' nor
'not-being' has any positive meaning unless taken in a specific
sense. Once again, the problem with the predecessors' views
on generation, and on motion generally, is that they proceed
from the assumption that being itself is some kind of substance
and as such also a ground for motion. By drawing a distinction
between the substance on the one hand and the categories of
being on the other, Aristotle is able to show that, as he puts it
in *De interpretatione*, "neither 'to be' nor 'not to be' signifies a
thing, nor does 'being' when uttered in isolation. Then taken
by themselves they are nothing, but they co-signify a synthesis,
which cannot be conceived without the things that are com-

bined" (16b22-25). It is certainly possible to say that something is, or in turn is not without qualification. But you will not explain the possibility of generation and destruction of substance by just saying that something first does not exist and then does exist, respectively that something does exist and later does not. In other words, there is no such thing as change from being or from not-being except in an accidental sense.

And here Aristotle agrees with his predecessors: generation cannot proceed from nothing, but there has to be some kind of substrate even of unqualified (*haplōs*) generation.

> We too say that nothing can be generated out of not-being in an unqualified sense, but that, nevertheless, something can be generated out of not-being in some sense, namely accidentally (for something can be generated out of a privation, which in itself is a not-being, even though the privation is not a consituent of that which has been generated; but this fills people with wonder, and they consider it impossible that something should be generated in this way, out of not-being) (191b13-17).

Moreover, the earlier philosopers were also right in saying that generation cannot proceed from being, although they did not realize that the problem disappears if we just add that generation is from being in an accidental sense, that is, insofar as some privation belongs to that which is.

It is common knowledge that Parmenides was of absolutely decisive importance to Plato, as a forefather as well as an antagonist. But it has not been sufficiently recognized, I think, that Parmenides plays pretty much the same role in Aristotle. The *Physics* is to a great extent a response to the Parminedean challenge, which is clear not only from its first book, but also from the fact that Aristotle devotes much time and effort to refuting Zeno's paradoxes concerning motion.[27] Parmenides is in a way

27. See book VI, in particular chapters 2 and 9, and book VIII, 8.

the father of logic: his ontology is based upon an extreme interpretation of the law of non-contradiction: being is, not-being is not. The early natural philosophers shared this view, but tried to escape from its devastating consequences as far as the possibility of motion and change is concerned, by suggesting that all motion really is alteration, not generation or destruction in the proper sense. To Aristotle, however, this is an entirely unsatisfactory move. We must be able to speak about generation and destruction: these are apparent phenomena in the world of nature. Moreover, if Parmenides is not defeated, then we cannot in fact account for the possibility of alteration either, since it too presupposes the presence of not-being within being itself.

When properly interpreted, however, the law of non-contradiction not only testifies to the necessity of distinguishing between beings on the one hand, and their different modes of being on the other hand, but it also lets us dissolve the absolute opposition between being and not-being. Once we realize that every attribution of a property to a thing simultaneously involves a negation of all other attributes of that thing, we see that things always *are* in some specific way, and consequently *are not* in numerous other ways. As long as you regard being and not-being as absolute opposites, such a view will seem to entail a contradiction: one and the same thing both is and is not. It is Aristotle's insight into the logical structure of language that enables him to see that this is not a contradiction. Moreover, the possibility of a certain communion of being with not-being is what makes motion and change possible: motion proceeds from a state of being to a state of not-being (or the other way round), but the initial state of being is also, in a specific sense, a state of not-being, and conversely. Everything depends upon the regard in which you take the thing in question.

Strangely enough, the very same logic, the law of non-contradiction, which forced Parmenides to deny the possibility of motion enabled Aristotle to demonstrate its reality. All that was required was a more generous interpretation of it.

On the Constructive Notion of Truth and a New Sea-battle Problem

Luiz Carlos Pereira[1]

1. The Constructive Notion of Truth: Prawitz and Dummett

A fundamental feature of verificationism in mathematics is that the notion of truth is replaced by the notion of proof/verification as the central/core semantical notion: truth-conditions are replaced by assertability-conditions in the analysis of the meaning of mathematical statements. A not so unusual constructive standpoint is that intuitionism could completely dispense with a notion of truth that would go beyond the correctness of an assertion, beyond warranted assertability. According to this standpoint a mathematical statement A is true if and only if we have a proof of A or we have an effective procedure to produce a proof of A (where the verb "to have" must be understood as a possession *de facto* and not just *in principle*). In the late nineties several constructivists argued that intuitionistic mathematics should have a notion of truth that were not reducible to the notion of warranted assertability. Dummett for example says:

> In my paper at Santiago I maintained that a semantics for intuitionistic mathematics needs a notion of truth, and not just one of warranted assertability, if it is to subserve a metaphysical account of the nature of mathematical re-

1. The author would like to thank CNPQ and FAPERJ/PRONEX for financial support.

ality. (Truth from a constructive point of view, *Theoria*, v. LXIV, 1998)

In the same vein, Prawitz argues that not only in applied mathematics but also in pure mathematics, intuitionism should have a notion of truth that would go beyond warranted assertablity:

> Also in pure mathematics there are phenomena that seem difficult to account for without such an objective notion of truth which does not refer to properties belonging to the speaker. We do not only assert sentences in mathematics, we also make conjectures and ask questions to ourselves. If we wonder whether there are infinitely many twin primes, we do not wonder whether this has been proved – we know already that it is not, that is why we wonder. [...] Similarly, he [the verificationist] may conjecture that there are infinitely many twin primes, and normally he is then not making the conjecture that it will be proved that there are infinitely many twin primes, which is a conjecture about future history.[2]

The general idea seems to be: to think of the content of a mathematical assertion as the claim that a proof has been found or that we have an effective method for constructing one is a misrepresentation of the mathematical assertion; as Prawitz puts it, "it is to put too much in the content."

I think it would be correct to say that such a constructive notion of truth should satisfy at least the following basic requirements:

1. It should be objective.
2. It should be constructive.
3. It should not collapse with warranted assertability.
4. If a mathematical statement is true, then there must be

2. Dag Prawitz, "Truth and objectivity from a verificationist point of view,"in *Truth in Mathematics*, edited by Harold G. Dales and Gianluigi Oliveri (Oxford: Clarendon Press, 1998), 47.

something (there must be some fact, some part of reality) that makes it true (Dummett's principle C).

Given that a mathematical statement is true if it has a proof or a method for producing one, and given that this condition seems to be the same condition for warranted assertability, how can truth not collapse in warranted assertability? A reasonable answer could be: given that warranted assertability implies truth (this is not subject to dispute), then the only way in which truth in mathematics could go beyond warranted assertability is through statements that are true (they have a determined truth-value) although we are not entitled to assert them. Dummett suggests that decidable statements are clear-cut cases of constructive truth going beyond warranted assertability. According to Dummett' proposal:

> It was intended to allow as true a statement for which we have an effective decision procedure that will *in fact* yield a positive result, even if we do not know this. For example, a statement that a certain large number is prime is decidable, and may, when we apply the decision procedure, turn out to be true. I was making the tacit assumption that it is already determinate how the decision procedure will turn out, because there is no room for any play in the process of applying it. Hence, if it would turn out that the number is prime, the statement that it is prime is, on the definition I gave, true, even though we have at present no proof that it is, and may never have one, though we possess what is in fact an effective means of constructing one. This differentiates a statement's being true from our being entitled to assert it.[3]

Dummett's idea is that if the outcome of an algorithmic procedure is determined independently of the application of the

3. Michael Dummett, "Truth from the Constructive Standpoint," *Theoria* Vol. 64, Issue 2-3 (1998): 123.

procedure, then the truth value of the statement that would be verified (or refuted) by the outcome of the procedure is also already determined. Hence that statement would be true (or false) without our knowing it, without "our being entitled to assert it." It is certainly interesting to observe Dummett's use of temporal indicators: "will *in fact* yield," "when we apply," "it is already determinate," "will turn out," "if it would turn out," "we have at present," "may never get," "though we possess" [present]. At least in the case proposed by Dummett, *time* plays a very important role in the explanation of how truth goes beyond warranted assertability: we may have an algorithmic procedure and even if we do not apply it, the (future) results of applications are already determined before these (future) results are obtained. In this case it is legitimate to say that the statement that a large number n is prime, for example, has a truth-value, although we do not know yet what this truth value is (an epistemic point that could be made by classical mathematicians in all cases), and for this reason we can neither assert that the statement is true nor assert that its negation is true.

Another way of thinking about constructive truth going beyond warranted assertability is through the propagation of truth to the past, and in fact this is the way Dummett seems to understand Prawitz' proposal for a constructive notion of proof:

> In his paper given to the conference at Santiago Dag Prawitz (without collusion between us) also argued that constructive mathematics needs a notion of truth that goes beyond warranted assertability; but he was prepared to go a great deal further beyond it than I had. Contrary to what I had attempted to maintain, he argued that, when Wiles proved Fermat's Last Theorem, we cannot say that the theorem was not previously true: Wiles showed that it had always been true. Hence, he reasoned, a constructivist must identify the truth of a statement with our capacity to prove it; more exactly, with the existence of a proof which we can recognize as valid. Here a proof is not

to be said to exist only when we have it in hand; rather, when a proof is given, it is thereby shown that there has always been such a proof to be found. After all, the reasoning contained in the proof must be of a kind that we have all along been disposed to recognize as cogent; and so we must already be capable (in principle) of proving everything which at any future time we prove.[4]

I am taking the expressions "*was* not *previously* true," "it *had always been* true," "there *has always been*" and "we *must already be capable*" as an indication of temporal effects produced by the existence of the proof. The temporal effect that will be discussed below is the already mentioned propagation of truth to the past. According to this line of thought, it would be as unreasonable to think of mathematical truths as temporally indexed, as it is unreasonable to say that a mathematical statement is true for John and false for Paul, or to say that A is a theorem in Stockholm but not a theorem in Rio de Janeiro. It would be unreasonable to think that Fermat's last conjecture was not true in 1993 and became true at noon in July 1994. Even from a constructive point of view, mathematical statements, if true, are necessarily true, impersonal and not time-dependent. The existence or non-existence of proofs for mathematical statements are obviously temporally determined – Wyle's proof did not exist before 1994 – but mathematical truth itself is impersonal, necessary and should not depend on time. (We must always remember that we are not talking here about contingent statements: the statement that the building is 30m high doesn't become true in the past even if the building is now 30m high. We are talking here about mathematical statements and hence about propagation of truth concerning necessary statements).

Let us consider a mathematical statement S and let us also assume that although S was stated as a conjecture in 1662, it was only proved in January 2009. According to the view of construc-

4. Dummett, "Truth from the Constructive Standpoint," 127.

tive truth that we are now considering, the proof of S makes S *Omni*-temporally true – as Dummett says, "always true," true in the present, in the future and in the past, including the year of 1662. We can now say: "look, S was true, but they didn't know that." They were not entitled to assert it because they did not have a proof of S in 1662 (the assertability conditions for S were not satisfied in 1662), but S was in any way true since it is now proved. As we have already said, we can see here another case of truth "going beyond warranted assertability": S *was* true, but its assertion was not warranted!

We have seen that the explanations given above for the sense in which truth goes beyond warranted assertability made use of considerations that explicitly involved considerations about *time*: the *future* in the first case, the *past* in the second case. In particular, the second explanation appealed to a notion of atemporal truth that is conceived in terms of *Omni-temporal* truth, i.e., true in the present, true in the past and true in the future. This relation between necessary truth and *Omni-temporal* truth clearly invites into the discussion Aristotle and the sea-battle problem.

2. The Sea-battle Problem

In chapter 9 of *De Interpretatione*,[5] Aristotle presents and discusses a fatalist argument in order to immediately reject it. This argument, commonly referred to as the *sea-battle problem* or the problem of contingent futures, is probably the most discussed, mentioned, criticized, and analysed argument in the domain of logical fatalism. Before I present in more detail the problem of contingent futures, let me try to situate chapter 9 in the broader context of the treatise. I think that we can say with some confidence that one of the main aims of Aristotle in *De Interpretatione* is to establish the thesis that, in the domain of (single and simple) statement-making sentences, to every affirmation there corresponds a negation and to every negation there corresponds

5. Aristotle. *De Interpretatione*, trans. J. L. Ackrill (Oxford: Clarendon Press, 1963).

an affirmation, forming a pair of contradictory opposites:

> Thus it is clear that for every affirmation there is an opposite negation, and for every negation an opposite affirmation (*De Int*. Ch.6).

Between chapters 7 and 13, Aristotle examines different forms of (single and simple) statement-making sentences in order to establish pairs of oppositions (or relations of oppositions): statement-making sentences composed of a name and a verb, statement-making sentences containing a third element, statement making-sentences where a universal is taken universally, statement-making sentences where a universal is not taken universally, statement-making sentences containing modalities, and singular future statement-making sentences about contingent matters. Thus, according to this view, chapter 9 is not a *strange body* in the structure of *De Interpretatione* but simply another case of statement-making sentence that has to be considered. This is the case of "particulars that are going to be":

> For if every affirmation or negation is true or false it is necessary for everything either to be the case or not to be the case. For if one person says that something will be and another denies this same thing, it is clearly necessary for one of them to be saying what is true – if every affirmation is true or false; for both will not be the case together under such circumstances. For if it is true to say that it is white or is not white, it is necessary for it to be white or not white; and if it is white or is not white, then it was true to say or deny this.
>
> When the subject, however, is individual, and that which is predicated of it relates to the future, the case is altered. For if all propositions whether positive or negative are either true or false, then any given predicate must either belong to the subject or not, so that if one man affirms that an event of a given character will take place and an-

other denies it, it is plain that the statement of the one will correspond with reality and that of the other will not. For the predicate cannot both belong and not belong to the subject at one and the same time with regard to the future.

Thus, if it is true to say that a thing is white, it must necessarily be white; if the reverse proposition is true, it will of necessity not be white. Again, if it is white, the proposition stating that it is white was true; if it is not white, the proposition to the opposite effect was true. And if it is not white, the man who states that it is makes a false statement; and if the man who states that it is white is making a false statement, it follows that it is not white. It may therefore be argued that it is necessary that affirmations or denials must be either true or false

Now if this be so, nothing is or takes place fortuitously, either in the present or in the future, and there are no real alternatives; everything takes place of necessity and is fixed. (18A 28).

We can summarize what the problem is for Aristotle in the following way. A problem for a classical logician: given a strong reading of the principle of bivalence, contingent statements about future events would commit us to some form of *determinism*. If the characteristic note of statement-making sentences, the note that distinguishes this species of sentences from other species of sentences (prayers, orders, promises), is that a statement-making sentence is either determined true or determined false, then statement-making sentences about contingent matters in the future already have a truth value at the moment they are stated, and hence, one can conclude, the future is already (and has always been) determined. It is not hard to see, Aristotle concludes, the ethical consequences of this line of thought.

3. A Short Digression on Logical Fatalism

Fatalism can be roughly described as the doctrine that the future is already determined. If something happens in the future there is nothing we can do now to prevent its occurrence, and if some event does not occur in the future, there's nothing we can do now to bring it about. Fatalism in a certain sense breaks with the asymmetry between the fixity of the past and the openness (indetermination) of the future. To say that the future is open does not mean of course that our present actions have no effect at all on what will happen, as if everything that happens just happen by chance; quite on the contrary, indetermination here is totally compatible with "depending on what we have done in the past or on what we do in the present." Fatalism restores the symmetry between past and future: we are as impotent to change the past as we are to bring about the future. As S. Cahn puts it, if we look back at the past we may regret not having done some things, that we took a wrong course in our lives, that some events that should not have occurred did in fact occur, but there is nothing we can do now to undo what is done; we cannot prevent an event from occurring in the past. But if we look at the future we could think of it as containing some open possibilities, but not according to fatalism:

> As a man looks toward the future, he may hope that certain events will occur, but he can do nothing now to prevent the occurrence of any event which will, in fact, occur and he can do nothing now to bring the occurrence of any event which will not occur.[6]

The consequences of fatalism to the problem of free will are well known and its importance to various areas of thought is undeniable (religious thought, law, the science of history, for example). Logical fatalism (a.k.a logical determinism) is the doctrine that fatalism can be established on purely logical grounds, that the laws of logic alone suffice to prove it. If fatalism can be logically proved, "one could deny it only by denying the laws of logic."[7] Greek philosophy presents us with two very famous logical fa-

6. Steven M Cahn, *Fate, Logic and Time* (New Haven: Yale University Press, 2004; first. publ 1967), 9.
7. Cahn, *Fate, Logic and Time* , 8)

talist arguments: the aforementioned Aristotle's' *Sea-battle Argument* and Diodorus Cronus' *Master Argument*. These fatalist arguments can be considered as matrixes for most of the existing logical fatalist arguments.

4. A New Sea-battle Problem

We have now all the elements to propose a new sea-battle problem. Remember that in the original sea-battle problem, our classical logician faces problems with respect to the unrestricted validity of the principle of bivalence and singular statement-making sentences about contingent matters in the future. If we are talking here about a new sea-battle problem, a first natural movement is to replace future time by past time. A second natural movement is to replace contingent statement-making sentences by necessary statement-making sentences – after all we are in the realm of mathematics and thus in the realm of necessity. A third movement is the replacement of the principle of bivalence by the principle of non-contradiction (it's impossible that the same attribute pertains and does not pertain to the same subject under all circumstances and at the same time). Let's also assume the *Omni-temporal* understanding of necessity, i.e., a statement-making sentence S is necessarily true if and only if S is true and S was true and S will be true. Let me fix these replacements in a chart:

General principle and definition
- Principle of bivalence (temporal reading): every statement-making sentence (is and/or was and/or will be true) or (is and/or was and/or will be false).
- Necessary statement-making sentences: sentences that are/was/will be true.

SEA-BATTLE	NEW SEA-BATTLE
Future time	Past time
Contingent statement-making sentences	Necessary statement-making sentences
Principle of bivalence	Principle of non-contradiction

Let us now construct a new sea-battle problem. Let us assume that in 1662 a mathematical statement S was proposed as a conjecture and that S was first proved in 1994. Thus we can say (in 1994) that, given that the assertability conditions for S are fulfilled, S is true. Furthermore, if our constructive notion of truth admits propagation to the past, we can also say that S was already true in 1662 (it was true but "they did not know it"). In fact, with the proof of the statement in 1994 we conclude that the statement is *atemporally* true, in the sense of *Omni*-temporally true (it was true, it is true and it will always be true). The assertability conditions for S were clearly not satisfied in 1662, but S was nevertheless true in 1662, and that is the reason why any assertion of S in 1662 was incorrect/unwarranted.

We saw in the beginning of this paper that one of the conditions a constructive notion of truth should satisfy is Dummett's principle C, the principle that states that if a statement S is true, then there must be something in terms of which S is true, there must be some "piece of reality" responsible for the truth of S. Classically one could say that this "piece of reality" is a mathematical fact, a necessary fact that exists objectively in a objectively existing mathematical world/reality, a world that exists independently of our access to it. But this answer is obviously unacceptable in a constructive setting: there is no such mathematical world that exists independently of our access to it, a world that determines what is true or false independently of our knowing what is the case. But then, what would this constructive piece of reality responsible for the truth of a mathematical statement be? To this, the constructive mathematician answers: the *de facto* existence of a proof or the *de facto* existence of a method to produce/find one. That's how mathematical truths depend on reality.

In the case of the statement S we can say that principle C was not satisfied in 1662, since there was neither a proof of S nor a method for producing one then, but nevertheless it was true. But how can this be so? How can a statement be true without some piece of reality responsible for its truth? If we say that S was true *then* (in 1662), then there must be something responsible for its truth *then* (in 1662), otherwise how could it be true *then*? Given that S has a proof in 1994, S is true in 1662 (propagation of truth to the past), but given that there is no proof of S or a method to produce one in 1662, then there is no "piece of reality" responsible for the truth of S in 1662 and hence S is not true in 1662. We could certainly say, as Dummett understands Prawitz' proposal, that "there has always been such a proof to be found," and hence that there was a proof in 1662, but it is not easy to see how this existence statement would cope with Principle C. This is the new sea-battle problem.

5. Conclusion

My aim with this text was very modest, it was simply to suggest a new sea-battle problem: while classical logicians have to face problems with respect to contingent singular statements concerning the future and the principle of bivalence, given a certain reading of what it is for a statement-making sentence to be atemporally true, intuitionist logicians would have to account for problems concerning the past, necessary statements and the principle of non-contradiction. It is true that I have said nothing about possible solutions to the new sea-battle problem, for example, solutions based on variation of McFarlane's notion of relative truth. It is also true that my proposal heavily depends on the *Omni* reading of atemporality and that I have said nothing about an understanding of atemporality that would simply reject the possibility of any temporal indexation to mathematical propositions:[8] if a mathematical proposition is true, then this "is" must be read in a *strong* atemporal sense, in the sense that it makes no sense in saying of a mathematical statement that "it *was* true but they did not know." The right thing to be said in this case is: the statement *is* true but they did not know. These interesting developments of the subject have problems of their own. In any way, I do think that this structural *reversal*

8. This is in fact Prawitz' official proposal for the nature of mathematical propositions as far as time is concerned.

of the *old* sea-battle problem can teach us an interesting lesson about some connections between logic and time.

Aristophanes in the Cratylus

Luisa Buarque

Introduction

Much has been said about the formal specificities of the *Cratylus*: we know the dialogue has a strange and particularly asymmetric composition, and, above all, we know that this asymmetry is marked by a comical tone. The fact that Socrates spends at least two thirds of the text utilizing etymologies without credibility, which are normally considered ridiculous, has made it the target of the most varied number of interpretations. Above all, this fact has generated a significant discussion in relation to Plato's alleged lack of seriousness when composing the *Cratylus*.

More recently, we find a tendency to overcome the long opposition between the comic and the philosophical that has dominated interpretations of *Cratylus'* comicality. Interpreters nowadays tend to recognize the playfulness as a characteristic of the dialogue, which does not stop it from being philosophical. In this sense, the identification of a comical note ceased to generate the perplexity that derived from the idea that philosophical topics should be approached in a serious manner and in superior language. As many of the commentaries opposing the tendency to exclude the comic from the philosophical point out, Socrates was already renowned for bringing day-to-day language to philosophical investigation, and Plato can be as good a writer of 'comedies' as of 'tragedies'.

On the other hand, in the same way that they identify the comical as an inherent characteristic of the *Cratylus*, these commentaries usually abandon its thematization, given that it stops being an enigma and thus stops generating interpretative problems. What I suggest here is a resurgence of the deliberation related to the comic tone of the *Cratylus*. I will attempt, briefly, to develop the perspective that the comedy of the *Cratylus* is not merely one characteristic among others, but is indeed at the very heart of its conception. Put differently, its comical streak is found not only in certain passages – namely, the etymological section and, correspondingly, Euthyphro's inspiration – but that it is part of the architecture of the text itself. In short, the playful tone of the *Cratylus* seems to be structural.

According to the observations above, the hypothesis which will be developed here, in relation to the comical role in *Cratylus*, is that it is possible to discern an Aristophanic inspiration in the dialogue's formal composition. This hypothesis can be demonstrated in at least two complementary ways. Firstly, by showing some Aristophanic characteristics in the strategies Plato uses here to expose and develop its theme – especially in the choice of its main characters, Cratylus and Hermogenes, and in the relation they bear to the central subject of the dialogue, namely, the correctness of names. Secondly, it can be shown that Plato employs, at the very core of his dialogue, certain words that are extracted from Aristophanes' language. This postulation shall be demonstrated in two distinct sections.

A) Hermogenes and Cratylus

Hermogenes and Cratylus are the two Socratic interlocutors of our dialogue. With both of them, Socrates discusses the topic of the correctness of names. In fact, as the beginning of the *Cratylus* makes clear, they were already discussing this topic when Socrates arrives. It is the arrival of Socrates that leads Hermogenes to recapitulate what was being said, and to profit from the occasion, to ask Socrates whether he could clarify some enigmatic observations that Cratylus makes, which he is not capable of understanding. Cratylus, according to Hermogenes, speaks through oracles (perhaps, we could add, imitating his master Heraclitus). He states that his name is, in effect, Cratylus, and that Socrates' name is indeed Socrates, but that Hermogenes is not the name of his interlocutor, although everyone refers to him as such. It is thus established a matter whose comical exploration shall pervade the dialogue, reappearing, by no mere coincidence, at important moments of the text, and bringing with it different meanings every time: is Hermogenes' name really Hermogenes, or not?

Firstly, this issue evokes a problem in relation to the ancients: the authority of the prophetic and poetical word, the concreteness of proper names and of speeches, and their power to replace reality. Hermogenes' name, however, does not replace his reality (the historical Hermogenes, for all we know, cannot be considered someone who belongs to the *genos* of Hermes, since his characteristics do not correspond to that of the God – gain and eloquence). For this reason, affirms Cratylus, it cannot be his name, given that for him false names do not exist. It can be, at most, someone else's name, or not be a name at all, but merely a sound. It is possible to observe in these introductory lines the establishment of a bond that links sophistic themes – namely the impossibility of speaking falsely – to the more traditional behavior of the Hellenic culture in relation to names.

Secondly, but in first place in terms of its importance to the current hypothesis, it is possible to observe in the problem regarding Hermogenes' name a strong reference to the Aristophanic use of characters' proper names as descriptions of their personalities, their characteristics and the role they play in the text. This kind of resource can be found in nearly all of the comic writer's works, where names become true epithets: *Philocleon* (Cleon's friend) and *Bdelycleon* (he who fears Cleon) in *Wasps*, *Pisthetairos* (loyal friend) and *Evelpides* (good hope) in *Birds*, *Fidipides* (lover of horses) and *Strepsiades* (he who turns the situation to his own benefit) in *Clouds* and many others. It is also true that the matter of the significant name has, in Greece, traditional strength, thus not being an Aristophanic exclusivity. Besides the previously alluded problem of the concreteness of proper names, the significant name also dates back to the tradition that goes from Homer to tragic poetry.[1] If analyzed more closely, however, the allusion to the etymology of Hermogenes' name reproduces specifically the Aristophanic ability to play with tradition. Like the etymologies of Aristophanic names in general, the etymology of 'Hermogenes' is absolutely simple and clear – it can be understood immediately by anyone and does not require additional explanations. It brings with it a network of references, thus making it apt for comic use (especially if we think about the huge distance between these references and the characteristics of the historical Hermogenes). In short, it becomes a direct element of comedy, exactly as the names of Aristophanes' characters, and in opposition to the names of Homeric and tragic heroes. As a result, it is possible to say that in this dialogue what Plato achieves, through the example of Aristophanes, is the comic appropriation of a feature that reverts to Homer, the poets in general, the tragics and the sophists. It is this good-humored exploration of a general feature of Greek literature that makes us think of a reference of philosophy to the reference of comedy to epic poetry, to tragic poetry and to sophists. It is, therefore, a frame of references of overlapping layers, i.e. one more example of those literary palimpsests with which Greek literature appears to be full.

Moreover, it is not only at the moment in which he baptizes his characters that Aristophanes plays with proper names and makes a play on words. It is also, for instance, upon the occasion of an aggression, which often results from the modification of the names of the people being insulted.[2] Aristophanes knows uniquely well how to extract the comedy inherent from language games, frequently adding the so-called "verbal comedy" to "situation comedy," and playing with elements such as

1. Cf. Gregory Nagy, *The Best of the Achaeans: Concepts of the Hero in Archaic Greek Poetry* (Baltimore and London: The John Hopkins University Press, 1979) specially the references to the etymologies of the names of Achilles, Patroclus, Heracles and others.
2. Just in *Wasps*, we can find at least six examples of puns with proper names: Philoxène, 83/84, Diopheíthes, 380, Drakontídes, 438, Khairéas, 687, Krobúlos, 1267 and Karkínos, 1502.

double meanings, the malleability of the words and their un-
foreseen meanings which break the expectations of the audience
in relation to the use of usual expressions, and extract the comic
from the flexibility of language itself. Plato, for his part, seems
to have noticed the comic potential of Hermogenes; and, in fact,
it is difficult to find an explanation for his presence in the dialogue, other than the puns made on his name. In conclusion –
and since the choice of the character whose name is opportune
to comedy is one of the most important formal aspects of the
dialogue – we could say that the Platonic games with the name
of Hermogenes across the *Cratylus*[3] are a primary and strong
indication of the interlocution with Aristophanes in terms of
dramatic composition, understood as the relation between the
theme dealt with and the manner in which it is engaged.

One cannot forget, however, that the Hermogenes of
Aristophanes would probably be someone that would indeed
belong to the *genos* of Hermes, gifted with cleverness for gain
and for speech, and that Plato's Hermogenes, as already said,
is the opposite of this. The philosopher, consequently, chooses
as his character he whose name means the exact opposite of his
most prominent characteristics, not by chance in a context in
which properties of names will be examined: comical torsion
of the comical resource of choosing meaningful names for the
characters.

More could be said regarding this topic. The introduction of
Hermogenes, of eloquent name, and the corresponding Platonic
lark, will insert into the dialogue precisely the theme of proper
names which, from that point onwards, shall be explicitly approached in various moments throughout the composition.
Already at the very beginning the theme shall emerge in three
crucial moments, as if to state a point of view by which the *ono-
mata orthotés* will be examined. Firstly, at the moment in which
Hermogenes, defending his thesis, remembers that names of

3. Plato, *Cratylus*, trans. C. D. C. Reeve (London: Hackett Publishing, 1998),
384c7, 408b8 and 429c2.

slaves can be changed arbitrarily, according to the wish of their owners;[4] then it will appear in the initial part of the etymologies, dedicated to the analyses of names of the Gods, so that the etymologic investigations which then follow will give continuity to the same line of rationale developed in the etymology of divine names;[5] and also, further ahead, at the moment in which, to prove to Cratylus that it is possible to make false statements, Socrates illustrates his proposal with the possible exchange of names between the two characters with whom he dialogues.[6] Notwithstanding, apart from the examples, what is important to note is that in the *Cratylus* the proper name works as a paradigm, not only of common names but of words in general. This becomes particularly clear when certain sections are examined, such as the following:

> SOCRATES: Similarly, someone who knows about names looks to their force or power and isn't disconcerted if a letter is added, transposed, or subtracted, or even if the force a name possesses is embodied in different letters altogether. So, for example, in the names 'Hector' and 'Astyanax', which we were discussing just now, none of the letters is the same, except 't', but they signify the same anyway. And what letters does 'Archepolis' – 'ruler-of-a-city' – have in common with them? Yet, it expresses the same thing. Many other names signify simply 'king'; others signify 'general', for example 'Agis' ('Leader'), 'Polemarchus' ('War-lord'), 'Eupolemus' ('Good-warrior'); and still others signify doctor, for example, 'Iatrocles' ('Famous-healer') and 'Acesimbrotus' ('Healer-of-mortals'). And we might perhaps find many others, which differ in their letters and syllables, but which have the same force or power when spoken. Is that plain to you, or not? Hermogenes: Certainly. Socrates:

4. *Crat.* 384d.
5. *Crat.* 401a-408d.
6. *Crat.* 429e.

Then those that are born according to nature should be given the same names as their fathers. Hermogenes: Yes. Socrates: What about the ones that are born contrary to nature, those that are some form of monster? For instance, when a good and pious man has an impious son, the latter shouldn't have his father's name, but that of the kind to which he belongs, just as in our earlier example of a horse having a calf as his offspring?"[7]

What can be noted in this passage is that the proper names and the common names seem to be completely interchangeable, and that there is an unrestricted application, to common names, of conclusions drawn regarding proper names. The discussion starts by the example of Hector and his son Astyanax, whose names mean more or less the same, thus sliding towards the observation that each animal should be named according to the species and genre to which it belongs – as if both cases were similar. This being the case, proper as well as common names are seen as eponyms: they say something about the referred person or thing, and give information regarding the origin of the being, exactly like Aristophanic proper names.

Nevertheless, the Platonic subtlety is put into practice here with rare mastery; as the same passage indicates, births against nature can also occur. The enemies of the Gods can be called Theophilo,[8] which means that names are not similar to nicknames, given to someone only after being met and according to the person's most striking characteristics – by the way, Proclus reminds us that the nick-name 'Plato' was adopted by Aristocles – but are instead given in advance. Either they are an expression of a "hope,"[9] or a reflection of the belief that children are similar to their parents (as a colt is similar to a horse) or shall develop the same activities as them. This does not occur in most cases, leading individuals either to correspond to the content of their

7. *Crat.* 394b1-e1.
8. *Crat.* 397b5.
9. *Crat.* 397b4.

names or not: nothing can assure us of this. Only in the case of a playwright who might do it on purpose, and with intent, could this be guaranteed; which would take us precisely to the *onomatourgos* hypothesis. What can be noticed, in few words, is that the *Cratylus* plays specifically with the theme of the eponymy[10] of names, as if to show that names can be treated as epithets – or even small definitions – of the people or things which they name, but should not always be so, for they are given matter-of-factly (or haphazardly) rather than with justification. So, words can be, but are not always (and indeed, in most cases, are not) Aristophanic.

Many of the etymologies illustrate specifically this observation regarding names of fathers and sons, and births against nature. They toy with the possibility that – just as certain names of epic and tragic heroes potentially contain the plot of their lives and the overview of their destiny, and also as the great majority of the comical names summarize the main quality of their bearers – the etymological work of decomposition of common names might be able to reveal their intimate and essential sense; as if the words in general contained encrypted messages which are ready to be decoded. However, it results in also showing that this procedure forces the name beyond its possibilities, enabling all types of content to be extracted from a word, depending on the will of whoever is conducting the etymology.

Subsequently, we would need to affirm that Hermogenes' only name (badly assigned eponym or no-name, in each case and according to each interpretation) already lends itself to the development and the strengthening of many of the dramaturgical, formal, thematic and philosophical intentions of Plato in the *Cratylus*. It is also possible to show how much the reference to the Aristophanic relation between proper names, the characteristics of the characters they refer to, and the thesis that they embody appear in these good-humored pages.

10. Cf. Gérard Genette, *Mimologiques: Voyage en Cratylie* (Paris: Éditions du Seuil, 1976), 17-24.

Regarding Cratylus, we could say that, as a character, he does not lag behind Hermogenes in terms of comical evocation, even if his relation specifically to Aristophanic comedy is not as strong as Hermogenes'. In any case, Cratylus is fairly comical, and this is, as we know, due to the fact that he is well-known by the extremism narrated by Aristotle: it is not possible to even once enter the river of Heraclitus. The correction of the master's thesis silences him; the most unpretentious assignment of a name would correspond to the attempt to stabilize an unstable reality.[11] So as to avoid determining a world in constant transformation, he merely points the finger, which is his way of showing the individual being at a precise moment. In actual fact, in this act of pointing out a straight connection with the theme of the dialogue is observed, since pointing out would correspond gesturally to naming; we always point to individual things, in occasional moments and, in the *Cratylus*, the acts of calling and naming (*kalein* or *onomázein*) are what make up the investigative tone.

Another Cratylic anecdote mentioned by Aristotle states that, according to Aeschines, Cratylus gesticulated very much whilst talking (supposedly before his period of terminal aphasia and economy of gestures, where only the pointing was kept), yet another citation in comical tone.[12] The fact that they are mere anecdotes only serves to re-enforce that Cratylus' personality was inclined toward the comical. Cratylus is, as it were, a ready-made joke. His Heraclitean extremism represents a comic and rough caricature of Heraclitus' thesis.

In the Platonic dialogue many aspects indicate that Plato used and consciously manipulated this data, or similar information, regarding the character. With this in mind, it is possible to point out the fact that his first citation of the famous sentence of Heraclitus (which made famous the flux doctrine) may manipulate the words to favor the Cratylic correction and its sub-

11. *Metaphysics*, 1010a10-15.
12. *Rethorics*, 1417b1-3.

sequent linguistic abstention. If the fragment that is most large-ly accepted as originally Heraclitean is that which affirms that "to those entering the same rivers other and other waters shall flow,"[13] the Platonic citation which reads "it is not possible to enter twice into the same river,"[14] which transforms the plural (same rivers) into singular (same river), highlights the change of the very same thing we name as river, thus leading to the conclusion that it is not the same on the occasion of a second bath. Which also leads to the quick conclusion that it should not be called by the same name. In Cratylus' extreme point of view, if someone is to be faithful to his master's teachings, he should abdicate speech, given that speaking presupposes the existence of realities which have a minimal stability in order that they can be named. In other words: if the first fragment suggests that the names of things are to be maintained specifically because they correspond to a space-time identity, which in turn covers – and is even enabled by – the constant transformation (other and other waters: change in which the continuous passage would be permanent, thus corresponding to the same rivers – riverbeds, paths, and names which to them are designated), the second can lead to the conclusion that the name of the object should not be kept, given that it is no longer the same thing. Put differently: in the first case there is an identity and a transformation, whereas in the second case the identity is completely annulled, leaving only transformation. This would easily lead to the conclusion that one cannot even name, let alone assert anything regarding reality. So, according to the Cratylic conception, it is not pos-sible to speak without violating the nature of things.[15]

13. Fragment XII.
14. Fragment XCI, whose authenticity is sometimes questioned by specialists precisely as deriving from Plato, who is not usually seen as a trustwor-thy source, given his tendency to use caricature as well as his strategic deformation of the thoughts which he seeks to examine. This discussion is not particularly relevant for me, since, whether it is or is not genuinely Heraclitean, the conclusions are the same.
15. It is also worth noting that either Plato manipulated the Heraclitean sen-tence or chose the version, original or not, which was the most favorable to his intentions. What matters is that the sentence seems to have been hand-

The above observations regarding the character that gives name to the dialogue lead to a wider understanding of the comicality within the Platonic text. On the one hand, Cratylus is someone known for his worries about problems regarding the correspondence between names and things. On the other hand, Plato makes of him someone who plainly contradicts himself: despite affirming throughout the dialogue that things always change, and that there are not even essences which stay stable (in spite of the diverse arguments that Socrates presents against this conception), he is the only one in the whole discussion who doesn't change. He isn't able to adopt another opinion or point of view, and tries no other theoretical position, thus staying stable, fixed, in the same place. Everything changes but Cratylus himself.

To sum up, we could say that both Cratylus and Hermogenes are characters who serve very well the two main characteristics of this platonic dialogue: its central subject – correctness of names – and its comic way of treating them. Moreover, as previously affirmed, it is within dramatic composition that the relation between the formal aspects of the dialogue and the theme to be treated can be most strongly observed. So in conclusion, some of its comic features, or at least those regarding Hermogenes, are directly related to that which, in Aristophanes' comedies,

picked. I would like to refer, in this context, to the discussion by Lucia Saudelli in "Heráclito Latino. Um caso de estudo" (*Anais de Filosofia Clássica*, vol. V, no 9 [2011]) regarding the different versions of the Heraclitic fragments with the river thematic. The doubts revolve around not only the differences between singular and plural but also around the term "twice," which one does not know whether to attribute to Plato or to Heraclitus. There is a citation, in particular, which becomes crucial in directing such doubts: Seneca in *Epistle 58*, which somehow united the "twice" of Plato and the singular "same river" with fragment XII by saying: "We go down, and do not go down twice, the same river." Shortly afterwards the author affirms: "In truth, the river maintains its name, but the water flows." Seneca's comment is particularly relevant to the present context, as it makes direct reference to the matter of the 'name' of the river. Additionally, what argues in favor of the probability of the expression 'twice' being Heraclitean is precisely the presumed correction of the historical *Cratylus* to the master, when it was changed to 'not even once' – and even if it's only an anecdote, the reference must be correct for the pun to work. Anyway, this real or fictional correction would not have occurred if the expression 'twice' had not already been present in *Heraclitus*.

point specifically towards the subject of names.

B) A Textual Comparison Between the Cratylus and the Clouds

As previously mentioned, the second part of the development of my hypothesis will focus on the identification of a more precise textual indication that, in the *Cratylus,* echoes the writing of Aristophanes. The Aristophanic composition that has the most affinity with *Cratylus* is, not by chance, *The Clouds.* Here, to be brief, I will refer to only one of these affinities. Going directly to the point, it is possible to identify in the *Cratylus* an important recapture of a pun made by Strepsiades in *The Clouds.* In the play, the character makes a joke with the double meaning of the word *dínon,* which can mean either 'whirl' (whirlpool or whirlwind), or vortex, or (circular) dizziness, or a roundish object, in particular a type of clay vase made for drinking from. At the opening of the play, Strepsiades learns from Socrates that Vortex was the new God who had come to reign in the place of Zeus.[16] At the end, Strepsiades says: "Ah me, unhappy man! When I even took you who are of earthenware for a God!"[17] This pun not only indicates the lesson that the protagonist learns throughout the play, but also underlines the core of the matter approached by the comedy writer in this context: there, the criticism of Aristophanes targets most specifically the sophists and philosophers – specialists, in his eyes, in turning the art of the rational inside out, performing cartwheels in thought and managing to make the weakest argument defeat the strongest, causing dizziness to those who listen to them. And so Vortex becomes the new God: it was with him that the sophists seem to have learned their tumultuous and whirling procedures, and it is in a vortex that their listeners and apprentices are thrown. The title of the play itself points toward the same direction: clouds are divinities worshipped by the wise of the *phrontisterion* ("…

16. Aristophanes, *Clouds. The comedies of Aristophanes,* ed. William and James Hickie (London, Bohn: 1853), v. 381/382.
17. *Clouds,* v. 1475.

great celestial clouds, Goddesses of the idle: they offer knowledge and dialectic")[18] for being volatile and fickle, changing according to the smallest alteration in the circumstances ("Have you seen, looking up, clouds similar to a centaur, to a leopard or a wolf or a bull? (...) They transform themselves into what they wish.")[19] And, additionally, for being mere fog, smoke, steam; but with the great power to cause rains, floods, catastrophes. With this in mind, the analogy between whirlwind (air, nothing which can solve everything) and steamy, unstable clouds indicates the play's central themes: new gods required by the new attitudes in the face of knowledge, and characterization of this new attitude as something selfish, that changes at every moment for its own benefit. Summarizing, it turns arguments according to circumstance and the slightest turn of the wind, uses "subtle wordings"[20] and confuses the unaware. These observations show that Strepsiades' pun, which links the beginning to the end of the play, has much more importance than it initially appeared to have.

The text of the Cratylus seems to toy very ably with the same 'vortex' idea, and this notion plays a role as important in the dialogue as in the play itself. The word that explicitly links the two contexts is *díne* – used by Plato in *Cratylus*, 439c – from the same family as the Aristophanic *dínos*, and even more usual than that. If the latter has a double meaning explored by the comedy writer, the Platonic *díne* is its synonym in terms of the meaning of 'whirl' (of water or wind), moving circularly and rotationally. However, even if Plato has substituted the double meaning of the first for the univocal sense of the second, all the notions linked to the term that appear in Aristophanes' play re-appear in the *Cratylus*. The term *díne* is used by Plato at the end of the work in one of the crucial moments of criticism of Heraclitus, namely at the point in which Socrates says that the authors of the Greek names, just as the Heracliteans, have fallen into a type

18. *Clouds*, v.316-317.
19. *Clouds*, v. 347-349.
20. *Clouds*, v. 365.

of vortex in which they confuse themselves and where they also plunge us into.[21] This affirmation is directly linked to two others where the term does not appear, but where the same notion is active. One of them is passage 411b, where Socrates detects the fact that both the ancient establishers of names and the wise men of their days go around in so many circles in an attempt to investigate the nature of beings, that they end up being carried off by a dizzy-making bewilderment (*eiliggiosin*, from *eiliggos* or *iliggos*, which also mean vortex, spin etc.), later transferring their own confusion and vertigo to the topics they investigated, and finally concluding that everything moves incessantly.[22] The second is a passage that appears soon after the one in which the word *díne* is explicitly used, and gives continuity to the treatment of the Heraclitean theme. Here, Socrates positions himself clearly against the thesis that everything flows, affirming that the tenant of this conception "condemns both himself and the things that are as totally unsound and all flowing like leaky pots, or believe that things are exactly like people with runny noses, or that all things are afflicted with colds and drip over everything."[23] Even if not utilizing the same term used by Strepsiades, the philosopher presents the same comparison – potentially contained in the double meaning of the term chosen by Aristophanes – between the rotary movement of the thoughts and of the arguments of the wise and the spinning movement of the manufacturing of ceramic – and adding to it the comic image of the running noses. And, finally, in the set of the three passages mentioned above it is possible to note the intense recurrence of the theme of *Clouds*: the circular vertigo of the wise in general and the vortex into which they throw their listeners with their blather.

Upon examining the passages, we clearly observe that

21. *Crat.* 439c7.
22. Curiously, in this passage we find the term *strephesthai*, go round, turn, spin (which is what the wise do in order to investigate the nature of the beings), verb from which the name of Strepsiades derives.
23. *Crat.* 440c9-d3.

there is a Platonic utilization of notions similar to those that Aristophanes developed in *Clouds,* and that, moreover, such utilization has analogous ends: it is the bearer of a criticism to the pretentious wise who, with their vaunted knowledge, end up by confusing themselves and bringing others into a state of confusion. However, what Plato refutes in Aristophanes's *Clouds* is the fact that Socrates can be thrown into this large bag of wisdom. Maybe we could say that what he really does is changing to Heraclitus the main target of his criticism, since, as we just saw, more than the wise in general, it reaches the Heracliteans in particular. The vertigo of the Heracliteans – and perhaps also of the first Greek name-givers, and with them a big part of Hellenic culture – corresponds to the reign of the vortex in the *phrontisterion*, which turns out to be a mere reign of the leaky pots. In *Cratylus*, as in *Clouds*, the biggest part of the wise men see the world as a giant gyration rather comparable to the wheel that turns the ceramic, without the knowledge that the vortex is indeed within them, and not in the things they investigate.

Conclusion

The good-humored and jestful tone of the *Cratylus* is presented to the reader since its initial pages, with plenty of jokes and humorous references to the vocabulary of others (beginning, actually, with the very subject of the dialogue, *onómaton orthótetos*, an up-to-date expression which is frequently attributed to Prodicus). Its composition, in formal terms, was carefully treated to enable the use of comical weapons in general, and Aristophanic weapons in particular. What we should still question here is the Platonic goal in the use of this strategy. To conclude on this theme, I shall make just a few general comments about the alliance between humor and *agon*, which may contribute to a future investigation of this problem.

It is well-known that the Old Comedy in general – of which style Aristophanes is for us the ultimate representative, given that he is the only one whose works have been partially preserved – performs a large-scale hyperbolic criticism that tars with the same brush the most diverse tendencies of thought and, transforming them into typical characters, exposes through laughter some politically and ethically relevant problems. It is possible that, if Plato really incorporates in the *Cratylus* the Aristophanic ways of criticizing and making himself heard, it is because his objectives there are closely linked to a hyperbolic criticism. In fact, Plato presents in this dialogue his own version of the caricature of some representatives of the most consecrated fields of knowledge in the Hellenic culture. Evidently, those whom his speech challenges the most are sophistry, poetry, religion, physiology. The oldest traditions and the current tendencies are toyed with through the mixture of the most varied elements in terms of intellectual formation parading before the reader, and from all these differences emerges their background, namely the epistemological, ethical and political consequences considered by Plato to be philosophically problematic.

In short, philosophical criticism of other types of speeches may have, according to Plato author of *Cratylus*, something to learn from comical criticism, even if comedy itself can largely be criticized by Platonic philosophy – otherwise Plato would not be Aristophanic enough. In conclusion, if this assumption is correct, even if it is not true that Plato kept copies of Aristophanes' comedies under his pillow, è ben trovato.

This Dust of Words[1]

Helena Martins

This text responds to the image in its title, a famous image by Samuel Beckett. I begin by dwelling on the expression for a while, as it gives me occasion to bring forth a certain Beckettian motif that is central to the thought I wish to pursue here.

This dust of words: in Beckett's landscape, the image might perhaps evoke the experience of being blinded by a cloud of dust, might lead one to think of words as forming a hindrance of sorts. In one of its familiar historical guises, language appears here as that which impedes access – access, in Beckett's terms, to whatever it is that "lurks behind, be it something or nothing."[2] In his writings words are indeed often brought up as this sort of haze through which one strives to see: "Less seen and seeing when with words than when not. When somehow than nohow. Stare by words dimmed."[3] Seeing with words is seeing *somehow* – a (vain?) wish to see *nohow* is avowed here and in many other passages in Beckett's oeuvre.

Another possibility is to conceive of words themselves as being dusty – old and feeble, devoid of any strength, like most of Beckett's characters. In a move that is hardly unusual in the modernist game of Beckett's time, *dust of words* could be a figure for the weariness or exhaustion of language, its yearning for renovation or else for silence. "I use the words you taught me," says exasperated Clov to Hamm, "If they don't mean anything

1. This is a modified version of the article "Words (mis)trusted", published in *Disorientations*, ed. Marcia Schuback and Tora Lane (Lanham, Maryland: Rowman & Littlefield, 2014).
2. Samuel Beckett, "'German Letter' to Axel Kaun," in *The Letters of Samuel Beckett 1929-1940 vol. 1*, ed. Martha D. Fehsenfeld and Lois M. Overbeck (Cambridge: Cambridge UP, 2009), 519.
3. Unless otherwise indicated, all quotations from Beckett's works are from *Samuel Beckett: The Grove Centenary Edition* (4 vols), ed. Paul Auster (New York: Grove Press, 2006), henceforth cited as GE, followed by number of volume and page. This passage: "Worstward Ho," GE IV, 482.

anymore, teach me others. Or let me be silent."[4] And in an early poem,[5] we hear a similar, if more radical, tone:

> Why not merely the despaired of
> occasion of
> wordshed
> is it not better abort than be barren

Quotes favouring this second way of taking the image *dust of words* could also easily be multiplied, giving salience to the notion that the words we have are out of work: "the mistake one makes is to speak to people."[6]

And moving further along this path we get perhaps to a third, no less compelling reading: one could think of words as being not merely dusty, but as being themselves reduced to dust, their integrity and differentiation lost – an image of language collapsing, falling apart, disintegrating. This reading is of course in perfect accord with Beckett's quite express and celebrated wish to create a *literature of the unword*, his ever growing predilection for *tattered syntax*:[7] over time Beckett's language grows indeed more and more tattered – torn up by baby talk, animal sounds, stuttering, maddening repetitions, conventional and unconventional onomatopoeia, jerky interjections; lack, excess or even the invention of prepositions and conjunctions, the shortage or absence of punctuation marks, disruption of verb transitivity and tense, unimaginable inflections, and so on. Two (quite explicit) examples out of a multitude:

> that's how it will end, in heart-rending, inarticulate
> murmurs, to be invented, as I go along, improvised as I
> groan along, I'll laugh, that's how it will end, in a chuckle,

4. "Endgame," GE III, 122.
5. "Cascando," GE IV, 33.
6. "First Love," GE IV, 234.
7. See Banfield, A. "Beckett's Tattered Syntax," *Representations*, vol. 84, no. 1 (2003).

chuck, chuck, ow, ha, pa, I'll practice, nyum, hoo, poo, plop, psss, nothing but emotion, bing bang, that's blows, ugh, poo, what else, oooh, aaah, that's love, enough, it's tiring... [*The Unnamable*, GE II, 401]

Back try worsen twain preying since last worse. Since atwain Two once so one. From now rift a vast. Vast void atween. With equal plod still unreceding on. That little better worse. Till words for worser still. Worse words for worser still. ["Worstward Ho," GE IV, 482-3]

In this drive toward the inarticulate words do seem to scatter like dust. The radical modes of pulverizing syntax in Beckett's writings, hardly made clear in the brief list of procedures and examples given above, are to be distinguished from, say, the attacks on language performed by his so-called "artistic father," James Joyce. Acting on his impulses to dissolve the "terrifyingly arbitrary materiality" of the surface of language, Beckett wished to adopt a "scornful attitude vis-à-vis the word," one that deliberately had nothing to do with what he described as Joyce's "apotheosis of the word": Beckett's own programme, as it is often said and quoted, had to do with tearing up the fabric of language, with drilling in it "one hole after another."[8]

Moreover, this disintegration of language is not self-contained; in Beckett, it overflows, it is everywhere: "no nominative, no accusative, no verb ... no 'I', no 'have', no 'being'."[9] This brings us, at last, to the actual text from which my image title comes. Here is the famous passage, pulled first from out of the loose-tight weave of *The Unnamable* by Maurice Blanchot:[10]

...I'm in words, made of words, others' words, what oth-

8. "German Letter," op. cit., 518-9.
9. Interview to Israel Shenker, 1956 in *Samuel Beckett: The Critical Heritage*, ed. Lawrence Graver and Raymond Federman (London: Routledge, 1997), 162.
10. Maurice Blanchot, "The Unnamable (1953)," in *Samuel Beckett: The Critical Heritage*, op. cit., 132.

ers, the place too, the air, the walls, the floor, the ceiling, all words, the whole world is here with me, I'm the air, the walls, the walled-in one, everything yields, opens, ebbs, flows, like flakes, I'm all these flakes, meeting, mingling, falling asunder, wherever I go I find me, leave me, go toward me, come from me, nothing ever but me, a particle of me, retrieved, lost, gone astray, I'm all these words, all these strangers, *this dust of words, with no ground for their settling, no sky for their dispersing*... [*The Unnamable*, GE, II, 379-380, italics added]

An emphasis seems to be placed here on the now very familiar theme of the merging between language and world, language and self, language and life – and in this case it is *we* who are this dust of words, we and everything else are somehow the residue of language. This imagination may lead us to think of language (and life) under the curse of aporia – to conceive of life and language as an aporetic commotion or tumult, an afflicted suspension, an endless and hopeless state of waiting-until-the-dust-settles. We find ourselves perhaps before a sense of confinement, a sense of language imposing very strict double-binding limitations: no settling, no dispersing; no grounding, no disappearing. Language is at once demiurgic, the great maker, and unfathomable, everything yields, opens, ebbs, flows. I can't go on, I'll go on.

The brief excursus through Beckett's universe we have just taken in the company of an image, *dust of words*, may have brought forth a certain motif: that of language mistrusted, disgraced, in disrepute. Language is that which blinds, or that which is exhausted or even dead beyond resuscitation, that which disintegrates (itself and everything else) – it is a trap, a curse. A very young Beckett was already quite explicit in this regard: "since we cannot dismiss it [language] all at once, at least we do not want to leave anything undone that may contribute to its disrepute."[11]

---

11. "German Letter," op. cit., 518.

What provokes this text is a wish to attend to the following perplexity: what can we make of the motif of *language in disgrace* within Beckett's own *glorious language*? How can we, readers of Beckett, trust his words so profoundly, even as these words declare again and again that language is not to be trusted? Where is the beauty or the force in taking language's disrepute to its extreme? I turn now to these issues with a very specific and limited strategy. Assuming that mistrust for language is an attitude or theme that manifests recurrently both in literature and in philosophy, I explore the possibility that the questions I have just posed might be well approached through a punctual dialogue between a literary and a philosophical endeavour – more specifically through a comparison between Beckett's own brand of mistrust for language and that of a particular philosopher for whom he has often shown a sort of cannibal attraction: Descartes.[12]

Let me begin, however, by sketching a backdrop for this brief exploration, one that highlights two among the principal historical manifestations of philosophical mistrust for language. First: as we know, language has been repeatedly taken as an *imperfect instrument*. The following lines, written by such different writers as Plato and Locke, may suffice metonymically here:

> [N]o man of sense will like to put himself or the education of his mind in the power of names: neither will he so far trust names or the givers of names as to be confident in any knowledge which condemns himself and other existences to an unhealthy state of unreality; he will not believe that all things leak like a pot, or imagine that the world is a man who has a running at the nose [Plato, *Cratylus* 438e].[13]

12. About that, see the entry "Descartes" in *The Grove Companion to Samuel Beckett,* ed. Chris J. Ackerley and Stanley E. Gontarski (New York: Grove Press, 2004).
13. Plato, *The Collected Dialogues of Plato,* trans. Benjamin Jowett, ed. Edith Hamilton and Huntington Cairns (Princeton: Princeton University Press, 1969), 474.

Words are used for recording and communicating our thoughts.
(…) [I]t is easy to perceive what imperfection there is
in language, and how the very nature of words makes it
almost unavoidable for many of them to be doubtful and
uncertain in their significations [J. Locke, *Essay*, III, IX].[14]

These quotes are not of course metonymies of Plato's or Locke's
general take on language – to say the least, both authors have
also praised the marvels of words more than once, in these very
books and elsewhere. In deliberate suppression of their own internal and external complexities, these passages are introduced
here just to exemplify instances of mistrust – a certain kind of
persistent mistrust. They are likely to point to the now widely
critiqued perception that language is a sort of invention, an artefact with a vocation; they reinforce the tacit notion that it has
one (main) function, supposedly an obvious one: as a collection of names, it is devised to represent (things, states of affairs,
thoughts). More to the point here, it is taken as an imperfect
instrument which can moreover be imperfectly used. As a potentially defective means of representation and expression, it
is an artefact to be handled with the utmost care. Words leak,
they are doubtful and uncertain: that which they are supposed
to represent, however, should be protected and exempt from
these defects; thought and the world, in their life apart from
language, are ultimately dependable, grounded (and grounding). So mistrust for language here is mistrust toward a self-
contained thing, endowed with its own ontological citizenship;
a thing, in short, that is or at least can be put under the watchful
control of its masters.

Contemporary attacks on this instrumentalist and reifying
view of language abound and are well known, but often do little
or nothing to improve its reputation: they tend sometimes, I
believe, to yield (or at least to self-diagnose) the second kind of

14. John Locke, *An Essay Concerning Human Understanding* (Amherst, NY:
Prometheus Books, 1994), 385.

mistrust that I have wanted to indicate here. Language can no longer be taken as a *thing* to be trusted or mistrusted: deprived of ontological citizenship, it is now everywhere and nowhere – it is a volatile, indefinite and irreducible array of heterogeneous and discontinuous practices, with no *telos* and no permanent anchor whatsoever – neither in reality nor in thought nor in the brain nor in society nor in God. Mistrust here may take the form of helpless and utter disappointment: language is no longer an imperfect but ultimately redeemable instrument; it is now a *false* one – it does not ever deliver whatever it promises to deliver; it falsifies and forges while pretending to represent. Language is now not only deprived of its separate ontological sphere – it seems to abolish ontology itself.

"It is this way with all of us concerning language," says Nietzsche, "we believe that we know something about the things themselves when we speak of trees, colours, snow, and flowers and yet we possess nothing but metaphors for things" – metaphors, he adds, "which correspond in no way to the original entities."[15] Equally suspicious of language's deceitfully unproblematic appearance, Derrida will insist, for example, that "'everyday language' is not innocent or neutral" – that it is, rather, "the language of Western metaphysics," carrying presuppositions "which, although little attended to, are knotted into a system."[16] And in *Discourse on Language*, we hear Foucault famously speaking of the *logophobia* that is prone to seize us once we stop believing that a "primary complicity with the world" enables us to speak of it – once we realize that "no pre-discursive fate disposes the word in our favour," and that things do not "murmur meanings our language has only to extract." Our societies, says Foucault, live in the company of an abiding and barely suppressed fear – a mute fear "of this mass of spoken

15. Friedrich Nietzsche, "On Truth and Lies in a Nonmoral Sense," *Philosophy and truth: selections from Nietzsche's notebooks of the early 1870's*. ed. and trans. Daniel Breazeale (New Jersey: Humanities Press, 1979), 82-3.
16. Jacques Derrida, *Positions,* trans. Alan Bass (Chicago: University of Chicago Press, 1981), 19.

things," of everything in language that is "violent, discontinuous, querulous, and perilous"; a terrifying fear that discourse may after all be no more than "incessant, disorderly buzzing."[17]

Here again I bring a few illustrative passages that do not – in any sense – reduce or exhaust their authors' different and insightful takes on language. But they *are* occasions in their writings that point to a common scene, a scene that is likely to reappear in many other pages, of many other authors. It is a scene of language being *exposed* for something it tends to conceal: its failure to reach outside itself, its arbitrary yet coercive historicity, its dangerous powers – even its own absence, its seemingly perverse propensity to mother us only to leave us orphaned, deprived of the ties with which it had somehow promised to hold us to a world, a self, whatever.

If we now start to think of Descartes and Beckett against this very rough backdrop, it may be natural and tempting to promptly identify the first with eventual doubts about the reliability of language as an imperfect artefact; and the second with the perception of language as an altogether failed, false and falsifying non-thing; the lines by Beckett quoted above (and a multitude of other possible ones) seem indeed to point in that second direction. However, as Beckett himself has once warned us, "the danger is in the neatness of identifications" – which are sometimes to be avoided despite their being soothing, "like the contemplation of a carefully folded ham sandwich."[18] In this case, of course, Beckett here; Descartes there. Without exactly disputing these opposing identifications, I would wish to make them a little less neat.

Beckett's first separately published work is a poem called *Whoroscope* (1930):[19] it was based on the life of Descartes, whose works and biography had been catching his quite obsessive in-

17. Michel Foucault, "Discourse on Language," in *The Archaeology of Knowledge and the Discourse on Language*, trans. A. M. Sheridan Smith (New York: Pantheon Books, 1972), 228-9.
18. "Dante... Bruno. Vico... Joyce," GE IV, 495.
19. GE IV, 3-7.

terest by then. The fact that a year earlier he had written an essay on Joyce's *Work in Progress*, where, among other things, he reflected with similar keenness on Vico's theories of history, language and poetry, is something that speaks perhaps for the atopic and non-sectarian nature of Beckett's philosophical interests. He did, it is true, more than once manifest publicly a guarded if not hostile attitude towards philosophy: asked by an interviewer about possible philosophical influences on his work, he claimed that "I never read philosophers... I never understand anything they write"[20] – a lie that is exposed not only by his biographers but also by the highly allusive thread of his works, where the voices of an indicative number of philosophers are heard, from the pre-Socratics, to Augustine, to Descartes and Vico, to Schopenhauer, to Fritz Mauthner, and many others, together, of course, with Homer, Dante, Shakespeare, Proust, and Joyce; and Freud, The Bible, the Marx Brothers etc. James Knowlson, the biographer, tells us that Beckett kept notebooks where he constantly jotted down lines he read that impressed him (many of them philosophical), lines that would surface somehow in his texts, this being such an endemic procedure as to allow attribution to Beckett of a "grafting technique."[21]

In any case, if we are to comprehend how the writings of Descartes are grafted onto Beckett's works, it will be useful to attend to the paradoxical vigour of a drive to the philosophical that is always coupled with, let's say, a non-philosophical vehemence – "I wouldn't have had any reason to write my novels if I could have expressed their subject in philosophic terms... I'm no intellectual."[22] So perhaps cannibal is after all a fitting adjective to describe Beckett's attitude towards Descartes and other philoso-

20. Interview to G. d'Aubarede, 1961. In: *Samuel Beckett: The Critical Heritage*, op. cit., 239-40.
21. James Knowlson, *Damned to Fame – The Life of Samuel Beckett* (London: Bloomsbury, 1996), 109. Deidre Bair observers that in 1926 Beckett filled three loose-leaf notebooks with his and others' thoughts and impressions on Descartes, whom he had read voraciously by then (*Samuel Beckett: A Biography* (New York: Harcourt Brace, 1978), 52.
22. Interview to G. d'Aubarede, 1961. In: *Samuel Beckett: The Critical Heritage*, op. cit., 240.

phers, as it places emphasis in a disposition to seize and consume, that is not however (overly) cognitive or doctrinaire. If I insist on this point it is mostly to clarify my very circumscribed concerns here: I am not primarily interested in discussing Beckett's literary stand *with respect* to Descartes' philosophy, or vice-versa.

This means that, in the brief lines that follow, I am going to be relatively deaf to questions that have often animated interesting reflections on the relationship between these two authors – questions such as "is Beckett's principal concern with investigating the human condition or with deconstructing it? (...) Are his works written after the death of God, or after the death of Man? (...) Does Beckett's literature mime a Cartesianism founded on the *cogito* or does it undermine that Cartesianism?"[23] These questions (especially the last one), posed by Richard Begam some fifteen years ago, are prone to sound at least slightly misplaced to contemporary ears – and this is perhaps due to the fact that Beckett tends to be, in the apt words of Ackerley and Gontarski, a "barometer of critical change."[24] Begam's questions might breathe an atmosphere that is still intermediate between that of the fifties or sixties, when Beckett had been attributed a sort of Cartesianism by such important readers as Hugh Kenner and Samuel Mintz, and the most recent critical climate, favouring almost imperially the verdict of an utterly antagonizing appropriation of Descartes in Beckett's works, one that would invariably point to a tragic or comic subversion, if not destruction, of Cartesian rationalism.

That – Cartesianism or Anticartesianism in Beckett – is not my concern here. For my purposes, it may even prove more fruitful to side with one of Hugh Kenner's early insights: for him, Descartes' works should be read as *spiritual autobiographies* – *novels* – and Beckett was perhaps the first to have read them like this.[25] Leaning more on Kenner's perception of the way

---

23. Richard Begam, "Samuel Beckett and Antihumanism," in *Literature and Philosophy*, ed. Herbert Grabes (Tübingen: Gunter Narr Verlag, 1997), 300.
24. *The Grove Companion to Samuel Beckett*, op. cit., 263.
25. Hugh Kenner, *Samuel Beckett: A Critical Study* (New York: Grove Press,

Beckett read Descartes – and less on the implied imperative that Descartes should (always?) be read like this – I would like to draw attention to a fictionalized *life experience* that brings them together, let's call it a fictional affinity, one that has direct impact on the subject of this text – language (mis)trusted.

The Experience Of Groundlessness

By the end of his *First Meditation*, let us recall, Descartes announces his disposition to embrace hyperbolic doubt:

> I shall think that the sky, the air, the earth, colours, shapes, sounds and all external things are merely the delusions of dreams (...) I shall consider myself as not having hands or eyes, or flesh, or blood or senses, but as falsely believing that I have all these things.[26]

The sheer intensity of the experience that is presented here is prone to be effaced or mitigated under the weight of institutionalized readings that have been produced around it, readings that prepare us beforehand for pacifying outcomes, two of them at least: either, in Descartes, radical doubt is methodological, and is fated to be overcome. Or, *pace* Descartes: radical doubt is unsurpassable, but one might find some consolation in the fact that reaching this conclusion is after all a form of *final lucidity* (Descartes himself rejected but anticipated this latter – sceptical – possibility: "even if it is not in my power to know any truth, I shall at least do what is in my power, that is, resolutely guard against assenting to any falsehoods, so that the deceiver (...) will be unable to impose on me in the slightest degree").[27] In both scenarios, the terrifying threat of losing ground, on the

1961), 82.

26. Descartes. "Meditations on First Philosophy," in *The Philosophical Writings of Descartes Vol. II*, trans. John Cottingham et. al. (Cambridge: Cambridge Univ. Press, 1984), 15. All quotes from Descartes' works are from the three volumes of this edition (Vol. III, 1991). Henceforth cited as PWD, followed by number of volume and page.

27. "First Meditation," PWD II, 15.

verge of madness, a threat so conspicuous in this passage, is somehow contained or suspended.[28]

Reading the *Meditations* "as a novel," Beckett might have been less numb to the horror (and the courage) in the life experience that is being depicted. The restless, deracinated figure in *The Unnamable*, the afflicted unstoppable mouth without a body in *Not I* are but two instances of the sort of fictional rapport that I am suggesting here. When, in the *Second Meditation*, Descartes goes on to describe the state in which he was thrown in face of the task he had committed himself to, we can again, perhaps, evoke Beckett's daring, intensive and vertiginous ventures:

> So serious are the doubts into which I have been thrown as a result of yesterday's meditation that I can neither put them out of my mind nor see any way of resolving them. It feels as if I have fallen unexpectedly into a deep whirlpool which tumbles me around so that I can neither stand on the bottom nor swim up to the top [PWD II, 16].

Many and very well-known are the available explanations for how Descartes may have pulled himself out of this fearsome whirlpool – for how he, after all, has thought to have managed to stand again on the bottom and swim up to the top. Without dwelling on them, in the limited circumstance of this text, I would like to consider the predicament in view of Descartes' attitude towards language. I shall attend specially to a further passage in the Second Meditation, where he seems awaken to the unreliability of language as an instrument, a passage that can be

28. Whether *madness* has or has not been silenced in Descartes' *Meditations* is the object of the famous debate between Foucault and Derrida. I side here with the second when, against Foucault, he argues that Descartes' stated wish to dissociate himself from "the insane" does not amount to a Cartesian exclusion of madness as possible grounds for doubting; for the possibility of the *malicious demon* opens his own rationality to the reach of doubt (PWD II, 15), see Jacques Derrida, "Cogito and the History of Madness," in *Writing and Difference*, trans. Alan Bass (New York: Routledge, 1978), 36–76.

placed in striking contrast to the praise language receives, say, in Part V of the *Discourse on The Method* ("it is quite remarkable that there are no men so dull-witted or stupid – and this includes even madmen – that they are incapable of arranging various words together and forming an utterance and from them in order to make their thoughts understood");[29] or in a letter to More, where he will go so far as to say that "speech is the *only* certain sign of thought hidden in a body."[30]

The particular lines I wish to consider appear in connection with the famous discussion of the ever changing piece of wax – does the same wax remain when it melts, when its smell is exhaled out of it etc.? Trying to make the point that the answer – yes, it is the same – depends not on senses but on thought, Descartes feels compelled to warn us against the deceiving powers of language:

> But as I reach this conclusion I am amazed at how weak and prone to error my mind is. *For although I am thinking about these matters within myself, silently and without speaking, nonetheless the actual words bring me up short, and I am almost tricked by ordinary ways of talking.* We say that we see the wax itself, if it is there before us, not that we judge it to be there from its colour or shape; and this might lead me to conclude without more ado that knowledge of the wax comes from what the eye sees, and not from the scrutiny of the mind alone. But then if I look out of the window and see men crossing the square, as I just happen to have done, I normally say that I see the men themselves, just as I say that I see the wax. Yet do I see any more than hats and coats which could conceal automatons? I judge that they are men. And so something which I thought I was seeing with my eyes is in fact grasped solely by the faculty of judgement which is in my mind. [PWD, II, 21, italics added]

29. "Discourse on the Method," PWD I, 140.
30. "Letter to More, 5 February 1649," PWD III, 336, italics added.

As in the passages of Plato and Locke quoted above, language, or at least ordinary language, is taken as a potentially imperfect instrument, one that will condemn the fate of words like "see" or "same" to a state of hesitance, uncertainty or impurity with respect to the silent thoughts they are supposed to represent – indeed they are depicted as unwelcome intruders, noisy disturbers in this otherwise silent medium. They trick. But only almost:

> However, one who wants to achieve knowledge above the ordinary level should feel ashamed at having taken ordinary ways of talking as a basis for doubt. So let us proceed and consider on which occasion my perception of the nature of the wax was more perfect and evident [PWD, II, 21].

Words, inadequate and clumsy as they may be, do not after all halt the movement of thought ("let us proceed"). They do not lend their volatility and imperfection to thinking – conceptual life may be disturbed by but is ultimately immune to the impurity of language. If it is true that Descartes is fighting the threat of scepticism, it appears that, for him, this is a threat that reaches the *external world* (is the wax there?) and *other minds* (are they people like me or automatons?) – but not language. Even the madmen, as we have seen, possess language and use it to express their mad thoughts; language itself, however, is exempt from madness.

Now a neat explanation here would be to say that the very failure to entertain the possibility of *linguistic scepticism* is the tacit and spurious manoeuvre that allows Descartes to proceed to the certainty of the *cogito*. Had he considered the possibility that language, as an instrument, is failed beyond redemption, had he acknowledged the chance that the silent medium of thought is never silent after all, and that words are not the unwelcome intruders but rather the landlords there – had he considered, in short, language itself as the great trickster, he would have had to yield to the sceptical, being left with the consolation of being able to "do what is in his power," that is, suspend judgement, "resolutely guard against assenting to any falsehoods, so that the deceiver (...) will be unable to impose on me in the slightest degree."[31] That is all very familiar: just one more metaphysician whose greatest sin has been to overlook the unlimited reach of language's irreducible volatility. We hear the (by now) old tale of language and its domino effect: all our partitions – ontological, moral, psychological, esthetical etc. – are language infused; the use and the abuse of language cannot be separated; language is not presided over by rationality, it is not under control, it contaminates everything with its arbitrariness and obscurity: words leak, so does the world, so does the self, etc. Just as neat, perhaps, would be to ascribe to Beckett a sort of literary manifestation of this brand of linguistic scepticism.

What neatness seems to sacrifice here is again: intensity – the intense experience of groundlessness. For doesn't the blind commitment to reach an intellectual outcome, sceptical or otherwise, tend to have a placating effect here?

I have fallen unexpectedly into a deep whirlpool that now tumbles me up and down; I cannot reach bottom or surface. I'm all these words, all these strangers, this dust of words, with no ground for their settling, no sky for their dispersing. The very life in these two scenes of grounds lost seems to drain away when they are taken as allegories of a tumultuous moment preceding the peace of an intellectual conclusion – *there are truths, grounds*; or else: *there are none.*

If we look at Beckett and Descartes with other eyes, perhaps a more interesting unlikeness may catch our gaze, a difference that does not so much manifest itself in the realm of abstract grounds or of truths affirmed or denied, regained or foregone – rather, a difference in life. For, perhaps more radically than Descartes, Beckett seems to have been open, in his fiction, to the ineluctable *truth in life* of the experience of groundlessness. This

31. "First Meditation," PWD II, 15.

would be a truth that does not oppose the false or the illusory. "What is more true than anything else?" Beckett once rhetorically asked – only to add, as if talking directly to the Descartes of the whirlpool: "To swim is true, and to sink is true. One is not more true than the other."[32]

It is useful here to retrace a possible source for this sombrely marvellous image: swimming, sinking. Beckett may have derived it from a dialogue that is supposed to have taken place between James Joyce and Carl Jung. Joyce's daughter, Lucia, had been diagnosed with schizophrenia, and was Jung's patient. Devastated and reluctant to accept the verdict, Joyce urged Jung to acknowledge that Lucia's random and uncontrollable associations, her nonsensical expressions, were no different from his own artistic ventures and explorations in language, that they were in fact probably even better. Jung is said to have answered something like "that may be true: but where you swim, she sinks." The episode helps me to turn now to the final part of this text: for it portrays a scene of groundlessness, and madness, in language. We are this dust of words, dust that never settles: Beckett's own deep whirlpool is somehow *of words*.

Unlike Descartes, he did seem to have acknowledged in language, far from a tricky but ultimately manageable instrument, something much more dangerous and powerful – something that gains indeed, at least sometimes, the contours of a *malignant demon*:

Vile words to make me believe I'm here, and that I have a head, and a voice... ["Texts for Nothing," 11, GE IV, 332].

The mind betrays the treacherous eyes and the treacherous word their treacheries. Haze the sole certitude ["Ill Seen, Ill Said," GE IV, 466].

---

32. "Interview with Tom Driver, 1961," in *Samuel Beckett: The Critical Heritage*, op. cit., 242.

> No, no souls, or bodies, or birth, or life, or death, you've
> got to go on without any of that junk, that's all dead
> with words, with excess of words, they can say nothing
> else, that here it's that and nothing else, but they won't
> say it eternally, they'll find another nonsense, no matter
> what... ["Texts for Nothing," 10, GE IV, 328].

Words make me believe in what is not there – an I, a head, a
voice, a soul, a body, life, death. They are treacherous: being
able to say nothing other than *here it's that and nothing else*, they
won't stay put, but will manage eternally to come and deceive
again, to find another nonsense, no matter what. Silence and
rest: impossible.

But, again, if the radical experience of grounds lost in the
whirlpool of language is here converted into a *conclusion about* language, this experience is already debilitated, pacified. Language
will have been reified, no matter how earnestly our theories may
still want to proclaim it to be a *non-thing*. Moreover, it will have
been converted into a *treacherous* something, against which I can
now "resolutely guard," much as Descartes would have deemed
possible – "so that the deceiver ... will be unable to impose on
me."[33] Yet the language of such vertiginous experience is perhaps not the language of lucid and ultimately protective conclusions, positive or negative. I am being tumbled up and down
inside a deep whirlpool – I do not conclude, articulate: rather, I
scream, I groan, I stutter, syntax weakens or even takes its leave.
Life and language whirl together.

When, to make their appearance here, lines from Beckett are
extracted and halted away from the intensive movement of their
original texts, they are (some more some less) prone to suggest
themselves as self-contained statements about a something else,
language, life. However, especially when brought back with
their restless adjacencies, these lines make us aware that even
as Beckett is taking language – its disgrace – as a motif in his

33. "First Meditation," PWD II, 15.

writings, he is at the same time *doing* something – un/doing language, not as thing but as life, in life. Blanchot is right: in Beckett, "language does not speak, it is."[34]

So it might prove insightful to bring into friction, for example, the theory of (linguistic) *scepticism* to a passage such as:

> I'm in words, made of words, others' words, what others, the place too, the air, the walls, the floor, the ceiling, all words, the whole world is here with me, I'm the air, the walls, the walled-in one, everything yields, opens, ebbs, flows, like flakes...

Or, the theory of *solipsism* to:

> I'm all these flakes, meeting, mingling, falling asunder, wherever I go I find me, leave me, go toward me, come from me, nothing ever but me, a particle of me, retrieved, lost, gone astray...

Rather than – or together with? – statement, theory, concept: rhythm, repetition, paradox, restless movement, vertigo. We are left with perplexity, rather than scepticism; solitude, rather than solipsism – with the inscrutable, rather than with the illusory.

When we say that, by taking language's disgrace and disrepute to its extreme, by drilling in it one hole after the other, Beckett is at the same time doing language, it is in the sense that he is creating or enacting a form of life, something that he does, paradoxically, by almost managing to make language, taken as a separate thing, disappear – disappear (back?) into life. We are after all promised to see without words, to see *nohow* – but not in the sense of seeing through the wordless eyes of a God or of a pure mind. Rather perhaps, seeing nohow is here akin to *living nohow*, in the absence of words grounded, in the absence

---

34. Maurice Blanchot, *The Book to Come*, trans. Charlotte Mandell (Stanford, CA: Stanford University Press, 2003), 216.

of grounds – accepting, not so much in mind as in action this very absence, this very nothing as a sort of groundless, restless, ground. Maybe Beckett had something like that in mind when he said: "there is more than a difference of degree between *being short*, short of the world, short of self, and being *without* these esteemed commodities – one is a predicament, the other not."[35]

We seem to be short of the world, short of self. It's all dead with the excess of words, Beckett says: even life and death are dead with words. But if we are able to trust words that say again and again "mistrust me," "I am dead," it is perhaps because the movement of these words, their action, shows something that is somehow at odds with what they say. For instance, that trusting need not be so cognitive or intellectual a thing, that it may have something to do with music, with terror, with humour, with habit, with absurdity. Or, with Nietzsche, that turning away from horror and death and groundlessness is also turning away from life, rapture, motion. Or that sinking and swimming are equally, dangerously, true. Or that madness and disintegration in language and in life may have something to do with liberty. Or that living short of the world is different from living without it.

What it shows, in any case, is not a solution, an explanation, but a form of life, its dread, its chance. A life of speaking beings, thrown without any guidance into the "vast void *atween*"[36] – and the very remote possibility that living as dust of words, with no ground to settle and no sky to disperse, be no longer living in an endless *between* – ground and sky; body and soul; word and meaning; life and death. A chance of living perhaps *atween* all this? In proud indigence?

We are, it is certain, before Beckett's own dreamed-of art – "an art unresentful of its insuperable indigence and too proud for the farce of giving and receiving."[37] And yet this is an art whose radical refusal to participate in the farce does not after all amount to the adoption of a *guarded attitude*, not even against

---

35. "Three Dialogues with Georges Duthuit," GE IV, 561.
36. "Worstward Ho," GE IV, 482, italics added.
37. "Three Dialogues with Georges Duthuit," GE IV, 559.

the great trickster it ceaselessly names, in paradox: language. On the contrary: Beckett has the freedom a writer who, while refusing to reduce his own writing to a means of expressing a meaning – while radicalizing the disgrace of words in this respect – manages at the same time to gloriously (un)do language, its life. In the felicitous words of Georges Bataille, Beckett has, in short, the freedom of a writer who is able "to respond to possibilities present, though chaotically mingled, in those deep currents that flow through the oceanic agitation of words, yielding to the weight of destiny, in the *amorphous* figure of *absence*."[38] Absence at the eye of the deep whirlpool of words – or as we could say with Beckett: "silence at the eye of the scream."[39]

38. Georges Bataille, "Molloy," in *Samuel Beckett: The Critical Heritage*, op. cit., 62.
39. "Ill Seen, Ill Said," GE IV, 459.

Neo-, Post-, and Anticlassicism: Modernity in Early German Romanticism

Pedro Duarte[1]

Every time the present challenges the preceding tradition, the question of how we relate to the past gains strength. To consciously turn the form in which we are situated in history into a theme is, to this extent, already a sign that we do not belong to it in a natural way. In this sense, the formation of what we call modernity, the "new age," occurs simultaneously with the birth of antiquity, since the latter, before the former, could not exactly be ancient. In other words: what makes antiquity ancient is modernity, which, at the same time, is only modern because it places another time distinct from itself. Novalis, in his day, liked to say that Antiquity did not exist, but had only begun to emerge: it needed to be produced.

In its early stages, this historical consciousness came to light especially through the gradual confrontation with the Classical past. Is the present neo, post or anti-classical? In the chronological sense, the simple act of calling into question the relationship with Classicism denounces a post-classical context: we are no longer in it organically. However, this "post" may be neo or anti-classical when faced with the past. This duality marks the famous quarrel between ancients and moderns, which was only possible because both were situated after Classicism. Even

1. Author of *Estio do tempo: Romantismo e estética moderna* (Jorhe Zahar Ed., 2011), in which this article originally appeared as a chapter. I thank Carla Kasumi for its translation into English.

when the French, in the 18th century, and following the Italian Renaissance, proposed Neoclassicism, they implicitly conceded that they were outside the original Classicism. They are "neo." They may have wished to remain faithful to the Greco-Roman tradition, but, as it is a wish and not a certainty, they were already outside that original belonging. In this sense they are modern, despite their desire to be like the ancients.

On the other hand, it was common to see the romantics, in the 18th century, as part of the search for an anti-classical formation, on account of their rehabilitation of the Middle Ages, as well as various oriental cultures, and above all their apparent opposition to Classical values. By praising exaggeration and not restraint, the subjective and not the objective, chaos and not order, excess and not sobriety, transgression and not stability, and night over day, the romantics would be judged to have declared war against the atmosphere of Apollonian Greek culture. Actually, they were already, before Nietzsche, suggesting that the Greeks were, in addition to Apollonian, Dionysian too. This, however, is another story, to which we will return later.

In fact, the biggest problem in placing Romanticism in opposition to Classicism is that, in doing so, we cannot explain how the Greeks remained central to the romantic thought thus hailed as the original source to which culture should turn its gaze. Not by chance, in respect of the Classicist character of Schiller and Goethe in their maturity, which was experienced in the city of Weimar, there are more convergences with their romantic Jena contemporaries than divergences, despite the comments of both. So much so, indeed, that it is common to accuse the romantics of nostalgia or of being under the tyranny of Greek culture,[2] which, strictly speaking, is not the case. It is true, however, that the early romantics sought for the modern formation, in the words of Friedrich Schlegel, "the perspective

2. Cf. Jacques Taminiaux, *La nostalgie de la Grèce à l'Aube de l'Idealisme Allemand* (La Haye: Martinus Nijhoff, 1967), and Eliza M. Butler, *The Tyranny of Greece over Germany* (London : Cambridge U.P., 1935) respectively.

of a Classicism growing without limitations."[3]

The matter at hand here is, as Hölderlin says, the perspective through which we should view antiquity: "We dream of formation, piety, etc. but have none," he said, adding that "they are just pretentions – we dream of originality and autonomy, we believe we state the new loud and clear, but it is nothing but reaction, a kind of gentle revenge against the slavery that rules our relationship with antiquity." His conclusion is the following: "It seems that, actually, there is hardly any choice other than to allow oneself to become buried by the assumed, the positive, or else with the most violent arrogance counter with our life-force everything that has been given , learned, to all the positive."[4]

What is Hölderlin saying here? We dream of building a culture of our own time, with our own formation. We wish for autonomy, in other words, we wish to give ourselves our own law, of our own time, instead of borrowing it. However, this intention collides with the solidity of the "already assumed," with the positivity of the given, which eclipses the opening onto negativity of that which is still "not." Even while seeking the new, the moderns are dominated by reaction – becoming, still, slaves to the Antiquity that they wish to deny, because in the effort to overcome it, they end up retaining it as a contrasting guidepost for the present. This is the historical crossroads at which the education of modernity found itself: whether to assert the present over the past or to leave it subordinated to the latter, whether to oppose with "violent arrogance" the force of the current to everything that has been made or "to allow oneself to be buried" by what is already formed?

This "all or nothing" approach was rejected by the early romantic thinkers, as well as by Hölderlin. Friedrich Schlegel, for example, diluted the opposition of modern Romanticism towards Classic Antiquity when he stated that "only when we find

3. Friedrich Schlegel, *O dialeto dos fragmentos*, trans. Márcio Suzuki (São Paulo: Iluminuras, 1997), 64 (*Athenäum*, Fr. 116).
4. Friedrich Hölderlin, "O ponto de vista segundo o qual devemos encarar a antiguidade," in *Reflexões* (Rio de Janeiro: Relume-Dumará, 1994), 21.

the point of view and the condition of absolute identity that existed, exists or will exist between ancient and modern, can we say that at least the contours of science are prepared."[5] Hence, it is not strange that, in Romanticism, praise for the Greeks abounds. So much so, indeed, that in formulating a canon, the romantics gave them the first position. When talking about "epochs of poetic art," for instance, they praise Homer: "In the Homeric plant we see also the rise of all poetry; but the roots are removed from view, and the flowers and branches of the plant spring inconceivably beautiful in the night of antiquity."[6] Passages such as this one raised the charge of "Greco mania" towards the romantics, although, for Schlegel, it is clear that "one should never evoke the spirit of Antiquity as an authority."[7]

Praise for the Greeks did not mean that the romantics wished to revive the Ancient culture. It was not a matter of returning to the Greeks, but of turning their eyes to them. This is where things start to become complicated, and at the same time interesting. Although they admired Greek art, the romantics were not buried by antiquity, thanks to the pioneering importance they gave to history. According to Friedrich Schlegel, "the science of art is its history."[8] This historical perspicacity kept the early romantics, even while worshiping the Greeks, from placing them as a model outside time to be copied. If praise of Antiquity does not allow us to conceive Romanticism as anti-Classicism, the historical sense places them far from Neoclassicism. No recreation of Greek culture was possible or even recommended by them, since it would rob them, in advance, of the possibility of the singular emergence of modern culture, even if it had to be considered through reference to antiquity. It is at this boundary between identity and difference with Classical antiquity that German romantic philosophy conceives modern formation.

5. Schlegel, *O dialeto dos fragmentos*, 71 (*Athenäum*, Fr. 149).
6. Friedrich Schlegel, *Conversa sobre a poesia*, trans. Victor-Pierre Stirnimann (São Paulo: Iluminuras, 1994), 35.
7. Schlegel, *O dialeto dos fragmentos* 27 (*Lyceum*, Fr. 44).
8. Schlegel, *Conversa sobre a poesia*, 35.

The discussion between moderns and ancients had already commenced during the pre-romantic period. Their attachment to Shakespeare, for instance, was linked to the fact that the English playwright was synonymous with modernity, because his work was free from Classical rules. Around him, the pre-romantics gathered to establish the creation of the original art of the present, facing the "curse of the difficulty for us of thinking like the ancients,"[9] as Herder, leader of the pre-romantic movement, asserted. Searching for ancient rules to form modern art, by trusting them to be universal and timeless, it is forgotten that, elevated as they might be, these rules were created at a specific time to which they belong. It would be necessary, therefore, to find an original, modern form to deal with modern themes, far from the "aesthetic chatter in which thought is treated separately from expression," as Herder also said. To him, "the poet that wanted to reign over expression should remain faithful to his land; in it he may plant powerful words, because he knows the country; there, he may harvest the flowers, because the land belongs to him." His conclusion is that "the true disposition is only impressed in the mother tongue." This metaphorical approximation between the exploration of language, in writing, and in the country through geography, dear to the rhetoric of the pre-romantics, aimed at indicating a point of reference for poetry other than the ancient Greeks, as well as other traditions formulated not universally, but locally. For this reason, many fictional tales of German Romanticism are magical or fantastic incursions into folklore.

Friedrich Schlegel, who shares the problem of Herder, but not his solution, speaks of the "strange predilection of modern poets for Greek terminology in designating their products."[10] In his return to local tradition, seeking inspiration for the production of an original art, the pre-romantics sometimes denied the Classics. The early romantics, even though they opened up

9. Johann Gottfried Herder, "Da terceira coleção de fragmentos," in *Autores pré-românticos alemães*, ed. Anatol Rosenfeld (São Paulo: EPU, 1991), 31, 33.
10. Schlegel, *O dialeto dos fragmentos*, 27 (*Athenäum*, Fr. 45).

the range of sources acceptable to modern creation uncovering alternatives to Greco-Roman tradition, never abandoned it. On the contrary, as we saw, they held Antiquity in high regard and never forgot its poetic richness. Neither, however, could they avoid submitting it to the scrutiny of history.

As early as 1794, Friedrich Schlegel thought of art as being based on history in his essay *On the Study of Greek Poetry*. In this text there was no lack of praise for antiquity, in which we could "enjoy sheer beauty," find "unpretentious perfection." For Schlegel, "Greek poetry truly reached the ultimate limit of the natural formation of art and taste, the highest peak of free beauty." These comments bring up the feeling of superiority of ancient over modern, which lacks the firm solidity of Greek culture: "This state is called the golden age," writes Schlegel. But he continues by stating that "the pleasures that the works from the Greek golden age provide, certainly admit increment." How could perfect works be enhanced? Their perfection was not timeless, but relative to their own historical reality, because "an absolute maximum in their continuous evolution is not possible; but a relative maximum, conditioned, a permanent approximation, insurmountable, is possible," says Schlegel. Thus Antiquity is not an absolute maximum, but a maximum relatively conditioned to its time. Its art was an "example that includes the unreachable idea, that becomes here, essentially, completely visible."[11] The romantic study of Antiquity sustains itself in this historical sense that "art is infinitely perfectible," as Schlegel wrote. Shakespeare was proof of this perfectibility, taking art to heights that even the Greeks could not have imagined. As good as it was, the Classical beauty would not refuse a thinking that went beyond it, so much so that the moderns look to the ancients to create beauty beyond theirs.

Although the essay in question continues to maintain a certain respect for rules and for the laws of poetic construction that

11. Friedrich Schlegel, "Über das Studium der griechischen Poesie," in *Kritische Schriften*, ed. Wolfdietrich Rasch (Munique: Carl Hanser Verlag, 1970), 184 (298), 175-6 (287-288).

originate with the Greeks, the young Schlegel, who had at that time a Classical proclivity, had already set forth his revolutionary considerations on antiquity, which would be consolidated a few years later with his participation in the Jena romantic group. His approach begins with the modern situation and hopes to contribute to its improvement. Not for nothing does his text open with these words: "It is obvious that either modern poetry has not reached the objective for which it strives, or that this striving does not possess an established objective, and its formation, no specific direction."[12] This was the seed of the transformation in the way of thinking about the relationship of the moderns towards the ancients, a thinking that recognized their aesthetic quality without depriving it of its historical nature and forcing it into a timeless position. We must emphasize the word "study" in the title of the text by Schlegel. It is the discussion about how Greek art will be seen and studied that matters in order to understand the challenges of the present.

If the early romantics were not opposed to classical antiquity, they were, however, opposed to the Neoclassical study of Classicism, which turned it into an eternal standard, and – making use of Aristotelian poetic lessons – intended, thus, to decipher the secrets of good production and the correct evaluation of all art. Therefore, whilst he maintained a high regard for Classical Greek art, Friedrich Schlegel could not accept that from it derived the normativity intended by Neoclassicism. He claims that "the most unfortunate idea ever had – and many of the traits of their overall prevalence still persist – was this: to assign to Greek criticism and art theory an authority that, in the realm of theoretical science, is completely unacceptable," adding that "it was believed that the real philosopher's stone of aesthetics had been found; isolated rules of Aristotle and Horace's epigrams were used as powerful talismans against the evil demon of modernity."[13] Even Goethe, so critical of the romantics, joined

12. Ibid.
13. Ibid., 218.

them on this point by saying that "fragments of the treatise on the art of poetry provide a strange view of Aristotle," because it would be necessary "before all things, to make contact with the philosophical thinking of this man to understand how he considered this artistic manifestation."[14]

It was this Neoclassical appropriation of the Aristotelian lessons that, sometimes, made the early romantics turn to another direction of the ancient Greek thought: to Plato. Although in his famous considerations on art, Plato had expelled the poets from the ideal republic he imagined, his doctrine seemed more philosophical than the normative tradition that the Romans and Boileau derived from Aristotle. By "philosophical" we mean speculative reflection, instead of rules and determinations on practical poetic action. From this comes the romantic attraction for Platonic reflection on the metaphysical, not empirical, nature of beauty, which gave wings to its own philosophy of art. It is interesting here to emphasize that this challenging of Aristotelian poetry sought to disqualify French Neoclassical aesthetics, and thus, takes from antiquity the very values of the model to be imitated.

At this point, the romantics followed the fight waged by the humanism of Lessing, despite his Enlightenment values, which separated them. A pioneer in the challenge to French Neoclassicism, Lessing admitted that the Germans did not yet have a consistent dramaturgy in their time. But he continued: "I really think that not only we Germans, but all those who boast of a hundred-year-old theater, that brag about having the best theater in all Europe, that also the French still do not have a theater."[15] French theater, in fact, was like a copy of Greek theater, according to this view: it paid the price of lack of originality in order to satisfy the Neoclassical requirements.

Behind this nationalist provocation by Lessing, was the

14. Johann Wolfgang von Goethe, *Máximas e reflexões*, trans. Marco Antônio Casanova (Rio de Janeiro: Forense Universitária, 2003), 142-3.
15. Gotthold Ephraim Lessing, "Dramaturgia de Hamburgo," in *De teatro e literatura,* trans. J. Guinsburg (São Paulo: EPU, 1991), 82.

drama of the "imitation in the *second degree*,"[16] as Philippe Lacoue-Labarthe and Jean-Luc Nancy called it: the Germans saw themselves forced to imitate the imitation that France and Italy exported from the ancients, remaining deprived not only of their own identity, but even of their own means of imitating. To re-edit that Classicism would not be enough to form a new theater. It would be necessary to challenge the predominance of Molière, Corneille and Racine to value the English poetic genius Shakespeare, an example of freedom from ancient rules, since he did not depend on Greek tragedy as an empirical model for his creation.

The early romantics found in Winckelmann the suggestion of thinking of the matter of imitation in another way. He was a pioneer in that he placed passion for the ancient Classical world below the demand of contributing to the formation of the modern world. In his *Reflection on the Imitation of Greek Works in Painting and Sculpture*, of 1755, he claimed: "The only way to become great and, if possible, inimitable, is to imitate the ancients."[17] In this way, he recovered the Classical definition of poetry as imitation, but twisting it, because the objective is the opposite: to become inimitable. For the early romantics, his paradoxical formula represented a challenge for them to become inimitable in their modernity, but, at the same time, to reach an originality in their formation exactly by copying the ancients.

In the modern artists, capable of creating their own work, the enthusiasm for the ancients, therefore, does not mean that they are used as models, but rather as stimulus and nourishment. In this way they avoided the sense that, in general, "the study of the ancients was inevitably perverted," as August Schlegel had said. Their works did not result in school exercises – correct in the final analysis but without spirit, evoking merely a "frigid

16. Philippe Lacoue-Labarthe and Jean-Luc Nancy, *O mito nazista*, trans. Márcio Seligmann-Silva (São Paulo: Iluminuras, 2002), 36.
17. Johann Joseph Winckelmann, *Reflexões sobre a arte antiga*, trans. Herbert Caro and Leonardo Tochtrop (Porto Alegre: Editora Movimento, 1975), 39-40.

admiration." As steeped as they were in the Classics, they would bring the seal of original genius, contrary to the monotony of the copy. If Shakespeare was the paradigmatic case of this situation, the early romantics, however, gave other examples, such as Dante. According to August Schlegel, recognizing Virgil as his master, Dante produced works that are radically different from the *Aeneid*. And this was not an isolated case: "What keeps the heroic poems of a Tasso or a Camões alive until today in the hearts and lips of their fellow countrymen is not, in any way, their imperfect resemblance to Virgil, or even, to Homer," says Schlegel, "but in Tasso, the delicate feeling of courteous love and honor and, in Camões, the incandescent inspiration of heroic patriotism." In this sense, we consider that "mere imitation is always sterile; even when we borrow something from others, for it to assume true poetic form, it must be born with us."[18]

These examples are mobilized to highlight the value of originality in works of art. From this comes the role of the artistic genius, as it had been theorized in the aesthetics of Kant: "the genius opposes completely the spirit of imitation." To imitate means here to emulate only. However, Kant himself signals that, still, the products of geniuses are "exemplary." To imitate now takes on new meaning. Every artist may follow another's example, as long as he does not simplify this operation into the form of a faithful copy. Kant admits that "it is difficult to explain how this is possible," but he does not waive stating that such products of geniuses are "the only means of guidance to lead art into posterity."[19] To imitate, therefore, is the basis of the historicity of art, thanks to which it reaches posterity, but only when this continuity happens through successive original productions of genius that do not take the example as norm, but as a teaching that inspires.

18. August Wilhelm von Schlegel, *Vorlesungen über dramatische Kunst und Literatur* (Bonn: K. Schroeder, 1923), Vorlesung I.
19. Immanuel Kant, *Crítica da faculdade do juízo*, trans. Valério Rohden and António Marques (Rio de Janeiro: Forense Universitária, 1995), 153-5 (183-186).

The romantics considered that "antiquity as a whole is genius."[20] Keeping Kant's theory of creation in mind, they did not search in Ancient art models to copy, in just the same way that, in Aristotle's poetic lessons, they did not look for practical requirements. What they sought there were examples – of originality. The Greeks themselves did not copy anyone, as the Dutch thinker Hemsterhuis said, who "knew how to define beautifully the modern scope through the Ancient simplicity,"[21] according to August Schlegel. Hemsterhuis observed that "the Greeks never copied the works of the Egyptians, and that one may consider that the arts were born in fact among them."[22] So to be like the Greeks, who never copied anything, we also could not copy them. To imitate them would be, at the same time, not to imitate them, since they never imitated anyone. To be faithful to the spirit of the Classics, we could not be faithful to the simple appearance of their empirical products.

In this sense, ancient art is esteemed in Romanticism as a source of exemplary poetic inspiration. "For us, moderns, for Europe, this source is found in Greece," said Friedrich Schlegel. "There was an incessant source of all-moldable poetry, a powerful flow of representation where every wave of life is poured over the other." To transform this powerful sea of life of Greek poetry into norms and rules would be to betray it, to turn the beautiful arabesque that combined varied figures from the chaos of creative fantasy into a simple directive of some general fixed and boring order. "This chaos formed in a stimulating way is the seed from which the world of Ancient poetry organized itself," wrote the romantics of Jena, revealing that "as well as the wise men who sought in water the beginning of nature, so too does ancient poetry display fluid features."[23]

Notice that as they changed the way they looked at antiquity,

20. Schlegel, *O dialeto dos fragmentos*, 91 (*Athenäum*, Fr. 248).
21. Ibid., 95 (*Athenäum*, Fr. 271).
22. Frans Hemsterhuis, "Carta sobre a escultura," in *Sobre o homem e suas relações*, trans. Pedro Paulo Pimenta (São Paulo: Iluminuras, 2000), 33.
23. Schlegel, *Conversa sobre a poesia*, 35.

the romantics discovered at the same time another landscape, different from that forged by tradition. The Greeks are not seen as stable and solid, but fluid and even chaotic. They not only constituted the sun people of the day, but they were equally a culture whose source was hidden in the dark night. There they put down the roots of their art and the relevance of the tragic dramatic form. "Equally mixed in the mind of Sophocles was the divine intoxication of Dionysius, the profound creativity of Athena and the calm prudence of Apollo,"[24] wrote Friedrich Schlegel in 1794. Thus they broke with the exclusively Apollonian ideal of "noble simplicity and calm grandeur," still defended by Winckelmann, for example. The romantics also uncovered the Dionysian dimension of Greek culture, later revisited by Nietzsche.

This discovery had the consequence, that once Antiquity, is not conceived unilaterally by the Apollonian solar principle of harmonic order, it no longer provided, objectively speaking, a fixed light to guide the moderns. Their Dionysian principle of excess took away the equilibrium and measure, because the ancient night was the source of its beauty. This ambivalence corrupted the necessary solidity of an image that wished itself to be prescriptive. Far from being a stable model, antiquity is now seen as fluid. Hence, it cannot be copied. Its changeable art, contrary to all rigidity, may be appropriated in many ways. It is only one exemplary cultural formation, that cannot be repeated, but may be absorbed and thus, has much to teach – because there the Greeks knew how to give shape to the shapeless, keeping themselves on the thin line that separates and joins order and chaos, being and nothingness, detailing effectively how lofty the concrete creation of art may be. It must not be copied, however, in empirical objectivity, but imitated in its gesture towards the world.

In play, as Friedrich Schlegel observed, was the "perception of the absolute difference between ancient and modern."[25] In short, the historical profile of Romanticism is drawn from the

24. Schlegel, "Über das Studium der griechischen Poesie," in *Kritische Schriften*, 184.
25. Schlegel, *O dialeto dos fragmentos*, 71 (*Athenäum*, Fr. 149).

contrast between the ancient past and the modern present, at the same time that, in effect, this is how the profile of history itself is defined, according to Romanticism. Due to this contrast, it was necessary to discard the authority that tradition gave to the Aristotelian teachings on art, in so far as they were considered timeless, valid for any time. They served as an umbrella within the modern tempest. According to the metaphor, however, we could say that, for the romantics, whoever is standing in the rain ought to get wet. They run with time. They do not make eternal rules that are historical. This is why, after writing *On the Study of Greek Poetry*, Friedrich Schlegel, together with his brother August, would discard the idea of the Greeks as representatives of a golden age of culture. They speak of the "misleading image of a past golden age," because, they say, "if there was an age of gold, it was not exactly golden," after all "gold does not rust or erode."[26] Here, the matter of history emerges. If it was gold, keeping the metaphor, the age would escape time, because gold does not erode, it is safe from the movement of history. The fact that we are no longer Classical proves that the Classics themselves are not golden. They are not absolute. But the absolute may be expressed with them.

It would be necessary, therefore, to extend the articulation of the absolute with its concrete historical effectiveness. It was Hegel who, writing after the romantics, explained this articulation. For him, the absolute is not located outside history, but is realized in history and as history – which is valid for art. "We treat art as being born from the absolute idea itself and even indicating the sensible exposition of the absolute itself with its finality, (and) we should proceed with this panoramic vision," he says. In his courses on aesthetics, this panoramic vision must be the history that "shows how individual parts are originated from the concept of artistic beauty in general as an exposition of the absolute."[27] Owing to this systematization of art in time, the

26. Ibid., 90 (*Athenäum*, Fr. 243).
27. Georg Wilhelm Friedrich Hegel, *Cursos de estética I,* trans. Marco Aurélio Werle (São Paulo: Edusp, 2001), 86.

art historian Ernst Gombrich confesses: "Hegel is, to me, the father of art history."[28] However, perhaps the paternal affiliation of Hegel to art history might be misplaced. He seems more like the mother, who gestates and gives to the world a fully formed child – the historicizing of art. In the place of the father who inseminates, beforehand, would be the early romantics, who demanded, along with the "most profound speculation," also "a more erudite art history."[29]

However, despite their proximity, the differences between Hegel and the early romantics are great. This is because the romantic way of thinking history did not have the teleological sense that Hegel lent it, did not have this fixed north to which it tended a priori. Even less did the romantics think, as Hegel did, that the path of time had an end, a place in which, when reached, it would cease. Therefore, the presence of history in the understanding of art, with the romantics, was not totalizing. Even so, it changed the relationship of the modern present to the Classical past, since, to them, the ancients "do not possess the monopoly on poetry,"[30] as Friedrich Schlegel stated. Although from Hegel onwards the approach to art by history has become sometimes suffocating, at that time the feeling was the opposite: to historicize art was to give it the air that it lacked due to its subordination to Classicism as an eternal model to be obeyed. This is what the romantics did, but without the systematic closure of Hegel.

We may say that the romantics took the absolute from the ancients and placed the ancients in the absolute. This historicity resembles the simultaneous and paradoxical combination of a precarious Neoclassical wish with an anti-Classical position, although it is not exactly either one or the other. Neither the endorsement, nor the rejection of antiquity could serve to measure the vigor of modernity. The romantics did not seek to oppose Greece with a modern formation, but to construct a critical re-

28. Ernest Gombrich, "Hegel e a História da Arte," *Revista Gávea* 5 (1988): 57.
29. Schlegel, *O dialeto dos fragmentos*, 90 (*Lyceum*, Fr. 121).
30. Ibid., 34 (*Lyceum*, Fr. 91).

flection between them. In the post-Classical context, they re-
founded the relationship of modernity with antiquity through
a new path. Paradoxically, the advancement of the modern age,
according to the romantics, would arrive not from overcoming
the Greeks, but from the creation of a more living and intense
relationship with them. According to Ernst Behler, the singularity of the German romantic position is precisely the fact that
in it "Classicism and modernity entered into a strong interac-
tive relation, a communication which was absent in France, in
England and in all other treatments of the quarrel between ancients and moderns."[31]

Goethe was shrewd when he said that "Classicism and
Romanticism, corporate impulse and professional freedom,
maintenance and disintegration of fundamental soil: it is always
the same conflict, that generates, in the end, something new,"
therefore, "the most sensible procedure of the regent would be
to moderate this struggle in a way that, with no loss to either
side, he could balance himself."[32] This must have been the hope
of Hegel when he sought the happy synthesis of opposing dialectics. "However, this is not given to Man, and God also does
not seem to want it," says Goethe, closer to the romantics here.
To these, however, Romanticism is not only one of the terms
of the conflict, but the name of its acceptance. If they sometimes tried to be the regent that would moderate the struggle
towards equilibrium, they knew that the effort would not avoid
reestablishing, every time, the conflict. Nevertheless, Goethe, in
general, did not understand them thus, as the following passage,
in which he suggests that the origin of Classicist and romantic
notions would be in his own discussions, demonstrates:

> The concept of Classical poetry and of romantic poetry,
> that exists in the world today and causes so many discus-
> sions, came originally from Schiller and me. I followed

31. Ernst Behler, *German Romantic Literary Theory* (Cambridge: Cambridge
University Press, 1993), 4.
32. Goethe, *Máximas e reflexões*, 21.

in poetry a maximum objectivity and did not wish to accept any other. But Schiller, who saw everything subjectively, considered his attitude the only fair one and, to defend himself from me, wrote the essay on naïve poetry and sentimental poetry. It showed that I, against my own will, continued to be a romantic, and that my *Iphigenia*, owing to the predominance of feeling in her, was in no way Classical according to ancient taste, as one might suppose. The Schlegels seized the idea and launched it, to the point that today everyone speaks of Classicism and Romanticism, when fifty years ago no one remembered such things.[33]

This passage suggests that Goethe did not see that for the early Romantics it was not possible to resolve the relationship with the ancients through either affirmation or denial. They abandoned this duality in the search for a modern formation, which required a productive relationship with the Classics. Because "the great poets and artists," observed August Schlegel, "whatever the strength of their enthusiasm for the ancients and whatever the determination of their purpose to enter into competition with them, are compelled by their independence and mental originality to explore their own path."[34] It was what modernity needed. Only then, the romantics believed, "will graying antiquity become alive again,"[35] as Friedrich Schlegel observes. Only then, moreover, could the past be alive in the present.

In this context, the early romantics take their boldest step in their manner of imitating. Paradoxically, they wanted to overcome the ancients while imitating them. This was possible because they did not seek to repeat what Antiquity had been, but what it had not been. Modernity should look for what the ancients could never have been. Novalis said that with the study

---

33. Goethe, *Conversações de Goethe com Eckermann*, trans. Luís Silveira (Lisboa: Vega, 1990), 240-1.
34. Schlegel, *Vorlesungen über dramatische Kunst und Literatur*, Vorlesung I.
35. Schlegel, *Conversa sobre a poesia*, 52.

of the ancients, in his time, a Classical literature that the ancients themselves did not possess started to emerge. It is not a matter of saying that the copy is superior to the original, but that what it intends to copy from the original was what it was not, what the original left open as a possibility to be conquered. This is the originality of the discovery of antiquity made by the early romantics. Against the traditional concept of imitation, in its heart, was lodged not the copy, but the creation of the new, since it was a copy of that which it wasn't.

"This is the character of true imitation," says Friedrich Schlegel, adding that "the model, for the artist, is only the stimulus and means to individualize the thoughts that it wishes to create."[36] He proposed a non-exclusive communication between old and new, since "affectation does not emerge so much from the effort to be new, as much as from the fear of being old."[37] Simultaneously with the creation of modernity, the romantics also created Antiquity. To imitate was no longer opposite to one's own singular formation. Schlegel said that "to be able to perfectly translate from the ancients into the modern, the translator would need to master both the latter which, if necessary, could make all the modern, but at the same time understand also the ancient which, if necessary, could not only imitate it, but also create it again."[38] Imitation would be translation. No experience was as acute, in this aspect, as Hölderlin's translations of the Greek tragedies.

It is not, therefore, the consideration of content which decides the position that the early romantics take toward Classicism. They would like to be Classical, since, according to Friedrich Schlegel, "a Classical text never has to be completely understood" and "those who are cultured and cultivate themselves have, however, to want to always learn more from it."[39] This is the objective of the romantic writings. But, what

36. Ibid., 75.
37. Schlegel, *O dialeto dos fragmentos*, 35 (*Lyceum*, Fr. 101).
38. Ibid., 126 (*Athenäum*, Fr. 393).
39. Ibid., 23 (*Lyceum*, Fr. 20).

changes, and distinguishes them from Neoclassicism, is the way in which they regard what they look at: antiquity. This way is not one of blind obedience that merely copies the past model, but is rather a creative appropriation of a source for the future. It was the announcement of the birth of the aesthetic modernity of the vanguard.

"From what the moderns want it is necessary to learn what poetry should become; from what the ancients do, what poetry should be,"[40] said Friedrich Schlegel. The future (the 'should become') comes into contact with the past (what should be) in the present (which is in between both). This relationship of the ancients with the moderns, for the romantics, was that in which "the master seriously disciplined the disciple, but also left him, with the sweat on his face, with a solid base as inheritance, over which the follower should advance forever more, with grandeur and audacity, to finally move with freedom and ability at the proudest heights."[41] Goethe, despite his many criticisms of the romantics, seemed attuned to them when he wrote the following verses in *Faust.*

> What from your father you've inherited,
> You must earn again, to own it straight.
> What's never used, leaves us overburdened,
> But we *can* use what the Moment may create![42]

40. Ibid., 33 (*Lyceum*, Fr. 84).
41. Schlegel, *Conversa sobre a poesia*, 35.
42. Goethe, *Fausto: uma tragédia – primeira parte,* trans. Jenny Klabin Segall (São Paulo: Ed. 34, 2006), 85.

The Vicinity of Poetry and Thought

Sven-Olov Wallenstein

1. Heidegger's Turns

On the Way to Language contains texts and lectures from the 1950s, the last phase of Heidegger's path of thought, when the relation between language and poetry becomes decisive in a new way. The precise meaning of this relation is however less easy to pinpoint. What does it mean to be *on the way* to language, instead of having a theory *of* language, as in the case of linguistics and the philosophy of language, and in what sense could poetry guide us along this way? And if there is such an intimate relation between them, which Heidegger often talks of in terms of "proximity" or "vicinity," relating them not in terms of a subsuming or an identity, but rather in terms of a distance or difference that is just as small as it is radical, what is this relation, and in what element does it unfold?

The way is a recurrent figure in Heidegger, and we encounter it not only in *On the Way to Language*, but in many other works, such as *Holzwege* and *Wegmarken*, and emblematically in the motto that he selected for the collected works: "Paths, not works" (*Wege, nicht Werke*). If "All is way" (*Alles ist Weg*),[1] this implies that we must retrieve another dimension of the movement of thought, in opposition to the modern idea of method that was developed from Descartes onward. For Heidegger, this

---

1. *Unterwegs zur Sprache*, *Gesamtausgabe* 12 (Frankfurt am Main: Vittorio Klostermann, 1985), 187. *On the Way To Language*, trans Peter D. Herz (New York; Harper & Row, 1982), 92. Henceforth cited as UZS (German/ English). I have often chosen to modify the translation. Other volumes in the *Gesamtausgabe* are cited as GA, volume and page.

modern method – of which the priority of the mathematical is only one, albeit central, aspect – depends on a technological view of thought that understands it as an instrument, as a means to an end. To retrieve the openness of the path as opposed to what method has become, is one of the basic meanings of being "on the way to…" – we are not on the way to some faraway goal that we one day may reach due to an increasingly subtle and discerning intelligence in the service of an increasingly precise science, but to a "site" (*Ort*) or "realm" (*Ortschaft*) where we already are, although without being able to see it. "If in what follows we reflect, then, upon the way of thoughtful experience with language," Heidegger writes, "we are not undertaking methodological considerations. We are even now walking in that region, the realm that concerns us" (UZS 168/75).

This return to the closest and yet most distant and unknown site will however not be simple, and even the figure of the circle, recurrent in Heidegger's earlier work, in fact seems too limited: it is only a "particular case of the interlacing in question," and only imposes itself if we "consider language as information" (UZS 231/113). In a marginal note in the GA edition (230, note e), Heidegger expresses a distrust in both terms: if interlacing (*Geflecht*) is a "bad name," then circle is "worse," and instead he hints at "folding" (*Falten*) and "folding together" (*zusammenfalten*), as in "folding one's hands" (*Hände falten*), as other possible terms. In order to "bring language as language to language" (*Die Sprache als die Sprache zur Sprache bringen*, 230/112) – a formula that, as Heidegger notes, uses the same word three times, each time saying something different and yet the Same – we must not push the interlacing aside, but enter into it, abandon ourselves to it, and discern the "unbinding bond" (*entbindende Band*, 231/113) that traverses language and liberates it into its own dimension.

Heidegger's own path too, as it unfolds through his works, is just as little as the way to language a linear progression towards a goal, but rather a series of turns and returns, reinterpretations and reformulations of earlier problems in the light of later questions, all of which has generated a long and probably never-ending debate on the relation between various phases in his thought.[2] Here it may suffice to point to a few crucial signposts, where the idea of language and its relation to thought is transformed, and in this also the role of poetry and poetic language.

The project of fundamental ontology in the 1920s, as it is formulated in *Being and Time* (1927) and the lecture series from the same period, can be understood as a retrieval and transformation of the transcendental philosophy of Kant and Husserl. The task is to overcome – but in this movement also to *found* – epistemology, with its point of departure in the subject or in consciousness, and to develop an ontology based in the hermeneutics of the everyday, in the being-in-the-world of Dasein. In this, the analysis of speech or language (*Rede*) plays an important part, and Heidegger describes it as an articulation of our understanding, which grows out of an ante-predicative level. Pre-linguistic meanings (*Bedeutungen*) grow into words, and the subsequent judgments are a way of synthesizing and rendering explicit a more basic relation to the world. The judgment "S is P," resting upon the emphatic and apophantic *as* – to say something *about* something (*ti kata tinos*), and thereby to see something as something, ultimately "being as being" (*to on he*

---

2. Heidegger's own statements on this point tend to vary. In this context, where the issue is to chart the transformed relation to language in the later writings, the idea of "site" becomes crucial, i.e. something to which we return and which is at once close and far away. In the seminar in Le Thor in 1969, Heidegger distinguishes "three steps on the path of thinking": the question of the meaning of being, the question of the truth of being, and finally "the question of the site or region of being" (GA 15, 344), which in some of the later texts is described as a topology of being. The latter term first appears in a series of aphorism from 1947, and it is explicitly connected to poetry: "Thought's character of poetry is still concealed. / But where it shows itself, it for a long time looks like the utopia of a semi-poetic understanding. / But the thinking poetizing is in truth the topology of being (*Topologie des Seyns*). / This says to being the region its essence." "Aus der Erfahrung des Denkens," in *Aus der Erfahrung des Denkens*, GA 13 (Frankfurt am Main: Vittorio Klostermann, 1983), 84. For the development of Heidegger's term topology, see Otto Pöggeler, "Heideggers Topologie des Seins," *Man and World* Vol. 2, No. 3 (1969).

on), two formulas both rooted in Aristotle's logic and metaphysics – grows out of the preceding hermeneutic *as*, where we do
not grasp things as isolated objects, available for the predica-
tion of properties, but as "equipment" (*Zeug*) that forms a non-
thematic part of our activity. In *Being and Time*, language is not
directly in focus, but first and foremost part of an equipmental
totality (*Zeugganzheit*) comprising all entities that are part of
a particular use, which in turn means that it only in a secondary sense can be taken as a means to communicate thoughts or
mental contents that would precede it or exist independently of
our everyday activity. In what is rejected (Cartesianism, mental-
ism, a pure and non-worldly subject), there is an unmistakable
proximity between Heidegger and the later Wittgenstein, but
also a connection to pragmatism as a larger philosophical movement. This alliance has exerted a profound fascination on many
contemporary interpreters: language is part of life, or a life- or
world-form that we share with others, and not the expression or
externalization of representations that would first exist in some
inner, private, and mental sphere; the positive claims, particularly the attempt to found ontology in a new analysis of temporality, however tend to disappear in these interpretations, which
ultimately provide a distorted picture of Heidegger's project as
a whole.

In *Being and Time* we do not find the claim that would become crucial in many later texts, i.e. the priority accorded to
poetry, or better to the poetic dimension of language (which
need not be identified with a particular literary genre, poetry
as opposed to prose, or even with the modern idea of "literature"). On the contrary, in the framework of *Being and Time*
the poetic use of language would be a modification of everyday
equipmental use. Even though Heidegger never proposes it explicitly, we may here even see the possibility of an aesthetic – or,
using the Husserlian terminology that Heidegger employs with
respect to the other sciences, a *regional ontology* for the aesthetic
object, as an extension of the list of regions cited in § 3 – i.e.,
a particular investigation that would show how the equipmen-

tal character of language and its specific mode of disclosure is modified when used in a poetic fashion. This is hinted at in § 34, when Heidegger, almost in passing, notes that the communication of the existential possibilities of Dasein's disposedness (*Befindlichkeit*), occurring in the "tone, modulation, and tempo of speech, 'in the manner of speaking,'" may become the "proper goal of 'poetic speech'" (*dichtende Rede*).

Beginning in the early '30s, Heidegger turns away from the idea of a transcendental foundation, and eventually – in the published works explicitly in *Einführung in die Metaphysik* (1935) – also from the term ontology. This shift has been understood in highly diverse ways, but regardless of how it is seen, a decisive moment is the new conception of history, in which the "oblivion of being" no longer results from a structural and inescapable tendency of Dasein to understand itself in a reified fashion (a tendency that would be akin to Kant's "transcendental illusion"), and instead becomes a historical process beginning somewhere in ancient Greece and unfolding until it reaches its end in the modern world. This is a what Heidegger calls the "history of being," i.e. a sequence of epochs in which being gives itself to thought in a movement of granting and withdrawal, of "sending" (*Geschick*), which finally reaches its end and so poses the task of thinking the *end* of metaphysics rather than its re-founding through ontology. The challenge to thought is no longer to clear away sedimented layers of traditional interpretations so as to disclose a ground, but rather to reach into the non-ground, the abyss of the "unthought" (*das Ungedachte*) that permeates metaphysics since its inception in Plato, or even earlier, and to discern the possibility of that which returns to us as an other or second beginning (*andere Anfang*), hidden inside the first and merely chronological beginning (often referred to as *Beginn*).

This turn to a transformed sense of history also results in a radical new approach to the work of art. This first necessitates a critique of aesthetics, understood by Heidegger as a way to enclose the work in a subjective sphere organized around concepts like experience, taste, and pleasure, and to deprive it of its capacity for disclosing truth.[3] It is only by overcoming the aesthetic relation, which on one level is a correlate to modern subjectivity, that the thinking of art may reach the dimension of the truth of the work as disclosure of a world, and understand it as a event that not just takes place in history, but *founds* history. In Heidegger's interpretation, aesthetics is however not just a product of a subjectivist, Cartesian modernity, but more profoundly already set on its course by the Platonic divide between the sensible and the supersensible, where the *aistheton* is subjugated to the *noeton* as an imperfect and transient image, which renders the concept of aesthetics inapt for a thought that wants to overcome this separation. (Here we must note Heidegger never seems to acknowledge the specific trajectory of the very term "aesthetics" from Baumgarten to Kant, and even though this is arguably because his problem is to think the unthought essence of metaphysics and not to produce a history of concepts, it nevertheless produces a distorted and insufficient picture.[4])

To overcome Platonism in this particular respect means that we must return to the quarrel between philosophy and poetry to which Plato briefly alludes as the context of his debate with mimetic art in *The Republic* – in fact he claims to have inherited it from a more distant past, and qualifies it as "ancient" or "immemorial" (*palaia diaphora*, 607b). This quarrel, which

3. See for instance the postface to "Der Ursprung des Kunstwerkes," where Heidegger says that "experience" (*Erlebnis*), the modern, subjectivized, and aestheticized version of the Greek *aisthesis*, is the element in which art dies, even though this process may take hundreds of years to be completed. But, he adds in a marginal note, this does not mean that art would come to an end after having been domesticated by philosophical aesthetics, as in Hegel, only that we have to find another "a wholly different 'element' for the becoming of art" (*Holzwege*, GA 5 [Frankfurt am Main: Vittorio Klostermann, 1977], 67, note b).

4. "Western reflection on art begins (*beginnt*) as aesthetics," Heidegger writes, although "great Greek art remained without a corresponding thought and conceptual reflection, which need not be identical to aesthetics" (*Nietzsche I* [Pfullingen: Neske, 1961], 95). In the brief historical sketch outlined in the same volume, Heidegger moves directly from Descartes to Hegel, which seems to imply that aesthetics is only an effect in, a kind of inner fluctuation of, the unfolding of the metaphysics of subjectivity.

for Nietzsche, at the other end of metaphysics, appeared as a "raging discord" whose conditions he set out to reverse by proposing that art is worth more than truth, is one of the central themes in the lectures on "Nietzsche and Will to Power as Art" in 1936. Heidegger's interpretation begins in a positive fashion, and even though Nietzsche in the end remains a Platonist in spite of himself, his conception on perspectivism and the body as way of exploring the world are initially seen as opening onto a productive transformation of the hierarchy rather than simply an inversion of it. [5] As the lectures progress throughout the '30s, the Nietzschean opening seems to close, and in the last lectures, he is treated almost unequivocally negatively.

But if Heidegger's revocation of the Platonic verdict on the poets in the end parts with Nietzsche's affirmation of will to power, the then he just as little takes the other traditional route, i.e. to follow Aristotle in rationalizing their activity through a theory of poetics, which would prove that their use of *katharsis* and *mimesis* is in fact beneficial to the city in providing their audience with a stepping-stone on the way to philosophical reason. The implicit claim is rather that the attempt to free art from the yoke of aesthetics – which is present in different although complementary ways in Aristotelian poetics and Nietzschean affirmation – must begin by stepping back in order to reveal the connection between Plato's negative determination of art and the passage staged in his writings from truth as the fold of openness and concealment to truth as a presence posed in rela-

5. See *Nietzsche I*, above all 231-254. Earlier Heidegger also emphasizes the role of language, not only because "the founding words are historical" (171), but also, and with a dismissal of aesthetics that comes close to "Der Ursprung des Kunstwerkes," because of its materiality: "Since language as a sounding signification from its foundation roots in our earth, and places us in, and binds us to our word, reflection on language and its historical power is always an act that shapes our Dasein. The will to the originary, to rigor, and to providing measure to the word, is therefore not aesthetic play, but a work in the essential core of our Dasein as historical." (169) In spite of this, Nietzsche's own use of language in all of its sensuous, affective, rhetorical, etc, dimensions, play little or no role in the following interpretation, which mainly deals with how his claims are linked to a set of Platonic metaphysical theses on the conceptual level.

tion to a corrected, accommodated, and "ortothetic" gaze. It is only if we are able to retrieve the moment of *aletheia* inside Plato's *ortothes* that we can understand the truth that belongs to art, which is why Heidegger's reading of the allegory of the cave, even though not containing any references to art, can be taken as a necessary correlate to his attempt to twist art free from its Platonic imprisonment.[6] That Heidegger pays no attention to Aristotle's *Poetics* would then be due to his general view, at least in this period, of Aristotle as almost wholly dependent on Platonic concepts: it is as if, in the *Poetics*, the bets have already been placed, and in order to overthrow the game the rules themselves must be changed. If the attempt to think art outside of metaphysics and aesthetics is to succeed, it must return us to something like an originary scene, since it is only this that allows us to rethink the essence of art as inextricably intertwined with the essence of metaphysics. Platonism is one such scene, and perhaps the decisive, but it is not the only one – it echoes and repeats other earlier phases, as Plato himself acknowledged.

2. Mythos and Logos

From the point of view of a separation between philosophy and poetry occurring sometime in the archaic phase of thought, and of which Plato would be a consequence, the retrieval of the exchange as a positive possibility might take the form of a suspension of the difference between *mythos* and *logos*, between experience as narration of the origin, and the origin as timeless structure, principle, and order. In the introduction to *Being and Time*, Heidegger cites Plato's demand in *The Sophist* that we should not "tell a story" (*mython tina diegeisthai*, 242c) as one of philosophy's founding gestures, and he locates his own project in the wake of this injunction, understood as the demand that being should not be derived from a particular being. Later, after the turn away from ontology, *mythos* undergoes a reevaluation,

---

6. See "Platons Lehre von der Wathrheit," in *Wegmarken*, GA 9 (Frankfurt am Main: Vittorio Klostermann , 1976).

and the question of the origin instead returns us to a concept of originary myth that must be liberated from all of its traditional determinations. The origin is nothing "primitive," Heidegger emphasizes in *Einführung in die Metaphysik*, and precisely for this reason it remains outside of the grasp of history, anthropology, archeology, or any other positive science, and can only be understood as "mythology" (GA 40, 165).

In this proposal some have perceived a massive ideological claim. Myth, so Philippe Lacoue-Labarthe, is fundamentally political, and when Heidegger "without any hesitation utters the word mythology, I cannot avoid hearing the voice of, for example, rector Krieck."[7] Heideggerian mythology would then constitute an echo, perhaps a more subtle one and yet an accomplice, of all the other myths of Germany that were being proposed at the same time by the official party philosophers. But even though the political dimensions of the concept are often unmistakable, it seems misleading to establish a direct link to the contemporary party ideologues.[8] At first, Heidegger's vocabulary seems closely affiliated to early romanticism and the mythology envisioned in "The Oldest System Program of German Idealism,"[9] where it was determined as a temporary stage in the return from the divisions of modern philosophy and politics to a primordial, and thus also final, state. A few years later, Schelling, in his *System of Transcendental Idealism*, would simply call this state "poetry" (*Poesie*).[10] For the anonymous

7. Philippe Lacoue-Labarthe, *Heidegger: La politique du poème* (Paris: Galilée, 2002), 22.
8. For a detailed discussion of the term "mythology" and its various uses in Heidegger, see Sommer, C. *"'Nämlich sie wollen stiften / Ein Reich der Kunst'*: Zum Verhältnis von Kunst, Mythos und Politik in Heideggers *Der Ursprung des Kunstwerks* (1935/36) und *Hölderlins Hymnen* 'Germanien' *und* 'Der Rhein',*" *Internationales Jahrbuch für Hermeneutik*, vol. 11, 2002.
9. The text is anonymous, but contemporary consensus opts for Hegel as the most likely author. For an edition of the text with a series of commentaries, see *Mythologie der Vernunft: Hegels "Ältestes Systemprogramm des deutschen Idealismus,"* ed. Christoph Jamme and Helmut Schneider (Frankfurt am Main: Suhrkamp, 1984).
10. "If it is only art that may succeed in making that which that philosophy can only represent subjectively into something objective with universal validity, then it can be expected, to once more draw this conclusion, that phi-

author of the "System Program," the position of a *Mittelglied* meant that mythology here operated as a preparatory way of providing Kant's ideas of reason with a sensible presence, so that they could be given back to "the people," through the complementary means of the "polytheism of imagination" and the "monotheism of the heart." This conception remains within a Kantian framework, although with the view to ground it in a more profound unity based in poetry, in which the state and the political sphere are included. But while it is true that Heidegger's mythology undoubtedly echoes the "System Program," it nevertheless aims at something different: the difference between poetry and thought is not to be submerged into an "ocean of poetry," but rather *intensified*, so that the two acquire a deeper relation *through* this difference, while the exact location of politics seems more difficult to decide, at least in the proposals in *Einführung in die Metaphysik.*

In Heidegger, mythology appears as a tentative way to name an essential and consitutive connection between two terms, poetry and philosophy, it points towards an *element* that would be the origin of both poetry and philosophy, neither one nor the other, and yet not a undifferentiated unity. We find this unity in difference, this entanglement of terms that precedes their coming into their respective unity, in pre-Socratic thought, as in the Poem of Parmenides where philosophy and myth cannot be pried apart, in Greek tragedy, where concepts assume a plastic

losophy – in the same way that it once, in the infancy of science, was born out of and nourished by poetry – and with it all the sciences that through it are guided towards perfection, after their completion will flow back like so many separate rivers into the general ocean of poetry from which they sprang forth. It is in general not difficult to grasp what will be the internediary (*Mittelglied*) for the return of science to poetry, for this intermediary has existed in mythology, before the – as it now appears – irrevocable separation occurred. But how a new mythology, which is not an invention of a singular poet, but belongs to a race that we can only represent as it were in the image of an individual poet (*eines neuen nur Einen Dichters vorstellenden Geschlechts*), itself is to appear, this is a problem whose solution we can only expect from the future destiny of the world and the future course of history" (Friedrich W. J. von Schelling, *System des transzendentalen Idealismus* [Hamburg: Felix Meiner, 1962], 300 [SW ed. 1856, III 629]).

shape and become forces that confront each other on a stage –
and indeed still in Plato too, whose "dramatic phenomenology"
should caution us not to separate singular theses and claims
from the textual web if we are not to lose sight of their constitutive multidimensionality.[11] The question of such a common
element of philosophy and poetry can just as little be solved by
privileging one over the other, as by the creation of some new
and synthetic meta-genre, but can only be approached of we
find a different relation to the language within which we are
already situated – a relation that Heidegger later on, as we shall
see, particularly in *On the Way to Language*, will discuss in terms
of a vicinity or proximity between poetry and thought, whereas
the term mythology largely tends to disappear.

The interpretation of Plato's philosophy as an inception
of metaphysics that harbors a profound unthought, implicitly
opens a whole series of new questions, not least concerning tragedy, where the quarrel is as it were staged from the other end, on
the basis of poetry. In the readings of Sophocles's *Antigone* that
we find in *Introduction to Metaphysics* in 1935, and in the lecture
series on Hölderlin's *Der Ister* 1942-43, Heidegger opposes man's
knowing (*techne*) to the overpowering force of *physis*, which we
should not understand as "nature" in opposition to culture,
but as the power of being as such. The truth – the clearing of a
world and its order of reason – that man establishes in tragedy
is always fragile, and can only be upheld in a struggle against a

11. I borrow the term "dramatic phenomenology" from Stanley Rosen; see the
introduction to Rosen, *Plato's Sophist: The Drama of Original and Image* (New
Haven: Yale University Press, 1983). In the first volume of his re-reading of
Plato's dialogs, Rosen notes: "It may be that philosophy cannot suppress
poetry except by adoption of poetic means. This does not, however, entail
that poetry in the usual or Homeric sense triumphs over philosophy. It
does mean that we have to rethink the usual senses of both philosophy
and poetry, and thereby to arrive at a more satisfactory understanding of
philosophy as an activity that includes its own versions of *poiesis*" (Rosen,
Plato's Symposium. [New Haven: Yale University Press, 1968], xxvii). In spite
of Rosen's many critical comments on Heidegger's interpretations – most
systematically presented in *The Question of Being: A Reversal of Heidegger*
(New Haven: Yale University Press, 1993) – the perspective that his work
opens op seems to me to be highly useful for understanding Heidegger's
approach.

power that traverses him, and which itself is nothing human. If man in the first stasimon in *Antigone* (v. 332) is defined as the most "uncanny" or "homeless" (*to deinotaton, das Unheimlichste* in Heidegger's translation),[12] this is because the power of *physis* forces him outside of himself, and makes him into an errant and placeless being precisely when he appears to occupy the highest point of the *polis*. Unlike Plato's philosopher, who at the summit of the state exerts his dominion (*basileia*), Sophocle's man is fundamentally homeless and bereft of a secure place, and when he ascends over and above the *polis* in order to govern it, he becomes an outcast, *hypsipolis apolis* (v. 370, Heidegger translates: "hochüberragend die Stätte, verlustig der Stätte ist er").[13]

Tragedy can in this sense be taken to show precisely what is repressed in Plato's theoretical intuition of forms and the stabilizing of truth in ortothetic correctness, i.e. not only the openness of *aletheia* that is required for any intuition, but also that this openness is itself wrested from concealment (a process indicated by the privative *a-* of a-*letheia*), in a violent act of which man is never the master. If the duplicity and withdrawal of truth itself is withdrawn when truth is stabilized as correctness in Plato – thereby initiating the oblivion of oblivion that traverses the history of metaphysics – then tragedy allows us to experience this withdrawal and excessive violence before truth

12. The adjective used in Sophocles' text is in fact in a comparative form: *polla ta deina kouden anthropou deinoteron pelei* (Heidegger translates: "Vielfältig das Unheimliche, nichts doch / über den Menschen Unheimlicheres ragend sich regt").

13. See Martin Heidegger, *Einführung in die Metaphysik*, GA 40 (Frankfurt am Main: Vittorio Klostermann, 1983), 152-173. See also the more detailed commentary in the lectures on "Der Ister," *Hölderlins Hymne "Der Ister,"* GA 53 (Frankfurt am Main : Klostermann, 1984), 63-152, where Heidegger develops his analysis beyond the stasimon to the initial passages in the text. Already Antigone's first exchange with Ismene, Heidegger says, shows that she is "das höchste Unheimliche" (GA 53, 122-129), and such already from the outset condenses everything that will follow. This separates Heidegger from Hegel, where the conflict depends on Creon's and Antigone's equally valid conceptions of right, and Heidegger comes closer to Schelling, for whom the fate of the tragic protagonist in the face of existence is a highest act and affirmation of his freedom, and not, as in Hegel, a moment in a historical process. See Schelling, F. W. J. *Philosophie der Kunst, Sämmtliche Werke* (ed. 1859), 1/V, 693-700.

has been corrected by the mastery of the theoretical gaze. A reassessment of the relation between poetry and thought might thus take its cues from the affirmation of the finitude and laceration of thought in tragedy, which also gives us an access to the unthought of metaphysics.

3. The Encounter with Hölderlin

It could be expected that this return to the Platonic scene, before it had been regulated and domesticated by an Aristotelian poetic that subsequently would become a founding model for most classicist art theory, would have motivated Heidegger to a more detailed scrutiny of the philosophy of art in German idealism, where the quarrel between poetry and philosophy was brought to life again, and particularly so in the case of tragedy. In the wake of the eighteenth-century invention of a new experiential domain named "aesthetics," which in its first phase must have appeared as merely a series of marginal notes to the rationalist tradition, a radical interrogation of the very forms of thought evolved, where Kant's third Critique may be seen as an attempt to meet the aesthetic challenge by inscribing its unruly quality in a more encompassing economy of reason. But in the immediate aftermath of Kant, in Schlegel, Schiller, Novalis, Schelling, and many others, there emerged the possibility of testing a "step beyond Kant's line of demarcation" (in Hölderlin's words),[14] in which the new dialog between art and philosophy began to transform both into something else. Even though this is an implicit point of departure for Heidegger as well, he remains largely unappreciative of German idealism and its attempt to rephrase the ancient quarrel, since it for him represents the penultimate step (to be succeeded by Nietzsche) on the way towards the completion of metaphysics as absolute subjectivity.

14. Friedrich Hölderlin, Letter to Neuffer (October 10, 1794), in *Sämtliche Werke* Bd. 6, ed. Friedrich Beissner and Adolf Beck (Stuttgart: Cotta, 1959), 137. The interpreters however disagree fundamentally on where this line should be drawn: between Kant's aesthetic (subjective) idea and Plato's (objective) idea, as the letter seems to suggest, or between sensibility and reason, or between theoretical and practical reason.

Hölderlin, on the other hand, is located as the major exception, and for Heidegger, Hölderlin's step does not lead *beyond* in the sense of an intensifying and completion of modern subjectivity, but *back*: his "Schritt über" is a "Schritt zurück," a step back into another dimension where the unthought essence of metaphysics begins to appear,[15] even though Hölderlin takes this step as a poet, not as a thinker.

Already before *The Origin of the Work of Art* (1935-36), this is staked out in the readings of "Germanien" and "Der Rhein" in 1934-35, and it would become a constant theme in all of the subsequent lectures on Hölderlin: he is pivotal not just because he is assumed to have stepped outside of the horizon of German idealism, but also that of Platonism and of the inception of metaphysics. His poems are not "aesthetic," and they do not deploy "metaphors" – since this would mean to remain in the division between the sensible and the supersensible – but instead point in the direction of another thought, although remaining in the sphere of poetry. In this context it is highly significant that Hölderlin translates and comments on Sophocles, even through this work never becomes central in Heidegger's many interpretations. When Hölderlin, in the comments to his translations of *Oedipus* and *Antigone* speaks of the "ceasura" of tragedy, its "counter-rhythmic interruption" and "categorical turning," this may be read as another case of a disclosure of something in the Greek origin that resists being appropriated by philosophy (and indeed also, as many have noted, also resists Heidegger's own appropriation of Hölderlin).[16]

In the constellation of poetry and thought that Heidegger wants to discern in Hölderlin we find ourselves in a split time,

15. "The step back" is analyzed in relation to Hegel's completion of metaphysics, in Heidegger, *Identität und Differenz* (Pfullingen: Neske, 1957). To my knowledge, Heidegger never comments on Hölderlin's letter to Neuffer and its thesis of a step beyond Kant.

16. For a discussion of Hölderlin's theory of tragedy, developing through the three successive versions of *Empedocles* and culminating in the translations and interpretations of *Oeidipus* och *Antigone*, see Véronique Marion Fóti, *Epochal Discordance: Hölderlin's Philosophy of Tragedy* (Albany: State University of New York Press, 2006).

on the one hand marked by the flight of gods, on the other hand by an attitude of waiting. The call of the poet opens an intermediary time that on the one hand may be seen as melancholy and backward-looking, on the other hand perceives the origin as that which still has to return to us from the future. In this, Hölderlin shares something of the experience of the thinker who thinks the withdrawal of being, which the poet poetizes in the "basic attunement" of "holy grief" ("heilige Trauer") determined by the flight of the gods (the most systematic presentation can be found in the second chapter in GA 39, § 8-11). In both of these experiences, disappearance and withdrawal are given as modes of suspended presence: neither the gods of the poet nor the being of the thinker were once simply there in order to subsequently disappear, just as little as they at some future moment will reappear after having been absent, instead the structure withdrawal-return is mode in which being and gods are present in the now. Heidegger's many descriptions of this temporal loop in Hölderlin echo Nietzsche's prophesy of the death of God (which for Nietzsche too is an event in the past, although it has yet to reach us in all of its implications), but he also distances himself explicitly from Nietzsche, whose diagnosis of modern nihilism for Heidegger remains entangled in Platonism and thus is more of a symptom than a remedy.[17] Hölderlin, on the other hand, he suggests, thinks the "coming god" (or gods) in way that is removed from modern subjectivism and will to power, just as from every theological framework, Christian or non-Christian.[18]

17. Heidegger's evaluation of Nietzsche shifts over the years, although the general tendency seems to be that the initially positive view in 1936 becomes increasingly negative. On the death of God, see Heidegger, "Nietzsches Wort: Gott ist tot," in *Holzwege*, GA 5.
18. This is particularly emphasized in *Beiträge zur Philosophie*, GA 65 (Frankfurt am Main: Vittorio Klostermann, 1989). Heidegger here develops a vocabulary to speak of God (or god) and gods, the content of which is even more difficult to grasp than in the case of Hölderlin, where the Christian references can hardly be left out. It is difficult to see how these terms can be emptied of all theological content and yet remain operative, even as almost formal structures of temporality. Ways of developing these figures even further can be found in Derrida's "messiancity without messianism," although

But is it at all possible for thought to follow the trail of Hölderlin, and what does this imply for the relation between thought and poetry? If the poet names the holy in – or *as* – its own absence, is it then possible for thought to reflect this poetic experience without making into another objectified theme and depriving it of its strangeness? This possibility is crucial for Heidegger, and this is his ground for rejecting the idea of poetic images and metaphors, since they always imply the possibility of a translation into a proper meaning, i.e. the sublation of poetry's sensible images into the intelligible medium of the philosophical concept, as Hegel would say. Thus, to the extent that we at all may speak of a "connection of images" in Hölderlin, we should instead attempt to "receive it in its veiling power" (GA 39, 119), and such images "should not clarify, but veil, not render familiar, but strange, nor bring closer, but place at a distance" (116).

The reception of Heidegger's encounter with Hölderlin for a long time largely rested on the essays collected in *Erläuterungen zu Hölderlins Dichtung* (a first version was published in 1944, a second and enlarged one in 1951, and then several subsequent editions with new material). This volume however only gives an indirect picture of Heidegger's successive readings during the '30s and '40s, which can now be traced in the lecture series on "Germanien" and "Der Rhein" (1934-35), on "Andenken" (1941-42), on "Der Ister" (summer 1942), in the fragmentary series on "Dichten und Denken" from 1944, interrupted when Heidegger at the end of the was called into military service, and finally in the notes and unpublished manuscripts from 1939 onward, published under the title *Zu Hölderlin* (GA 75). Apart from the principal philosophical question, the relation between poetry and thought, these lecture volumes also evince much more clearly the strong political claims being made. Hölderlin

they are in the end just as ambivalent, and have generated a long debate about a possible religious turn in Derrida's late work. See, for instance Jacques Derrida, *Spectres de Marx* (Paris: Galilée, 1983) and *La religion,* ed. Jacques Derrida and Gianni Vattimo (Paris: Seuil, 2001).

has a message to the Germans of the present, and in poetizing a future Germany he asks whether the Germans are ready for his words, if they are able to enter into a fundamental history. Hölderlin's poetry, Heidegger says, is a "decision concerning time, in the sense of the originary time of different peoples (GA 39, 51).[19] Even though these claims about the originary are often presented in opposition to the political debates of the moment, they are still at crucial moments directly connected to immediate events, so that sudden raging attacks on the "American lack of history and self-destruction" that motivates the US entry into the "planetary war" after Pearl Harbor (GA 53, 68) may be inserted into explications of Sophocles. When Philippe Lacoue-Labarthe summarizes his extensive work on Heidegger, he suggests that it is these texts that we find Heidegger's proper political philosophy, and the "national aestheticism" that led him to understand the state as a work of art is developed above all in the dialog with Hölderlin.[20]

The tonality of these lectures shifts between the demand for heroic action and, as the war progresses, an increasing sense of desperation: the apocalypse, the dramatic decision concerning the fate of the West – often, though not always, identified with the fate of Germany – is close. At the end, in the final lectures from 1944, the question of nihilism and the death of God, as a question of the loss of direction and ground in the contemporary moment, finally settles on the constellation Nietzsche-Hölderlin, and the possibility to understand the sense of the "Now" (*was ist Jetzt?*), can only come through a more profound

---

19. The theme of historicity is central throughout the '20s, and after the turn it becomes a question of the history of being, which can no longer be thought on the basis of Dasein's existential structure. In the mid '30s it also becomes a question of the particular historical fate of Germany, as "metaphysical middle" (*metaphysische Mitte*) between the Soviet East and the American West. For the theme of historicity in the Hölderlin lectures, see Susanne Ziegler, *Heidegger, Hölderlin und die Aletheia: Martin Heideggers Geschichtsdenken in seinen Vorlesungen 1934/35 bis 1944* (Berlin: Duncker & Humblot, 1991).

20. See Lacoue-Labarthe, *La politique du poème*. The concept "national aestheticism" is fist discussed in Lacoue-Labarthe, *La fiction du politique: Heidegger, l'art et la politique* (Paris: Christian Bourgois, 1988).

understanding of their relation. There is a "peculiar necessity in the mutual historical relation" between Nietzsche and Hölderlin – "*Nietzsche*, who as a thinker is a poet," and "*Hölderlin*, who as a poet is a thinker" (GA 50, 96) – in such a way that they both go beyond us and our present, but in this also come toward is from the future. The first difficult in discerning their relation is that they are "infinitely separated," as if there would be an infinite difference "in that which is, namely being itself" (103), and it is only through this difference that we may understand what is hidden in the insignificant "and" that connects poetry and thought. The second difficulty is that the question is posed from the point of view of thought, and "that we, as thinking and re-flecting, when reflect on thought and poetry, already are placed on one side of the relation between thought and poetry, so that everything that is to be said in advance becomes one-sided." (145) The lectures end by stating these difficulties, and we seem have ended in an aporia.

The 1944 lectures thus mark the endpoint of the first phase in Heidegger's dialog with poetry, both in terms of external bi-ography and internal thematic development. When this thread is picked up again after the war, the tonality is different. This is also where many have seen a third phase in Heidegger's thought in general, where the key problems would no longer be the criti-cal thinking through of the history of metaphysics, but the es-sence of technology, man's possibility of dwelling in the world, and a transformed relation to language. Even though all of these themes are present earlier, there is undoubtedly a new approach, where the activist and apocalyptic attitude of the writings from the later '30s to the end of the war, which emphasized a set of concepts tinted by voluntarism, such as project, projection, deci-sion etc., is succeeded by a more meditative stance bases in lis-tening, waiting, letting-be (*Seinlassen*), and release (*Gelassenheit*).

The question whether the poet, in the words from "Andenken" that were chosen as the epigraph to the first Hölderlin lectures from 1934-35, can *found that which remains*, or *lasts*, depending on how we understand the German (*Was aber bleibt, stiften die Dichter*), now appears in a different light. Even though earlier interpretations too insisted on questioning, on the experience of waiting, expectancy, and absence, there is still a shift, where the founding of the poet is called into question. The seminal essay on Rilke in the immediate aftermath of the war, "Wozu Dichter" (1946), testifies to this. If Hölderlin, Heidegger reminds us at the end of the essay, is still the one who in advance sets the measure for the poet's search of the holy, "which is why no poet in our age can surpass him" (GA 5, 320),[21] then Rilke's attempts to grasp the holy in the form of the angel remains caught up in a Nietzschean philosophy of life. But at the same time, Rilke's attempt to follow the traces of the holy into an inner space – which for Heidegger, the poet's various turns notwithstanding remains a space of consciousness – seems to constitute our inescapable predicament, and in this sense Rilke points to a limit of the modern poetic project, also in Heidegger's own thought.[22]

4. The Later Dialog Between Poetry and Thought

The later essays that we find in *On the Way to Language* are not in the same way as the readings of Hölderlin inserted into a

21. In many of Heidegger's statements, Hölderlin remains the very model of the poet, although he no longer plays the same role as historical break with metaphysics, as can be seen by the rather sparse references to him in *On the Way to Language*. The key document in this transformation is the unfinished manuscript "Das abendländische Gespräch" (1946-48), *Zu Hölderlin; Griechenlandreisen*, GA 75 (Frankfurt am Main: Vittorio Klostermann, 2000). For a discussion of this shift in a general context, see Robert Savage, *Hölderlin After the Catastrophe: Heidegger, Adorno, Brecht* (Rochester: Camden House, 2008).

22. The ambivalent attitude in 1946 is a considerable displacement from the more unequivocally negative remarks in the lecture series on Parmenides 1942-43, where Heidegger wholly rejects all affinities between the openness in *aletheia* and "the Open" in the eighth Duino Elegy; see *Parmenides*, GA 54 (Frankfurt am Main: Vittorio Klostermann, 1982), 226ff. Heidegger and Rilke can be made to communicate in other and perhaps more fertile ways, for instance through the idea of "becoming-thing" (*Dingwerdung*) in Rilke's earlier work, and Heidegger's reflections on technology; see Christoph Jamme, "Der Verlust der Dinge," in *Martin Heidegger: Kunst – Politik – Technik,* ed. Christoph Jamme and Karsten Harries (Munich: Fink, 1992).

historical project to overcome metaphysics. Even though such claims are not entirely absent, as in the interpretation of Trakl in "Language in the Poem," where the motif of "going under" is understood as "going over" into an "early time," the dramatic overtones of a momentous historical decision have been considerably subdued. What is at stake here is not the dismantling of metaphysics, but rather what Heidegger later will propose in the lecture "Zeit und Sein" (1962), to "leave metaphysics to itself" and instead to approach the "clearing" (*Lichtung*), the appropriation, and openness as a constant possibility, which indicates an abandoning of the idea of something originary that would have been withdrawn from thought at some point in time.[23] Rather than a rereading of the history of philosophy in search of the unthought, the task is to approach the world and man's dwelling in it. The fourfold (*Geviert*) of mortals and immortals, heaven and earth, is the new constellation that describes our way of being in the world, and the exchange with poetry is conducted in order to elucidate this condition. If language, as Heidegger famously says in *Brief über den Humanismus* (1946) is the "house of being" (GA 9, 313) and thinkers and poets are its custodians, who bring the openness of being to language and preserve it in language, the question becomes how we should understand our dwelling in language, and what language must be if it is to give us guidelines for dwelling. Once more the poem leads the way, which is now explicitly a "way to language" as a site or place to inhabit. As we shall, this spatiality is not simply an analogy: if the dialog requires an openness, a vicinity that opens and holds together the in-between in which it may unfold,[24] then this will be connected in a particular and emphatic way with dwelling

---

23. See "Zeit und Sein" and "Das Ende der Philosophie und die Aufgabe des Denkens," in Martin Heidegger, *Zur Sache des Denkens* (Tübingen: Niemeyer, 1976).

24. The dialog would in this sense face the same problem as dialectics, since every *dia-legesthai* requires an In-Between, a *Zwischen*, as Heidegger notes in "Hegels Begriff der Erfahrung," *Holzwege* GA 5, 183, 201. That Hegel, at least as Heidegger sees it, finally forgets this in-between would be one of the reasons for the one-sided in his relation to the poem.

and the dimensionality of the world.

The conversation (*Gespräch*) or dialog (*Zwiegespräch*) takes place in language, but it cannot be governed by the rules of literary studies, linguistics, aesthetics, or some other discipline that studies our way of handling language; it belongs to thought, and even more to that which forces itself onto thought as a necessary task. This was emphasized already from the first lectures on Hölderlin onward, it recurs from one end to the other of Heidegger's work, and one of the last cases is the laconic preface to the third edition (1971) of *Erläuterungen zu Hölderlins Dichtung*: "The present *Elucidations* do not claim to be contributions to research in the history of literature or to aesthetics. They spring from a necessity of thought" (GA 4, 7).[25] In the earlier versions of this claim, this affirmation of thought's autonomy was made in the name of a historical necessity and destiny that governed the exchange between poetry and thought; later, it is based on the fundamentally different relation that thought has to language.

Many objections can and have been voiced against such claims. It is by no means self-evident that we must accept such a division of labor between literary studies and philosophy, or the kind of immunity here claimed by "thought" to philological questions and criticism developed on the basis of techniques of textual analysis. Modern phenomenological, hermeneutic, and deconstructive literary theories have developed many of Heidegger's themes in a way that opposes the one-sided nature of the exchange; others have shown how Heidegger's readings in many cases rest on philological decisions that cannot be justified simply by an appeal to the necessity of thought. Similarly, the determination of aesthetics that underlies Heidegger's claims – that it is a theory framing and specifying a particular type of experience of pleasure, for which truth is irrelevant – is by no means undisputed, as is demonstrated by Adorno's aesthetics, and in particular by the important role played by

25. English translation by Keith Holler, *Elucidations of Hölderlin's Poetry* (Amherst: Humanity Books, 2000), 21.

Hölderlin in Adorno's account of modern art. And as we noted earlier, Heidegger's own historical genealogy of aesthetics can be questioned on many points, not just because of lacking historical precision, but also because it neglects the transformative potential that exist in the early forms of aesthetics in the eighteenth century, and have accompanied modern philosophy as a constant subtext.

On the question of one-sidedness that Heidegger himself brings up, it may at first seem like a trivial necessity; Heidegger is a philosopher and makes no claim to be a poet.[26] And furthermore, the position accorded to thought in this exchange is not simply one of superiority – neither a conceptual subsumption nor a lifting up into the concept, as in Hegel – but one of listening in a particular way, so that a truth unfolds that belongs to neither of them as such, only to the in-between. In this Heidegger continues a line of thought originating in early German idealism, and that he extends as far as possible, which is what ultimately renders his meditations on poetry so refractory to discursive classification. Thought must reflect poetry in itself, not in order to master it though a reflective relation that only finds its own projections, but in order to be led along by the poetic word, and from the resonances created by the parallel of the two modes of saying extract something that it would not be able to say in its own. To be sure, there is a danger that thought overinterprets – but this danger, Heidegger says, above all lies in "that we will think to little, and reject the thought that the true experience with language can only be a thinking experience." And he continues:

26. Similarly to the lectures from 1944, Heidegger notes en passant that there are other types of dialogs, for instance the one between poets, which he here even calls "the true dialogue": "Only a poetic dialogue with a poet's poem is a true dialogue – the poetic conversation between poets." (UZS 34/161) Consequently, if only in order to complete the cycle of permutations, there might then be a dialog between poet and thinker occurring from the poet's point of view, and belonging exclusively to the latter without laying any claim to be thought. Heidegger provides no examples, but perhaps the latter might be exemplified by Hölderlin's writings, particularly those on tragedy.

But if what matters first of all is a thinking experience, then why this stress on a poetic experience? Because thinking in turn goes its ways in the neighborhood of poetry. It is well, therefore, to give thought to the neighbor, to him who dwells in the same neighborhood. Poetry and thought, each needs the other in its neighborhood, each in its fashion, when it comes to ultimates. In what region the neighborhood itself has its domain, each of them, thought and poetry, will define differently, but always so that they will find themselves within the same domain. (UZS 163/69)

Before we look more closely on the enigmatic vicinity of art and poetry, or on the element in which their unity in difference unfolds, we must pose the more general question of language as such – although, as we will see, the idea of "generality" is possibly misleading, and here too Heidegger's reflections on language articulate themselves through a reading of a particular poet. The essay that opens *Unterwegs zur Sprache*, "Die Sprache,"[27] is organized around a reading of one poem of Trakl, and although the themes extracted have an obvious bearing on the whole of his claims about the structure of the world, they remain attached to a particular interpretation, although one that, as we will see, constitutes an *example* with *exemplary* value.

One of the most common and traditional determination of man is that he is the *zoon logon echon*, the living being endowed with reason or language – this is what makes us human, as Humboldt once claimed. We are always speaking, Heidegger notes at the outset, we speak we are awake, in dreams, even when we are not uttering a single word, and in this sense language permeates out being beyond the linguistic in a limited sense. But what is man, so that language can belong to him in such an intimate way? Language is indeed in the "closest vi-

---

27. This text is not included in *On the Way to Language*, and is here cited in the translation of Albert Hofstadter, in Martin Heidegger, *Poetry, Language, Thought* (New York: Harper and Row, 1971).

cinity to the human being" ("die nachste Nachbarschaft des Menschenwesens," UZS 9/189), Heidegger says; but how are we to approach this vicinity and this essence? Traditionally, essence has been understood as generality, but Heidegger cautions us that we should not force any general framework onto language, since this brings it under the rule of framing and positing, of *Stellen* and *Vorstellen* – and thus ultimately under the rule of technology as framing, as *Ge-Stell*, which for Heidegger is the horizon of all modern philosophies of language and linguistic theories. The task for a thought that is "on the way to..." is rather to approach the site of language, which means to situate (*erörten*) it and thereby bring us closer to the site. In bringing us closer, it also shows how language approaches us as a gathering in the enownment or appropriation (both of which have been proposed as translations of *Ereignis*), that which makes possible a new relation to being because it has always been there as the unacknowledged background of all metaphysical representations.

This means that we must approach language itself, without attempting to ground it in something else,[28] for instance in the view that its source would be in us, since we are the ones who use it for our own aims. At first this reversal appears as an empty tautology: "Language itself is: language and nothing else. Language itself is language." ("Die Sprache selbst ist: die Sprache und nichts ausserdem. Die Sprache selbst ist die Sprache.") (10/190) This approach is however also the way in which language approaches *us*, its essence as presencing, or *es-*

---

28. Similar formulas are frequent in Heidegger's later work, for instance in the essay "Das Ding," where the thinghood of the thing is brought back to its own mode of presencing in the duplicative formula "the things things," *das Ding dingt*. Already in the 1919 lectures *Zur Bestimmung der Philosophie*, GA 56/57 (Frankfurt am Main: Vittorio Klostermann, 1987) we find an early instance of a similar verbal construction, "es weltet" (GA 56/57, 73), and in the published works it appears for the first time in the aftermath of *Being and Time*, in "Vom Wesen des Grundes" (1928), when Heidegger stresses that "Welt ist nie, sondern Welt weltet" (GA 9, 219): the world is never something that *is*, it "worlds," and must be thought on the basis of its own presencing instead of as a collection of objects.

sencing, according to Heidegger's understanding of *wesen* as verbal, "coming-into-presence." This is the *speaking* of language itself: "Language speaks" (ibid), in a formula whose duplication is even more striking in the German: *Die Sprache spricht* (ibid).

This overturning of the formula implies that we must neither understand language first and foremost as a tool among others, which was basically the conception of *Being and Time*, nor as an objective system that precedes the speaker's individual moves in the game, as in various structuralist theories, for instance Saussure's *langue*. Both of them would be different instances of a technological view of language that prevents us from seeing how we inhabit it as the ones who *addressed* by, caught in, the *Zuspruch* of its essence (*Zuspruch*, "address," can also mean "promise," as if the coming-toward-us of language is also a promise given to us in which we must trust).[29]

From the point of view of classical (and modern) foundationalist metaphysics, the step back from grounding and into presencing may seem like falling into an abyss. This was in fact how also language began to appear on the horizon of modern philosophy, most famously in Hamann's rejoinder to Kant, "Metakritik über den Purismus der Vernunft" (1784). As Hamann claims, any determination of a transcendental sphere already presupposes language, also in the empirical sense of natural languages, and Kant's a priori universalism necessarily draws on temporally and spatially located significations whose

29. Heidegger's dismissal of linguistics and modern philosophies language, together with the absence of "technical" rigor in his meditations, can of course give rise to a vast spectrum of criticism, of which he is not unaware. Ultimately it has to do with his stance on modern technology, which he in the case of language sees as embodied in "metalinguistics": "Metalinguistics is the metaphysics of the thoroughgoing technicalization of all languages into the sole operative instrument of interplanetary information. Metalanguage and sputnik, metalinguistics and rocketry are the same." (UZS 150/58) As Derrida notes, the insistence on language as always already there not only renders objectification and metalinguistics impossible, but also displaces the priority of the question, which had been a guiding motif throughout all of Heidegger's earlier writings. See the long note in Jacques Derrida, *De l'esprit: Heidegger et la question* (Paris: Galilée, 1986), 152ff.

priority seems impossible to account for in transcendental philosophy. In Hamann, this criticism however reflects an empiricist motif that is foreign to Heidegger, who cites a more dramatic letter of Hamann to Herder, where he speaks of the identity of reason and language as an "abyss," the key to which can only be provided by an "apocalyptic angel" (Hamann, cited in UZS 10f/191). The abyss, Heidegger suggests, however only appears as something negative if our quest is for a ground. If this is given up, the vertiginous hovering described by Hamann instead allows us to "fall upward, to a height," and to open up a new depth, both of which measure a "realm" in which we may feel at home, since the speaking of language constitutes the "dwelling place" (*Aufenthalt*) for mortal human beings (ibid/191f).

Before approaching this place, Heidegger briefly overviews a series of traditional conceptions of speaking, not in order to reject them, but rather to understand them as derived from a more originary level. The most basic view of language in modernity is that of an activity whose external side is made up of physiological features, but on the inside is in the service of the communication of inner movements of the human mind. In this is presupposed the idea of speech as an *expression* of an inside in an outside, that speaking is a particular human *activity*, and that man in his expressions *represents* and presents what is real or unreal. Other and more traditional conceptions emphasize a divine origin, or the basis in images and symbolism, so that theology, anthropology, poetics, and a host of other disciplines can be summoned to contribute to a study of man as a creator of symbolic orders. Both of them for Heidegger however belong to a traditional metaphysical view that has remained the same since antiquity, and which may indeed be correct (*Richtig*), precisely because it moves in the sphere of truth as correctness and correspondence established by Plato, but that does not reach the dimension of truth, language *as* language, which is the "oldest essential characteristic" (*die älteste Wesensprägung*, UZS 13/193).

5. The Exemplary Example

But how are we to approach this speaking? Here we find the claim for a priority of poetry, established in a series of moves that we must follow more closely. First, speaking can best be found in the spoken, where it has completed and gathered itself. But any random instance of the spoken cannot suffice, since it mostly appears as the past of an act of speaking, as a mere remainder. We must rather find something that is "spoken purely" (*ein rein Gesprochenes*, UZS 14/194), where perfection, Heidegger says, is also a *beginning* (which implicitly signifies a location outside of everyday temporality, although it is not developed here), as is the case in the poem. Further on, Heidegger suggests that poetry is not primarily a higher and more achieved form of everyday language – which would suggest that the poetic dimension, perfection notwithstanding, is an *extension*, and as such superfluous in normal use – but that everyday language is a "forgotten and used-up poem" (28/208) whose call can barely be perceived anymore. In a substitution reminiscent of Plato's *Symposium* – where Socrates notes that we often name the whole, *poiesis* as production in the most general sense, bringing something from non-being into being, after the most eminent part, *poiesis* as poetry – Heidegger's poetry (*Dichtung*) is not identical to literature or a genre of literature (*Poesie*), and yet it bears no other name than *Dichtung*. It is the *origin* of language, and not one its specific uses, which is why it unfolds in a time of its own that does not simply pass, but preserves the spoken as the possibility of new beginning.

But if "poem" does not denote a particular literary genre, and prose can be just as "poetic," why should then a particular poem be our guide? Is the selection of poetry, and furthermore of one specific poem, not simply arbitrary? Heidegger here performs a move that we can recognize from *Der Ursprung des Kunstwerkes*, in claiming that we must always begin at a particular place, in front of a singular work, which then opens up a truth that belongs to its own way of speaking. This is a circular movement in which we must trust, Heidegger says in *Der Ursprung*; here, he suggests that the speaking of language has already been thought *to* us (*zuge-*

dacht) in the manner of an approach that guides us onward. In *Der Ursprung*, van Gogh's painting was one example of how an artwork can open a truth, but also an *exemplary initial example*, in showing us the more general structure of earth and world that is subsequently developed in relation to the Greek temple. Similarly, in discussing Trakl's poem, "A Winter Evening," Heidegger traces, through its particular features, a spatial and temporal movement that describes the structure of the *world*, and that will be decisive for his further meditation on language as an opening onto the fourfold. From the first stanza that speaks of what is outside, to the second that sets up an opposition between those that are home and the "wandering ones," and the third that brings the two together by inviting the wanderer into the house, where the table is set with "bread and wine," the basic regions of the fourfold are outlined, and in this sense Trakl's poem too is an exemplary example with a general significance. And while it is true that the dialog intended by Heidegger to some extent can disregard the question of generality, if the latter simply would be derived from concepts given in advance – it does claim to be a general theory of literature, or an aesthetic that lays down general features of literary experience, but something like the record of a singular encounter that forces thought to respond – the choice of a particular poem as a guide to the general structure of the world still seems in need of further elaboration, also on the historical level. How, for instance, should we locate Trakl with respect to the lineage extending from Hölderlin to Rilke? Is Trakl a specifically *modern* poet, or does he occupy an even more exorbitant position than his two predecessors? Does Trakl's "purely spoken," outside of the flow of everyday occurrences, point to founding of that which remains, as in Hölderlin?

Heidegger stresses that we need to hold traditional concepts of the poet's individuality at bay if we are to grasp how the poem can constitute an opening to the world. If the poem just as little as language as such can be understood as an expression of "movements of the mind," i.e. an expression of the poet's inner states, neither can it be grasped on the basis of the imagination that "imagines" something in the domain of representation. But if expression, imagination, and representation as such are insufficient to situate the essence of language, and the only measure for this situating is given by the singularity of poem, then this in turn constitutes a limit for thought, a given that cannot be further explained, only experienced as a hint or indication: "The poem cited has been chosen because, in a way not further explicable, it demonstrates a peculiar fitness to provide some fruitful hints for our attempt to situate language" (USZ 17/198). There is something like a *logic of examplarity* at work here, where the example (the *Beispiel*) it at once only an example, something located alongside, even outside the movement of showing, and wholly essential, since its particular features is what orients the whole of this movement.[30]

The reading, which I here will follow in some detail, focuses on particular words and locutions of Trakl's poem, which reads as follows:

Window with falling snow is arrayed,
Long tolls the vesper bell,
The house is provided well,
The table is for many laid.

Wandering ones, more than a few,
Come to the door on darksome courses.
Golden blooms the tree of graces
Drawing up the earth's cool dew.

---

30. This "not further explicable" is akin to the intrusion of a seemingly insignificant "And yet" (*Und dennoch*) in *Der Usprunf des Kunstwerkes*. On one level we are caught in a aporia – the context of van Gogh's shoes is too indeterminate, we cannot go any further – and yet, there is a light that begins to glow from inside the shoes, and the following ekphrasis is just as much an epiphany, where we are transported "elsewhere," as Heidegger writes. The idea of exemplarity is developed in great detail in Derrida, and I borrow it from the reading of Kant's third Critique proposed in *La vérité en painture* (Paris: Galilée, 1974). Derrida is also attentive to the rhetorical details in Heidegger's van Gogh ekphrasis, though the idea of exemplarity is only hinted at; see whole of chap 4, "Restitutions," but especially 365ff.

Wanderer quietly steps within;
Pain has turned the threshold to stone,
There lie, in limpid brightness shown,
Upon the table bread and wine.[31]

The first stanza names both thing and world, and calls upon the mortals, and in this it prefigures the following. A founding claim of Heidegger's reading is that this naming of things bids, calls or summons them (*Rufen* and *Heissen* are uses throughout) into word and language, instead of being added to already given entities as linguistic ornaments. What is called into language is brought close, or rather placed in a particular proximity that includes both presencing and absencing, the near and the distant. These are given a new dimension in being brought into language: the falling snow and the evening bell in the poem are both *here*, although not in the same way as things in everyday life, and when Heidegger rhetorically asks which of the two modes of presence is the highest, we may no doubt read him as saying that the presence that unfolds in the poem is the eminent one. Even though the sentences in the poem, in using what appears like a determining "is," may seem like propositions that record or propose facts, they rather bring entities into presencing. (This, we might add, is what is insufficiently understood when one speaks of poetry as constitutive of an imaginary world, since this always is a modification, no matter how autonomous, of a real and already given world outside of language.) The call of the poem bids things to come, not simply as present things among other things, but to a different "place of arrival" (*Ort der Ankunft*, 19/199) – a place or site that will be fourfold.

31. Eng. translation by Hofstadter, from *Poetry, Language, Thought*. German original: "Wenn der Schnee ans Fenster fällt, / Lang die Abendglocke läutet, / Vielen ist der Tisch bereitet / Und das Haus ist wohlbestellt. // Mancher auf der Wanderschaft / Kommt ans Tor auf dunklen Pfaden. / Golden blüht der Baum der Gnaden / Aus der Erde kühlem Saft. // Wanderer tritt still herein; / Schmerz versteinerte die Schwelle. / Da erglänzt in reiner Helle / Auf dem Tische Brot und Wein."

After these initial remarks, Heidegger's reading will proceed to show how the three stanzas of the poem gradually unfold the structure of the world as the fourfold. The figure of Fourfold, which comprises heaven and earth, the immortals and the divine, is one of the decisive ideas in Heidegger's later work, and it may seem like a relapse into a crude mythology that simply takes leave of all recognizable philosophical explication, not least the element of phenomenological "showing" and "intuition," and instead extrapolates from particular types of poetry, or even particular poems. Most readers of Heidegger have attempted to derive this idea from Hölderlin, who uses many similar of not wholly identical expressions, and other sources in the philosophical tradition have also been cited, for instance Plato, Aristotle, and even Kant.[32] Regardless of what the sources may be, authors from the history of philosophy or particular poets or poems, in the present context it is important to follow how Heidegger, to be sure on the basis of a single poem, develops the new idea of world.[33]

As an originary unity, the fourfold revolves around the thing, which is not an object for a consciousness, but has an active way of presencing that Heidegger calls "thinging" (*dingen*). Thinging is what "gives world," i.e. allows to the world to appear to us as that of which we are already a part, also in a temporal sense that,

32. The relevance of this historical background has been argued in great detail by Jean-François Mattéi, *Heidegger et Hölderlin: Le Quadriparti* (Paris: PUF, 2001), and *L'ordre du monde: Platon – Nietzsche – Heidegger* (Paris: PUF, 1989). Here we must also note a shift from the earlier readings of Hölderlin that, as we saw, emphasized the absence and distance of the holy in terms of *grief*, whereas the fourfold seems to signal a kind of return, although in a way that transforms the earlier question rather than providing a response to it.

33. Unlike the concept of world in *Being and Time*, the fourfold can no longer be understood as a moment in the projective structure of Dasein and its temporality. There is also an important displacement in relation to *Der Ursprung des Kunstwerkes*, where the world as unconcealment was set against the earth as concealment. As can be seen in some propositons in *Der Ursprung*, and more clearly in the reading of Sophocles in *Einführung in die Metaphysik*, openness must be achieved through power or violence (*Gewalt*), whereas the world in the later texts is described in terms of release, stillness, and rest.

in consonance with the purely spoken in the temporality of the poem, points to the permanence and continuity of the world: things linger and abide (*währen*). The call of the poem is what calls things to thinging, i.e. allows this dimension to be seen and understood in showing us how things give a world by bearing it to us, giving birth to it, in what Heidegger calls their "gestures" (*Gebärde* here plays on the closeness to *gebären*, giving birth, both of which, as we shall see, signal the material, corporeal, and earthly dimension, and why the insistence on language is not a linguistic idealism). "Thinging, they gesture – gestate – world" ("Dingend, gebärden sie Welt," UZS 19/200), Heidegger writes in a compressed formula.

The second stanza begins from the point of view of the mortals. While death and mortality is not explicitly mentioned in the poem, which speaks only of "wandering ones," Heidegger interprets this as a mode of erring and straying connected to finitude. The wanderers are thus those who are capable of dying, of a death that "has already overtaken every dying" (UZS 20/200). The mortal ones are however not singular, isolated figures, riveted to their own fate, but reach out to the others, and in this they can be understood as figures of the poet that we can recognize from the earlier readings of Hölderlin, where the idea of poet as a mediator is a persistent theme. Their wandering and their relation to death are for the sake of the many, in order to show them that their belonging to a home and a place is illusory if it has not passed through the exterior and the foreign, i.e. has been exposed to the possibility of loss inherent in finitude.

The second part of the stanza moves on to name that which binds the four in the fourfold together to a world, the "tree of graces." Here we also encounter the moment of *beauty*, as a radiance (*Schein*) that belongs to the world and the poem alike, which indicates that it must be thought outside of aesthetics that reduces beauty to mere sensuous appearance.[34] Rather than

34. Heidegger refers the "golden" in Trakl's poem to Pindar, *Isthmian V*, and the radiance that permeates everything. Already in *Der Ursprung des Kunstwerkes* Heidegger referred to beauty as above all related to shining

an ornamental or accessory dimension, beauty's radiance is
what grants things their essencing, and is a dimension of the
way in which the poem bids thing and world to come together
into a unity. This unity is however not identity: world and thing
come together in that they both traverse a "middle" (*Mitte*,
22/202) through which they achieve unity, intimacy, or a common depth (*Innigkeit*).[35] The in-between (*das Zwischen*) makes
possible a being-together where the parts remain separated in
their unity and united in their difference: it is the *Unter-Schied*,
or the *dif-ference*. This dif-ference is of a unique kind: it is not a
general concept that subsumes particular differences; it not the
difference of distinction added by a reflection in representation,
or an empirical difference between objects, but that which ap-
propriates world and thing and releases them into their own;
it gives a dimension to thing and world, as both turned toward
and away from each other. It is *One*, unique and singular, in pry-
ing the middle apart and bearing world and thing onto each
other, which also means to decide their relations (this dual dimension of *tragen* is distributed to two terms, *zutragen* and *aus-
tragen*), or the *Diaphora* in the eminent Greek sense of the term,

and radiance, and in many places he would point to Plato's determination
of the *idea tou kalou* as the most shining and enrapturing, *to ekphanestaton
kai erasmiotaton* (*Phaedrus* 250d); see, for instance, the interpretation of
Hölderlin's "Wie, wenn am Feiertage…" in *Erläuterungen zu Hölderlins
Dichtung*, GA 4 (Frankfurt am Main: Klostermann, 1981), 53. Heidegger's
critique of Plato notwithstanding, the idea of beauty as that which gives
visibility and presence to worldly things is a motif that underlies his rejection of aesthetics.

35. The idea of a formative middle, a *Mitte* that unfolds as the poles of an
opposition, and this sense "hovers" between them, is of course a perva-
sive theme in German Idealism from the early readings of Kant in Fichte,
Schelling, and Hegel, and it is the guiding thread in Heidegger's reinterpretation of the concept of imagination as the middle ground or common root of reason and sensibility in *Kant und das Problem der Metaphysik*
from 1929. Already here, Heidegger however presents his own reading
as situated at the same level as that of idealism, although moving in the
opposite direction (§ 27, note 196). *Innigkeit*, on the other hand, while
a common term in religious language, here comes from Hölderlin, and
Heidegger understands it as a belonging together that preserves the difference. Heidegger comments on the theme at length in *Hölderlins Hymnen
"Germanien" und "Der Rhein,"* GA 39 (Frankfurt am Main: Vittorio Klostermann, 1980), § 19, esp. 248-259.

which takes us back through Heidegger's reading of Hölderlin's *das Eine in sich selber unterschiedne* to his interpretation of the inception of early Greek thinking in Heraclitus.[36]

The third stanza probes further into the middle of world and thing and how their intimacy is decided. It is the moment when the wanderer enters into the interior, through the gate that opens unto an inner stillness. But here the poet adds a line that marks a strong division between inside and outside, which is crucial for Heidegger's reading: "Pain has turned the threshold to stone" ("Schmerz versteinerte die Schwelle"). The pain belongs to the past (and it is also described in the poem by the only verb in the past tense), it precedes the moment of passing, but in this also determines it, and signals the decisive dif-ference inside the movement of the poem. The threshold is thus the very figure of the in-between, and its permanence and prevailing power is signaled by the stone, not as a mode of mere inertia, but of continuing presencing. The pain of dif-ference that has petrified the threshold is never simply past, but is equally active in the present: it rends and tears, it is the rift (*Riss*) that both tears apart and joins together, the "joint" (*Fuge*) of the intimacy of thing and world. In this sense, pain may be understood as that which holds the fourfold together and pries it apart, it is both *diastema* and *systema* in one, and cannot be reduced to an anthropological or psychological state. As dif-rence it determines the clearing of the world, it provides luminosity and radiance to the "bread and wine" that adorn the table inside the house, so that they may shine in their "onefold" or simplicity (*Einfalt*) and, as gifts of the gods to the mortals, gather the four of the fourfold and allow it to linger and acquire an abiding presence.

36. The traditional formula *hen diapheron heauto* stems from Heraclitus fragment 51: *ou xuniasin hokos diapheromenon heoutoi honomologeei. palintropos harmonie hokoster toxou kai lures* ("for they do not understand how that which of from itself differs accords; harmony turned against itself, like the bow and the lyre"), which was transmitted to posterity through the citation in Plato's Symposium 187a. The paraphrase *das Eine in sich selber unterschiedne* comes from Hölderlin's *Hyperion*, a work that in Heidegger's reading belongs to a phase when Hölderlin was still struggling to emancipate himself from German idealism.

This bidding, which gathers thing and world, is the essence of speaking, which as have seen presences in an eminent sense in poetry. Language speaks by bidding thing and world into the in-between of dif-ference, and in this it "expropriates" or "enowns" (*enteignet*) the thing into the repose of the fourfold, which however does not mean to deprive the thing of something, but to elevate it into its own. The dif-ference stills (*stillt*) the thing in the world, allows it to rest in the "favor" (*Gunst*) of the world, but it also allows the world to achieve satisfaction in the thing. Together, these two aspects make up stillness (*Stille*), which is not meant as a mere silence and absence of sound, but as a rest (*Ruhe*), itself more in motion than any particular motion.[37] Similarly, the bidding that calls thing and world into the rift of the dif-ference is not just simply the production of sound, but draws on something like the origin or condition of sounding, which Heidegger calls the gathered sounding of stillness, or the "peal of stillness" (*Geläut der Stille*, 27/207). This gathering sounding – which does not in itself signify anything in particular, but can be taken as the resource of all sense and signification – is nothing human, it is not something in our possession but rather something that possesses us. The human being is something linguistic in the sense that it has been appropriated (*ereignet*) out of the speaking of language, and thus handed or given over to (*übereignet*) the presencing of language. The peal of stillness "needs and uses" (*braucht*, 27/208) mortal speech for its articulation,[38] and only as belonging to a gathered stillness

37. These seemingly contradictory claims draw on Heidegger's many earlier readings of movement and rest in Aristotle, where *entelecheia* is not just a cessation, but an eminent gathering of the movement of *ousia* towards its *telos*, "having-oneself-in-the-end," as is the literal meaning of Aristotle's neologism. Similarly, *eidos* and *morphe* are not the outer limit, geometric contour or shape – as the Cartesian *forma* – but the defining moment that makes the thing into what it is. See, for instance, Heidegger, *Nietzsche I*, 404.
38. "Use" here first signals the reversal of the idea of man as the user of language, but in other texts it also refers to which in which worldly things are distributed in time and beings are related to being, as in the reading of the Anaximander fragment, "Der Spruch des Anaximander," GA 5; see also the texts assembled in *Der Spruch des Anaximander*, GA 73 (Frankfurt am Main: Vittorio Klostermann, 2012).

are we capable of articulated speech. Human speech thus always rests on the speaking of language, which is made invisible as long as we represent speaking as the articulation of inner states.

This however leaves open the more precise relation between the peal of stillness and human articulation, which necessarily breaks this stillness. In any case, Heidegger claims, voicing (*Verlautbarung*) cannot be decisive, and the articulation of speech rather comes out of the dif-ference of stillness in the form of a mode (*melos*), a particular form that exists against a background of that which has no particular form. In this way, the mortals speak by corresponding and responding (*entsprechen*), and they must first have listened to the bidding. Every word speaks out of a listening to language, which also implies a certain withdrawal, a holding back of saying, which marks everything said with a lack or absence.

6. Figures of Vicinity

In the above reading of Trakl's poem, a constantly underlying theme is the proximity of thought and poetry: both of them are moves in language, ways of listening and responding – to be sure not by merging thought and poetry into an indistinct unity, but nevertheless in such a way that something can be transferred from one to the other. This is as it were the condition for the exchange, and in order to elucidate it, we must attempt to approach the neighborhood or vicinity (*Nachbarschaft*) of poetry and thought, the region (*Gegend*) in which they unfold.

Earlier, this proximity was thematized as mythology, and occasionally this vocabulary recurs in the later writings, although it rarely brought to the fore as a historical hypothesis. An exception would be the lecture series *Was heißt Denken?* (1951-52), which belongs to same period as *On the Way to Language*. Here Heidegger once more returns to the relation between mythos and logos in the context of a discussion of Hölderlins "Mnemosyne" – one of the Titans, and according to Hesiod, the mother of the muses – and suggests that we must not understand the poem as "mythical" in a limited sense, but as that which allows the radiannce of presencing: "Mythos means: the saying word. Saying for the Greeks mean: to reveal, allow to appear, namely the radiant and that which presences in radiance, in its epiphany. Mythos is that which presences in its saga: the radiant in the address of its unconcealment."[39] The term mythology is here connected to the "saga" (*die Sage*), which is the term that will play an increasingly important role, also in *On the Way to Language*. The term is frequent also in the earlier texts, although it seems to have a more emphatic function in the later work.

For Lacoue-Labarthe, the saga is in principle identical to *mythos*, as it was put forth in *Einführung in die Metaphysik*, and thus only a verbal variation on the theme of national aestheticism. Even though a certain continuity cannot be denied, one should not overlook the differences. *Sage* should rather be understood as a way of relating the two types of saying (*Sagen*, which must be distinguished from *Sage*), i.e. poetry and thought; it is a way of approaching that which has not yet been differentiated, even though it only be rendered visible and come to language as already differentiated. Something similar applies to the term *Dichtung*, which in many cases does not refer to a particular mode of writing, but to a "linguisticality" belonging to all the arts, sometimes even in the form of an *Urdichtung* that also draws together poetry and thought.[40]

---

39. *Was heißt Denken?* (Pfullingen: Neske, 1954), 6. The same suggestions can be found in the 1942-43 lectures on Parmenides (GA 54, 89ff, 103f). In a later essay on Parmenides (1952), where Heidegger brings up the question whether we should understand the goddess as a personification, he proposes a distinction, and says that "we have hardly even considered the mythical, above all not that mythos is saga (*Sage*), while saying (*Sagen*) is the bidding bringing-to-radiance. "Moira (Parmenides, Fragment VIII, 34-41)," in *Vorträge und Aufsätze* (Pfullingen: Neske, 1954), III, 44.
40. For *Dichtung* as a category that includes the other arts, see the final sections of *Der Ursprung des Kunstwerkes*, GA 5, 59-65. The term *Urdichtung* appears in the interpretation of the Anaximander fragment: "Thought is nevertheless a poetizing (*Dichten*), but not just a poem (*Dichtung*) in the sense of poetry (*Poesie*) and song. The thought of being is the originary form of poetizing. In this, what first of all comes to language is language as language, that is, its essence. Thought says the dictation (*Diktat*) of the truth of being. Thought is the originary *dictare*. Thought is the originary poetizing

In order to become useful, *Sage* must be liberated from its everyday use, which Heidegger exemplifies by Grimm's dictionary, where it is defined as "witnesses of past events that lack historical credibility," or a "naïve storytelling and tradition, which through its transmission from generation to generation is reshaped by the poetic capacity of popular sensibility."[41] In the essay "The Way to Language," Heidegger comments:

> We have a tendency today to use the word "Saga" [*Sage*; the Eng. trans. here and in the following erroneously gives "Saying", which renders the whole passage incomprehensible], like so many other words in our language, mostly in a disparaging sense. Saga is accounted a mere say-so, a rumor unsupported and hence untrustworthy. Here "Saga" is not understood in this sense, nor its natural, essential sense as "legends of gods and heroes." But perhaps as in "the venerable saga of the blue source" (Georg Trakl)? In keeping with the most ancient usage of the word we understand saga on the basis of saying, in terms of showing, and in order to name the saga, to the extent that the order of language rests upon it, we use and old, well-attested although extinct word, *die Zeige*. (UZS 242/123)

The *Sage* is not a narrative, not even in the form of a "In the beginning was the Word," rather its role is to establish a bond between the two sayings, that which they must have in com-

(*Urdichtung*) that precedes all poetry (*Poesie*), but is also the poetical (*das Dichterische*) in art, to the extent that this turns into a work in the domain of language. All poetizing in this wider sense, in the more narrow sense of the poetical, is at bottom a thought. The poetizing essence of thought preserves the abiding of the truth of being." (GA 5, 328f) In the earlier use of the term in the '30s, where it is close to "mythology," *Urdichtung* signals a collective dimension, as in early epic poetry (Homer is the case in point), and Heidegger claims that "language is the *Urdichtung* on which a *people* poetize being." *Einführung in die Metaphysik*, GA 40, 180, my italics.

41. In vol. XIV (1893), cited in the article "Sage," *Lexikon des Mittelalters*, vol. 7 (Munich-Zurich: LexMA-Verlag, 1995), col. 1254-1257.

mon in order to pursue their respective paths. The way back to language, understood as showing (*Zeigen, Zeige*), which should be connected to the recurrent idea of "gesture," takes us into a region of communality that we *encounter*, to be sure not a standing-against, as the *ob-* of the ob-ject, the *Gegenstehen* of the *Gegenstand*, but as the openness that is the condition for all possible relations. This realm, Heidegger says, is a "region" (*Gegend*) that "encounters" or "comes up against" (*gegnet*) us, and in turn should be understood as a clearing that sets free, the differentiating tracing (*be-wëgen*) of the paths that belong to the region.

In the third part in the essay on Stefan George, "The Essence of Language" (the English title given in *On the Way to Language*, "The Nature of Language," is misleading) Heidegger directly addresses the possibility of such an experience, in which we are ti become acquainted with the "vicinity" in order to transform our relation to language. We are indeed already there, in the place which is our abode, and yet we are not there: we have yet to approach that which concerns our essence, and in this sense we must always be on the way to language, without ever assuming that we could ever fully posses it or become accustomed to it.

This is where the *Sage* shows us the way. It is that which presences in the different forms of saying, without itself being reducible to any of them; it is the possibility of separating and relating them, and appears as their vicinity. Poetry and thinking take on their respective forms in the proximity of the *Sage*. This is why proximity and *Sage* can be said to be the Same (*das Selbe*), which remains difficult to think, Heidegger notes, since it is not any determined content, nothing that is *said* in the *Sage*, which is probably also why the term mythology in the end appears misleading.

What more can then be said about the proximity that holds vicinity together? We must not understand it in terms of distances that could be measured numerically, Heidegger says, which may seem a superfluous remark, but once more links his mediations on language to the spatiality of the world, and to building and dwelling, which might seem to belong in a different context.[42] These themes are however fundamentally connected, also in showing that we are not enclosed in language in a way that would sever us from the outside world; that *language speaks* does not mean that our agency is transferred to an alien subject or power, or that we are caught in some "prison-house of language," as in some versions of structuralism and linguistic culturalism. Language is that which bears world to us, lets it presence, and the region is wherein we always move.

All measuring and calculating of distances that thinks proximity on the basis of metric magnitudes belong to the "parametric," a measuring of something via something else, and as long as parametric thoughts holds sway, the proximity of the vicinity remains closes to us, just as the proximity between poetry and thought. Proximity is thus not a distance between two things in the world, but belongs to the fourfold of heaven and earth, mortals and immortals. Just as little as the *Sage* does the fourfold offer a narrative or a particular content: it is the way in which the four regions open onto each other, the tracing of their being-together, their relation (*Verhältnis*, sometimes written *Ver-hältnis*, in order to indicate the appropriation that precedes the related parts; sometimes Heidegger prefers *Bezug*). If the *Sage* appears to be the final word on the essence of language, this means that it is the relation of all relations, that which holds the world together as a differentiated unity.

In relation to poetry and thought, the *Sage* is their unity and difference; it is the element of their belonging together, but also

42. These themes are developed above all in "Bauen Wohnen Denken" (1951), in *Vorträge und Aufsätze*. In his lectures at the Sorbonne in 1959-60, "Husserl aux limites de la phénoménologie," Merleau-Ponty connects the texts in *On the Way to Language* (largely focusing on "Die Sprache," whose first pages he discusses in some detail) in a productive fashion to Husserl's theory on the origin of geometry and the "orginary earth" as a ground for all ideal objects, and suggests that Heidegger's project is best understood as an attempt to show how the layer of linguistic signification cannot be understood without an embodiment that relates to the earth and to materiality, a "depth" or "verticality" that is the proper sense of the "abyss" that Heidegger speaks of in connection to Hamann. See Maurice Merleau-Ponty in *Notes de cours sur* L'origine de la de géometrie *de Husserl*, ed. Renaud Barbaras and Maurice Merleau-Ponty (Paris: PUF, 1998).

that which parts into two forms of saying, so that divergence is the relation – not a fusion of the two into one, not a form of mutual exchanges and borrowings, but a "delicate yet luminous difference" (*zarte und helle Diffferenz*, UZ 185/90) between two parallels. They are infinitely separated, and yet, as Heidegger somewhat enigmatically proposes, intersect "in the in-finite" (*im Un-endlichen*, ibid);[43] they intersect in a section that none of the make, just as they emerge out of *Sage* that splits – has always already split – up. They do not move into a proximity, a vicinity or neighborhood that preexists then, instead the proximity is the event (*Ereignis*) do their relation, letting them emerge, each for itself. Poetry and thought can neither be unified nor separated once and for all, since what is propriated or enowned, that which is the eventful in their relation, is their constantly changing separation on the basis of an impossible unity that guides their unceasing and mutual encircling.

43. The hyphenated *in-finite* (which has disappeared in the English translation) must obviously be distinguished from the *infinite*, and should probably be linked to Heidegger's claims that finitude must be thought through itself, without any relation to the infinite, which Heidegger somewhat surprisingly claims still was the guiding idea in the analytic of finitude in *Kant und das Problem der Metaphysik* (1929); see the seminar on "Zeit und Sein" (*Zur Sache des Denkens*, 58). In this sense, the negation "in-" would signal a transcendence that remains within an even more radical finitude that belongs to the *Ereignis*.